The Massacres at Mt. Halla

The Massacres at Mt. Halla

Sixty Years of Truth Seeking in South Korea

Hun Joon Kim

Cornell University Press
Ithaca and London

First published 2014 by Cornell University Press
Printed in the United States of America

Library of Congress Cataloging-in-Publication Data

Kim, Hun Joon, 1975– author.
The massacres at Mt. Halla : sixty years of truth seeking in South Korea / Hun Joon Kim.
pages cm
Includes bibliographical references and index.
ISBN 978-0-8014-5239-0 (cloth : alk. paper)
1. Korea—History—Chejudo Rebellion, 1948. 2. Massacres—Korea (South)—Cheju Island. 3. Cheju 4.3 Sakon Chinsang Kyumyong mit Huisaengja Myongye Hoebok Wiwonhoe. 4. Cheju Island (Korea)—History—20th century. 5. Transitional justice—Korea (South) I. Title.
DS917.55.K48 2014
951.904'1—dc23 2013027120

Cornell University Press strives to use environmentally responsible suppliers and materials to the fullest extent possible in the publishing of its books. Such materials include vegetable-based, low-VOC inks and acid-free papers that are recycled, totally chlorine-free, or partly composed of nonwood fibers. For further information, visit our website at www.cornellpress.cornell.edu.

Cloth printing 10 9 8 7 6 5 4 3 2 1

Contents

Acknowledgments

Many people and institutions have inspired, helped, and supported me as I researched and wrote this book. It is impossible to thank and acknowledge them all sufficiently. First of all, I am truly privileged to have conducted my research for three years at the Griffith Asia Institute and Centre for Governance and Public Policy at Griffith University, Australia. I thank my colleagues at Griffith University, especially Jason Sharman, Haig Patapan, Andrew O'Neil, Luke Glanville, Renée Jeffery, and Wes Widmaier. I am also indebted to the teachers and mentors who inspired me to write this book in the first place: Michael Barnett, Mary Dietz, and most of all Kathryn Sikkink.

I owe my deepest debt to the activists and researchers in the field who willingly shared their time, expertise, and ideas with me in the midst of their busy schedules. I am especially indebted to Kim Jong-min, Yang Jo-hoon, Yang Dong-yun, Kang Deok-hwan, Ko Chang-hoon, Park Gyeong-hun, Park Chan-sik, and Oh Seung-guk for their invaluable insights. I also thank Roger Haydon, acquisitions executive editor of Cornell University Press, who provided engaged and timely feedback on my manuscript, and Patrick Allington for his copyediting help in preparing my manuscript. I am very grateful to two anonymous reviewers who provided very useful suggestions for the final revision and to Katy Meigs who has provided invaluable copyediting help. Finally, I am grateful to my family members: my parents, my wife Ha Young, and my children Yejin and Gyujin for their endless love. This book was made possible by a grant from the Australian Research Council (DE120101026).

I dedicate this book to all those affected by the wars and armed conflicts in the Korean peninsula.

Introduction

Over the last three decades, a growing number of countries have undergone the transition from authoritarianism to democracy, and the recent wave of democratization in the Middle East and northern Africa suggests that this trend will continue into the twenty-first century. One of the novel features of this transition is that these new, democratically elected governments are increasingly being expected to address past human rights violations using a wide range of measures such as criminal prosecutions, truth commissions, judicial reforms, reparations, memorialization, exhumations and reburials, and the lustration of police and security forces.[1] This book relates one such story—the first truth commission in South Korea. A truth commission is an official government body temporarily set up to investigate a past history of human rights violations.[2] To date, thirty-five countries have instituted such commissions, with five new truth commissions created in 2009 alone.[3] The most famous examples are in Argentina (1983) and South Africa (1995), but there are many lesser-known examples worldwide, such as the National Commission for Investigation of the

Figure 1. Mt. Halla (Courtesy of Jeju Special Self-Governing Province)

Truth about the Jeju 4.3 Events and Recovering the Honor of the Victims (Jeju Commission) in South Korea.

The Jeju 4.3 events were a series of Communist armed uprisings and counterinsurgency actions that occurred between 1947 and 1954 in the rugged and precipitous region of Mt. Halla on Jeju Island.[4] The counterinsurgency strategy was extremely brutal, involving mass arrests and detentions, forced relocations, torture, indiscriminate killings, and many large-scale massacres of civilians. The conflict resulted in an estimated thirty thousand deaths, approximately 10 percent of the total population of Jeju at the time. The massacres, however, were systematically hidden from the public, and demands for truth and justice were totally ignored throughout forty years of anti-Communist dictatorial and authoritarian rule. With democratization in 1987, however, local students, activists, and journalists openly embarked on a movement to reveal the truth. After many painstaking years of grassroots advocacy, the Jeju Commission, South Korea's first truth commission, was created in 2000.

The official translation of the National Committee for Investigation of the Truth about the Jeju 4.3 Incident is a mistranslation because "incident" (*sageon*) downplays not only the scope and duration of the seven-year guerrilla warfare and counterinsurgency campaigns but also the gravity of the human rights violations involved. In Korean, *sageon* literally means an event that causes social problems and attracts social attention; it does not have the English connotation of a minor or subordinate event. It is more appropriate to understand *sageon* as "an event" in this context, and I use the term "events" to stress that the Jeju 4.3 events were complex and multifaceted and involved a series of large-scale massacres and other human rights crimes.

The Jeju Commission has gone largely unnoticed by scholars and practitioners around the world, and this is the first English-language monograph about the Jeju massacres and the truth commission.[5] This can be attributed, first of all, to research on truth commissions in Asia lagging noticeably behind that on similar commissions in Latin America and Africa.[6] The reason is largely historical. During the 1980s and 1990s states in Latin America, Africa, and Eastern Europe experienced transitions to democracy and, in the process, pioneered efforts to hold state officials accountable for past human rights violations. Although the creation of truth commissions has also been common in Asia, this region has attracted decidedly less scholarly attention.[7] More striking, studies on the region are heavily focused on Cambodia and East Timor, which suggests a lack of interest in cases that have not attracted attention from the international media or advocacy organizations.

This is a significant oversight. As the region that has most recently embraced the practice of truth commissions, following, developing, and modifying practices employed in the rest of the world, Asia has developed many of the most innovative, dynamic, and, at times, problematic processes. With at least ten truth commissions so far, South Korea is a leader in transitional justice in the region and provides an ideal research site. Apart from the 1980 Gwangju massacre, however, its large-scale atrocities have not yet been at the center of international scholarly research.[8] With the creation of the Truth and Reconciliation Commission of the Republic of Korea (TRCK) in 2005, however, scholars have begun to study atrocities that took place during the Korean War.[9] Nevertheless, the massacres in Jeju, which occurred before the outbreak of the Korean War, remain a blind spot.

Despite the lack of full-fledged research on the civilian massacres and the truth commission in Jeju, some scholars have been studying the Jeju 4.3 events, focusing on the armed uprising and military counterinsurgency operations. The first wave of studies started in the late 1960s and early 1970s when social scientists studying Communist movements and peasant uprisings briefly addressed the causes and background of the uprising in Jeju.[10] The second wave of research started in the 1980s with the release of US military and government documents. John Merrill made an in-depth study of the uprising and counterinsurgency operations; his work was the first substantial research on the Jeju 4.3 events not only in the United States but also in South Korea.[11] Bruce Cumings also addressed the Jeju 4.3 events in his book about the role of US occupation forces and military government in South Korea.[12] The most recent wave of research started in the twenty-first century when the US military's interest in irregular and guerrilla warfare increased. Military historians have rediscovered the Jeju 4.3 events and started to investigate the details of the uprising and counter-insurgency operations.[13]

Although all these studies provide important background information about the Jeju 4.3 events, they do not answer three important questions. First, why did the massacres of thirty thousand islanders occur in the course of the Jeju 4.3 events, and why and how was this kept secret for over forty years, until democratic transition in 1987? Second, why and through what process did South Korea establish the Jeju Commission in 2000? Finally, what has the Jeju Commission accomplished, and how has it affected South Korean society?

Questions and Approach

The Process of Establishing Truth Commissions

The South Korean experience poses an important puzzle for the study of truth commissions more generally. Earlier truth commissions, such as those in Latin America and Africa, were mostly set up immediately after a change in political power. Recent commissions, though, are investigating more historically remote cases, as we have witnessed in Uruguay, Panama, and Paraguay. Why is there a growing tendency for states to create truth commissions to investigate human rights violations that occurred in the distant past? Because truth commissions are a relatively recent phenomenon, scholars still know little about why and under what conditions they are established. I answer this question in part 1 of this book by closely examining why and how South Korea established the Jeju Commission a half a century after the outbreak of the events and how the total suppression of truth was possible for over forty years.

Conventional wisdom suggests that truth commissions are most likely to be created immediately after a political transition as a result of a power game between old and new elites.[14] Scholars have assumed that new governments are reluctant to hold past regimes accountable for human rights violations because of their concern for stability and that when states do establish a truth commission they usually do so shortly after their democratic transition. In addition, they have also believed that the demand for truth and justice is at its peak immediately after transition but is likely to diminish over time if not addressed by the incoming regime.

Since the mid-1990s, more and more states have willingly adopted truth commissions, and the demand for truth has become increasingly effective over time. Several factors have provided the necessary preconditions for this change: the end of the Cold War and the subsequent acceleration in the pace of democratization, the atrocities in the former Yugoslavia and Rwanda and the creation of ad hoc international criminal tribunals, the creation of an exemplary South African truth commission followed by the conferring of the Nobel Peace Prize on Nelson Mandela, and the accretion of human rights treaties and the development of related organizations.[15]

I argue, however, that strong and persistent civil society activism, mature democracy, sympathetic leadership, and indisputable evidence have been the key factors in facilitating the delayed establishment of truth commissions. Most important, persistent local activism was the single strongest foundation for the truth commission process in South Korea. After tracing over fifty years of persistent and rugged advocacy, I conclude that local social justice and human rights activists, students and academics, and journalists, who were mainly motivated by the pursuit of the truth, a sense of justice, empathy and compassion, and historical consciousness, were the pillars of this advocacy. Interestingly, activists sometimes strongly believed that it was ghosts—the spirits of the dead—who forcefully urged them to act and helped them throughout.

A range of domestic and international factors were significant, among them democratic consolidation, sympathetic political leaders, media, and international human rights and accountability norms. Nevertheless, these factors would not have come into play if not for the persistent struggle of local activists. Local activists made the most of these domestic and international opportunities to push for the creation of a truth commission by means of various timely and effective strategies. Each chapter in part 1 demonstrates how local activists were able to overcome the grave challenges they faced in the course of the movement.

My findings relating to local activists are significant because they show that local advocacy networks were the most important actors in the transitional justice process, facilitating favorable conditions, taking advantage of positive factors, and fighting hard against constraints and obstacles. Domestic or even local actors initiated most action, and they called for international pressure with a combination of confrontational protests and demands but also negotiations and compromise. This provides counter-evidence to those who interpret transitional justice as a kind of Western import that local populations simply tolerate or actively resent. My findings support social movement theory and transnational advocacy networks theory and thus draw our attention to the role of nonelite actors in shaping the transitional justice process.

The adoption of truth commissions has also been explained as a matter of global diffusion. Sociologists and experts in international relations have offered explanations for the diffusion of ideas, institutions, and policies in the realm of human rights.[16] In my earlier cross-national analysis, I also found strong evidence of a diffusion effect in the establishment of truth commissions.[17] In this book, I further trace the diffusion process by examining various diffusion mechanisms, such as individuals, advocacy groups, experts, and diaspora populations. The South Korean case further helps to explain why, when, and under what conditions the diffusion of truth commissions occurs. I found that the diffusion of truth commissions is caused mainly by similar cultures, histories, and political and international contexts. I also found that a diffusion effect is strong when local people have actively sought out the influence of foreign cases.[18] The influence of the Taiwanese case on the South Korean truth commission process, for example, had nothing to do with political developments in Taiwan. It was introduced, studied, and publicized by concerned journalists and activists, who were eager to make a breakthrough in the movement in South Korea.

The Impact of the Jeju Commission

This book also contributes to a decade-long debate over the effects of truth commissions by asking: What has the Jeju Commission accomplished, and how has it affected South Korean society? Many argue that truth commissions are ethically desirable and practically useful in deterring future human rights violations,[19] whereas others find that such commissions will not prove a deterrent to future violations.[20] Similarly, some scholars maintain that truth commissions help new regimes to achieve political legitimacy and garner popular support,[21] whereas others argue that such commissions cause instability and promote discord by instigating social dissent that is motivated by hatred and vengeance.[22] In addition to the impact of truth commissions at the societal level, scholars have revealed effects such as psychological healing for individual victims and family members,[23] or the reformulation of a community's collective memory.[24] Empirical evidence, however, is still insufficient to support either position adequately, as concluded in recent state-of-the-field essays.[25]

In part 2, I argue that the Jeju Commission has had a positive impact on South Korea, not only by revealing the comprehensive and historical truth about the Jeju 4.3 events and civilian massacres, but also by showing the nature of systematic suppression of the truth under the consecutive anti-Communist governments. The commission and the report it produced provided the critical evidence that made it impossible for the authorities to totally cover up the atrocities and indefinitely silence the victims. I trace the key changes the commission has made to South Korean society since the release of the final report, such as the presidential apology and participation in a memorial service, the revision of history textbooks and official documents, excavations and reburials, and the creation of a permanent institution for research and commemoration of the victims.

Three pieces of evidence support my evaluation. First, with the exception of declaring a national memorial day, the government has started to implement all the policy recommendations of the commission. Second, the Special Law for Investigation of the Jeju 4.3 Events and Restoration of the Honor of Victims went through a progressive revision in 2007, redefining the victims more widely and providing a legal basis for government-funded excavation projects and a permanent research and memorial foundation. Third, all major opposition to the commission's activities ventured by conservatives ended in failure.

A study of the Jeju Commission also helps us to understand two of the important debates about the institutional design of truth commissions. First, unlike many commissions created immediately after democratic transition, it was a full thirteen years after transition and fifty-two years after the massacres before South Korea established its truth commission. The question as to why it took so long is still unresolved and controversial.[26] In the South Korean case, I find both limitations and advantages to the delayed establishment of truth commissions. Certainly, the destruction of critical evidence over time (both intentional and unintentional); the aging and natural deaths of key witnesses, perpetrators, and victims; and a lack of public interest in pursuing the truth after a half century proved to be difficult obstacles. However, I also saw premature truth-seeking efforts, made under a weak and insecure democracy, get bogged down by endless ideological and emotional debates. The passage of time can allow for the development of one of the crucial preconditions for the establishment and success of truth commissions—mature democracy.

Second, the South Korean truth commission is unique in terms of its length of operation. Although the Jeju Commission's investigatory task was fulfilled with the release of its report in 2003, the commission, which was established in 2000, is still officially in operation twelve years later, still screening victims and carrying out various commemoration projects. Importantly, the commission published the white paper on the commission activities in 2008 and held its 16th plenary session in January 2011, identifying four thousand more victims and approving 12 billion Korean won (equivalent to $1.2 million) for commemoration projects. This is exceptional; usually truth commissions are in place for somewhere between six months and two years.[27] Moreover, all these recent accomplishments came under a conservative government, which does not necessarily support the core values of the commission. A comparative analysis of truth commissions around the world shows that the Jeju Commission is by far the longest-lived truth commission created to date.[28] A close look at the South Korean case is pertinent because many recent commissions—such as those in East Timor and Sierra Leone—have operated for longer than earlier examples.

I have found that such longer-term commissions have the potential to be highly effective and influential, but they also face the danger of creating human rights fatigue among the public, thus becoming easy targets for authoritarian backlash. The Jeju Commission has also met with strong resistance from the conservative and anti-Communist elements of South Korean society, especially from the military and police. These challenges existed before, during, and after the commission activities; and the major blows came from both inside and outside the commission. However, the commission, along with civil society, effectively defended its activities and accomplished its mandate. The South Korean case shows what kind of challenges existed throughout a decade of its activities and how the commission successfully overcame these challenges and criticisms.

Evidence and Approach

I employ several types of evidence, mostly from my interviews and field research in South Korea between 2005 and 2011. First, I collected and analyzed a vast array of primary and secondary sources on the Jeju massacres and Jeju Commission. The materials came from the government, libraries, the National Archives, the Internet, individuals, and relevant advocacy and research organizations. I was also able to obtain rare and confidential documents from individuals from advocacy organizations and government agencies.[29] Second, I conducted focused and semistructured interviews with relevant persons (activists, scholars, victims, perpetrators, state officials, lawyers, and politicians) regarding the processes and impact of the Jeju Commission. Since both the commission itself and research on it are relatively new, interviews are a critical source of information for the advocacy processes and commission activities. I identified 137 key figures and have interviewed 63 persons. These interviews covered the activities of 54 organizations out of 103 key organizations.[30]

The experience in Jeju—Communist guerrilla warfare, counterinsurgency actions, the suppression of truth, and the establishment of a truth commission after democratization—lies within a larger national and international political context. Coupled with decolonization, Communist challenges were common in the 1940s and 1950s in Latin America and Southeast Asia, and these efforts were often met with ruthless suppression by the newly independent states, overtly and covertly backed by the United States as part of its global strategy to contain Communism. Many military and authoritarian leaders were sustained under the Cold War system, with domestic repression justified in the name of national security and large-scale massacres rationalized as collateral damage in a war between Communist and counterinsurgent forces. With the end of the Cold War, these leaders were overturned in democratic uprisings, and there was a move toward holding individuals accountable for past human rights violations. Thus, in order to gain a comprehensive understanding of state violence, human rights advocacy, and transitional justice in South Korea since 1947, I situate the Jeju massacres and the subsequent political process within the context of similar cases, not only within South Korea but also around the world. However, I do place more weight on in-country comparisons than cross-country comparisons since the South Korean experience is less known than other country cases.

Overview of the Process

Although the civilian death toll from the Jeju 4.3 events was unprecedented in South Korean history, the massacres were systematically hidden from the general public, and calls for truth and justice were totally suppressed under consecutive anti-Communist military regimes until 1987. Following the transition to democracy, it took considerable time and effort to enact the Jeju Special Law of December 1999, which became the legal basis for the Jeju Commission. The path to the establishment of the Jeju Commission was long and arduous, as noted in the official report of the commission: "The transitional justice movement for the Jeju 4.3 events has proceeded in tandem with the development of democracy in South Korea."[31]

I have divided the transitional justice advocacy that led to the creation of the Jeju Commission and its activities into six distinct phases. The first phase covers the years from 1947 to 1987, when consecutive dictatorial and military regimes suppressed the memory of the Jeju 4.3 events and civilian massacres. Nevertheless, even during this time, a few courageous individual victims and activists made sporadic attempts to question, remember, and seek redress for the unjustifiable state violence. The second phase spans the years from 1987, the year of democratic transition, to 1992, when the forgotten massacres slowly regained local attention through the efforts of local university students, social movement activists, and progressive journalists. These efforts reached a climax with the excavation of

Darangshi cave and the discovery of the skeletal remains of eleven civilians, including women and children, which provided concrete evidence of indiscriminate civilian killings.

The advocacy for truth and justice became more collective and public in nature during its third phase, between 1993 and 1997. During this period, the Jeju provincial council successfully mediated demands from various local groups, including students, the media, activist organizations, and associations for the victims, and focused on investigating the massacres, organizing the united memorial service and leading the petition movement. The fourth phase of the advocacy was from 1998 to 2000, when victims and activists pursued the implementation of the Special Law passed by parliament and eventually the establishment of the Jeju Commission. During this period, activism shifted from Jeju to Seoul, the center of national politics, and the transitional justice advocacy movement began to attract the support of many outside sympathizers.

The fifth phase started in 2000, when the Jeju Commission launched its investigation, and ended in 2003, with the release of the commission's official report. Although the commission had three mandates—to investigate the truth, identify civilian victims, and restore the honor of the victims—the commission, between 2000 and 2003, focused on the investigation that laid the foundation for later accomplishments. The last phase of the movement covers from 2003 up to the present and starts with President Roh Moo-hyun's official apology in 2003, the first presidential apology for abuse of state power in South Korean history.[32] President Roh visited Jeju in 2006, participated in a memorial service for the victims, and issued a further apology for the abuse of state power. The government has also revised history textbooks and official documents to incorporate material about the state violence and civilian massacres in Jeju. Subsequently, the commission has focused on screening victims, exhuming the mass graves, and carrying out various commemoration projects, including the establishment of the permanent Jeju 4.3 Peace Foundation and the Jeju 4.3 Peace Memorial Park and Museum in 2008. The decade-long work of the commission is generally viewed as a success, and a dozen other truth commissions have been created in South Korea in the wake of the Jeju Commission, including the TRCK to investigate and reveal the truth about five major past human rights abuses, violence, and massacres that occurred in South Korea since 1910.

1

The Jeju 4.3 Events

Before 1950 no place suffered the political conflicts of liberated Korea like Cheju [Jeju]. . . . Cheju is a magnifying glass, a microscope on the politics of postwar Korea, for in no place else were the issues so clear and the international influence so tangential as in the peasant war on this windswept, haunted, magnificent island.

Bruce Cumings, *The Origins of the Korean War*

No one knows the exact number, but between 1947 and 1954 somewhere between 25,000 and 30,000 civilians were killed or wounded on Jeju Island. In March 2011, the Jeju Commission announced that 15,100 victims had been identified, of whom 10,729 (71%) had been killed, 3,920 (26%) had disappeared, 207 (1.4%) had been injured, and 244 (1.6%) had been imprisoned. The commission also identified 31,255 family members of the victims. As the population of Jeju was around 280,000 in 1948, what became known as the Jeju 4.3 events affected almost every family on the island. Most members of the local elite, whether on the ideological right or the left, were killed, disappeared, or fled, and this led to the self-deprecating saying that "the smart ones who were literate were all killed during the events and only illiterate persons like me survived."[1]

Of the individual cases, 84.4 percent of the harm was said to be caused by state agents such as the police, the military, rightist youth groups including the Northwest Youth Association; 12.3 percent was said to be caused

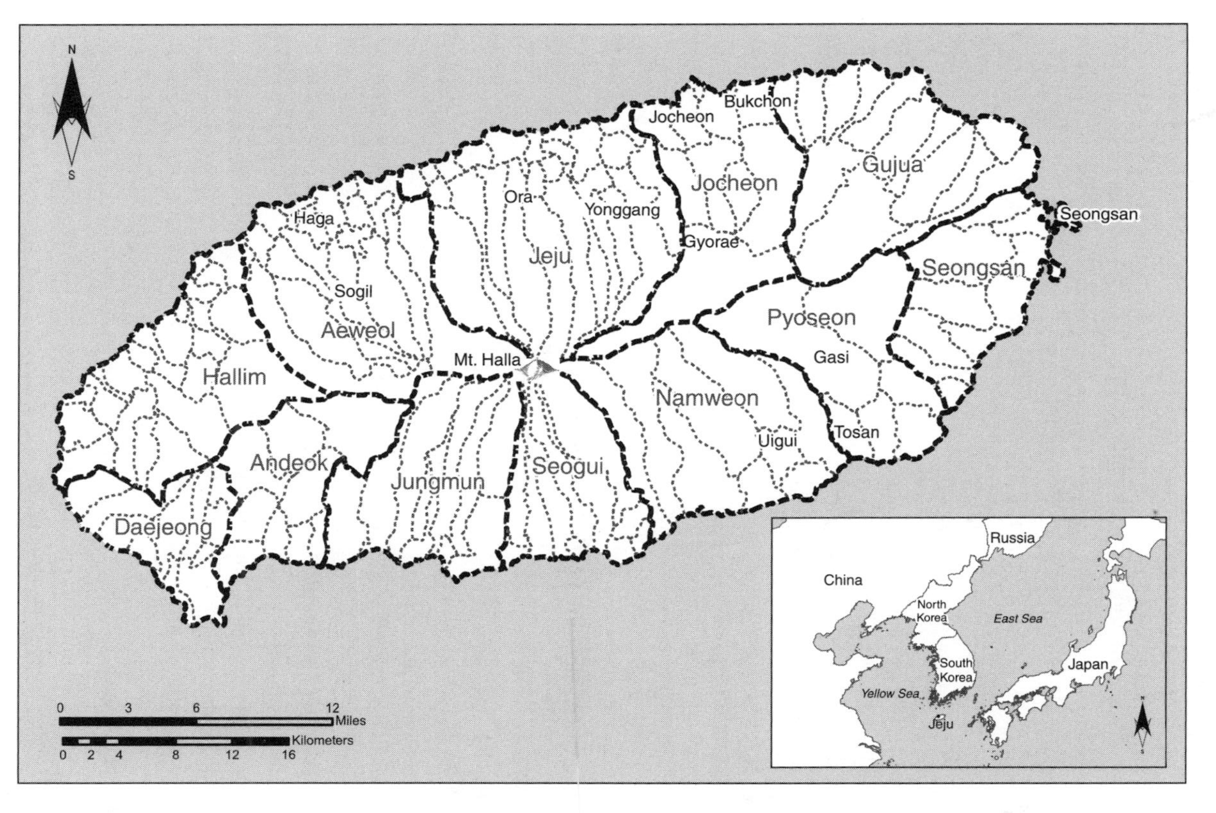
N
S
Jocheon
Bukchon
Gujua
Jocheon
Ora
Yonggang
Haga
Seongsan
Gyorae
Jeju
Seongsan
Sogil
Pyoseon
Aeweol
Mt. Halla
Gasi
Hallim
Namweon
Uigui
Tosan
Andeok
Seogui
Jungmun
Daejeong
Russia
China
North Korea
East Sea
South Korea
Japan
Yellow Sea
Jeju
0 3 6 12 Miles
0 2 4 8 12 16 Kilometers

Jeju Island

by the insurgents.[2] Most victims were in their teens and twenties, but 12 percent were civilians under ten years old (5.5%) or more than sixty years old (6.5%).[3] Of all civilian victims, 79 percent were male and 21 percent female. The percentage of children, the aged, and women among the victims suggests the indiscriminate nature of the killings. Most victims were killed in 1948 (53.1%) and 1949 (34.2%), within two years of the outbreak of the armed uprising. Mass killings were concentrated—with 63.4 percent of deaths—in the five-month period between October 1948 and February 1949, when the authorities set up their headquarters and carried out the most severe crackdown.

Civilian massacres took several different forms during the counterinsurgency campaigns. Most mass killings occurred in the mountain villages during the crackdown period. Anyone found in the interior of the island was considered a rebel and was summarily executed.[4] Many interior villages, such as Gyorae, Haga, Sogil, and Tosan, were wiped out. For example, in Gyorae, at 5 a.m. on 13 November 1948, the military closed in on the whole village and started to burn houses, killed everyone trying to escape from the fires, and then threw the dead bodies back into the fire to destroy all the evidence. Within one hour, soldiers killed twenty-five residents, including five children under ten years old and six people over sixty years old. Yang Bok-cheon, who miraculously survived the massacres, testified to the commission:

> I was at home with my nine-year-old son and three-year-old daughter. At dawn, I heard loud gunshots everywhere. I never imagined that they were killing villagers. When soldiers came to burn down my house, I begged them to spare our lives. But the soldier pushed me down and pulled the trigger; the bullet went through my side and made a big hole—about a size of an adult's fist—in my daughter's thigh, who was on my back. Immediately, my son rushed toward me screaming, "Mom!" Then, the soldier fired a gun at my son. I can still clearly remember soldiers saying to each other, "The little bastard is not yet dead!" My son's heart protruded through the skin since he was shot on his left chest. They were not human![5]

At Haga, soldiers killed another twenty-five residents, including Ko Sunhwa, who was in the last month of pregnancy. Kang Eung-mu testified about the death of her husband:

> Three soldiers rushed into the room and dragged him out. They gathered some spectators and shot him several times with an automatic gun. Several

> bullets penetrated him, but my husband was resilient. Then, one soldier cut my husband's head off with a sword and his blood splattered all over. I regarded them not as soldiers but as butchers.[6]

At Sogil, soldiers killed another 34 residents and burned the remains in order to destroy the evidence. At Tosan, soldiers killed around 150 residents over the two days of 15 and 16 December 1948. The military summoned all villagers and killed any male resident between eighteen and forty years old.[7]

Some families who had taken refuge in nearby mountain caves so they could save their livestock and crops were shot and killed. Several operations led to large-scale massacres such as that in Yonggang village, where one hundred villagers were killed and officially reported as insurgents. In a similar incident, four or five families—fifteen to twenty villagers—hiding in a cave were discovered and executed. Similar killings took place at Banmot cave, Darangshi cave, and Bilemot cave. On 16 January 1949, police killed sixteen residents whom they found taking refuge in a cave. The only survivor, Yang Tae-byeong, testified:

Figure 2. Refugees living in a temporary residence (May 1948) (US National Archives and Records Administration)

> In the cave, there were about thirty-six people who took refuge. Everyone felt relief since the entrance of the cave was very narrow and the cave itself was located in a very secretive place. However, I did not lower my guard but always sought out another hideout. One day, the police discovered the cave! All residents hid themselves deeply in the cave, but the military appeared, saying, "Don't worry, we will save your lives." Everyone else walked out of the cave, and, immediately, the military killed them all. The police even grabbed the legs of two children and brutally killed them by smashing them against the rocks. That is something a human could never do! I am sure that those murderers did not have a peaceful end to their lives.[8]

In other cases, whole families—and often whole villages—were wiped out, simply because one relative or villager joined the insurgents or merely went missing. For example, the police killed sixty-three family members and relatives of young people who disappeared in Hagui village. Ahn In-haeng witnessed and survived the massacre because his dying mother, who was covered in blood, wrapped herself around him. He testified:

> The police first summoned all villagers to the nearby hillside and then searched every house and found two persons, a seventy-year-old father and a thirty-five-year-old son. A policeman started to severely beat the son, and then the father begged for his son's life, and the other policeman started to beat the old man. The old man soon died, and the son ran away; immediately the police opened fire and shot him to death. Then, the police pointed out one woman—a twenty-five-year-old pregnant woman. The police first hanged her to a tree by putting a rope around her shoulders, and then three policemen stabbed her with swords. . . . Everyone turned his eyes away from the scene, but the police forced us to watch.[9]

Similarly, in Gasi village, residents were summoned by the military, who then identified families with members missing. They killed seventy-six villagers on the spot.

The military often deceived residents into applying for amnesty for simple misdeeds such as aiding, supporting, or not reporting insurgents, and then they arrested and executed them. In Jocheon, 200 residents turned themselves in to ensure their safety in the midst of the fighting;

150 of them were executed over the subsequent two weeks in December 1948. In many cases, the military and police disguised themselves as insurgents and lured villagers into supporting them before killing them all. In many mountain villages, the police and military had control during the day, but at night insurgents took over and killed those who cooperated. Residents were often sandwiched between the two combatant groups.

Around fifty members of the local elite, working in law, education, journalism, public office, and private firms, were detained and executed in the fall of 1948. Revenge killings were also frequent, and sometimes whole villages were targeted when counterinsurgency forces were discovered nearby. For example, on the morning of 17 January 1949, two soldiers were killed in a surprise attack by insurgents near the coastal village of Bukchon. Ten elders of the village, afraid of possible retaliation, brought the two corpses on stretchers to the military headquarters. The military

Figure 3. Residents at the foot of Mt. Halla (May 1948) (US National Archives and Records Administration)

executed all elders, except a close relative of one of the policemen, on the spot. By 11 a.m. the military had raided the village, driving the villagers from their houses and burning the houses down. They burned around four hundred houses, while summoning one thousand villagers, including the old and the weak, to the elementary school. For around five hours, the military searched for collaborators and informers, executing around three hundred villagers on nearby farms. They killed another one hundred villagers the following morning. Kim Byeong-seok, a policeman who witnessed the massacre as a driver of the police ambulance, testified:

> Then, the military burned all houses in Bukchon and summoned all residents to the Bukchon Elementary School. The commander of the battalion in charge first ordered the soldiers to "separate out the family members of the police and the military," and then they had a meeting with his staff in my car. Since my car was an ambulance, it had two side benches, and seven or eight officers sat at the benches. Officers suggested several ideas about how to kill the residents, and some even said, "Let's kill them all by striking them with several mortars." Then, one of them suggested, "Since there are still many soldiers who have not yet had the experience of shooting anyone to death, I think it would be good if each platoon takes their portion and then execute them by shooting." His idea was adopted, and I was frightened out of my senses.[10]

This massacre at Bukchon later provided Hyun Gi-yeong with a motif for his short story "Aunt Suni" ("Suni Samchon") in 1978,[11] which became turning point in the campaign to start an investigation.

The number of massacres declined dramatically after March 1949, when the insurgents were mostly defeated, but they increased again with the outbreak of the Korean War in June 1950. In order to avoid disruption and insurgency in a noncombat zone in the South, the police and military quickly arrested former Communists and anyone whom they suspected of being Communists or their supporters. They also took into custody anyone closely related to suspected Communists—spouses, siblings, or relatives. This illegal practice resulted in the detention of large numbers of civilians. From June to August, more than 1,100 suspects, including public servants, teachers, students, and housewives, were held in preventive detention centers. In late July most detainees were taken from the detention centers; they were never seen again. The families of the victims still do not know when and where they were executed. The testimonies of survivors and witnesses indicate that about five hundred victims were buried at sea near the port of Jeju, several hundred were shot dead and buried near the airport, and a couple of hundred were killed in a cave that had been used as an ammunition depot during the colonial period. However, there was one exception. Detainees who were under the supervision of the Seongsan police station survived, mainly because Chief Mun Hyeong-sun resisted the order to execute them all.

Mass arrests and civilian killings during the early phase of the Korean War were not confined to Jeju but were a nationwide practice. Within a three-month period, at least 300,000 people were detained and subsequently disappeared nationwide. In addition, immediately after the war, prison inmates were executed, and around 2,500 people who had been imprisoned in connection with the Jeju 4.3 events also disappeared. Most of these inmates were the victims of harsh suppression by the military operation that

Figure 4. Detainee camp at the Jeju Agricultural School (November 1948) (US National Archives and Records Administration)

included sweeping arrests and detention of residents in the mountain villages. Only 200 of those imprisoned were convicted in civilian courts; the remainder was convicted by court-martial, which was widely suspected of lacking objectivity and ignoring due process. Among those who were tried by court-martial, 350 were sentenced to death and were immediately and secretly executed and buried. The trial process was summarily concluded within two weeks. Judging by the simple fact that 871 people were convicted at twelve public trials in 1948 and a further 1,659 were convicted at 10 trials in 1949, it is highly doubtful that these court-martials followed due process. In addition, according to witness accounts, torture was widely used to extract confessions—in most cases, false—which were later used to justify convictions and executions.

Why did these gruesome atrocities against thirty thousand islanders occur? In order to understand the nature of the civilian massacres and surrounding debates, I start with the historical background of South Korea between 1945 and 1948, and then provide details of the armed uprising and counterinsurgency operations in Jeju. After democratization in South Korea various analysts and commentators in the fields of history, sociology, and political science tried to explain the Jeju 4.3 events. Most important are the key findings of the Jeju Commission and its final report, which as of 2013 has not been translated into English.

Historical Background

The modern history of South Korea started in 1945 with the country's liberation from thirty-five years of repressive Japanese colonial rule. Although the Japanese authorities pursued a conciliatory policy known as "culture rule" between 1920 and 1930, through most of the period the colonial authorities relied on coercion, terror, and surveillance to govern the Korean peninsula.[12] With the outbreak of the second Sino-Japanese War in 1937, the colonial authorities adopted an assimilation policy aimed at erasing Korean national identity and incorporating Koreans as second-class citizens of the Japanese polity. During this period, the colonial authorities effectively used many Korean collaborators from different walks of life to induce voluntary submission to their rule and suppressed all indigenous and independence movements. Korea also became a key source of manpower and resources for the Japanese military and industry during the Second World War. Some 140,000 Korean men and women were victims of forced labor, and thousands of women were forced to work as sex slaves, or "comfort women," for the Japanese military. This all came to a sudden end, however, when the Japanese emperor surrendered to the Allied Forces on 15 August 1945. The liberation came suddenly. According to Gregory Henderson, who pioneered the study of modern and contemporary Korean history, it "burst like a bombshell into the Korean world."[13]

Korean history between 1945 and 1948 was marked by a brief moment of enthusiasm for the new and unified Korean state, as well as by US and USSR military occupation, conflict and power politics between the left and right, terrorism and assassination, riots and revolutions, a failed attempt to reestablish a unified government on the Korean peninsula, and the creation of separate governments in the North and South. The Jeju 4.3 events, counterinsurgency actions, and civilian massacres all occurred within the context of this series of critical political events. In order to understand the political dynamic of this three-year period, we first need to examine the role of the US occupation forces, which later set up the military government and heavily influenced both the political and socioeconomic structure in South Korea.

Partly because independence movements had been sharply divided along ideological lines and partly because liberation came unexpectedly, there was no single group that could exert power and authority, concentrate political forces, and represent Koreans in the international community. Although the Korean Provisional Government, led by President Kim Gu, existed in Chungking, China, there were no iconic political figures who could unite the various political factions on the Korean peninsula.[14] At the time of the Japanese surrender, most independence movements were based in China and the United States. Japanese authorities, despite their police and military forces, fearing for their own loss of lives and property, approached the Korean leaders for protection. As a result, an interim authority, the Committee for the Preparation of Korean Independence (which later declared itself to be the Korean People's Republic) was set up and led by Yeo Un-hyeong and Ahn Jae-hong to maintain law and order until the establishment of a new Korean state or, at least, until the arrival of the Korean Provisional Government from Chungking. However, the interim authority officially lasted a mere twenty days until the arrival of the US Army on 7 September 1945. The US Army then established a US military government and declared it the only legitimate power. This government ruled the peninsula until the establishment of the Republic of Korea in August 1948.

However, the US occupation forces operated within a highly complex web of domestic social and political interests. In December 1945, five major political groups existed in South Korea, encompassing the full ideological spectrum and heavily dependent on personal leadership. According to Sim Ji-yeon, a prominent scholar of Korean party politics, the following major political parties existed in South Korea in 1945: the South Korean Labor Party (led by Park Heon-yeong), the Korean People's Party (Yeo Un-hyeong), the Korean Nationalist Party (Ahn Jae-hong), the Korean Independence Party (Kim Gu), and the Korean Democratic Party (Rhee Syng-man).[15] These parties were often identified by their ideological platforms and their positions on four highly controversial issues: collaboration, the Cold War divide, land reform, and form of democracy.[16] The rightist groups tended to be more generous toward those who were considered to have been collaborators and traitors during Japanese colonial rule, whereas the leftist groups took a harsher approach. The rightists were pro-American and anti-Soviet, whereas the leftists took the opposite view. The rightists were reluctant to carry out major land reforms, whereas the leftists actively supported such measures. The rightists pursued liberal democracy, whereas the leftists favored social democracy. In addition, the rightists opposed the indigenous nation-building efforts of the Korean People's Republic, whereas the leftists either actively participated in it or supported it.

After liberation, South Korean society leaned toward change, reform, and revolution, and leftist groups had widespread public support.[17] The leftism at this time was "almost synonymous with opposition to Japan and it made the Korean masses highly sympathetic to the left."[18] In contrast to the rightist groups that had collaborated, hidden, or fled under colonial rule, the leftist groups were sincerely admired by many for their unflagging underground resistance. However, this all changed with the political struggle over the Moscow Agreement of January 1946. In Moscow, foreign ministers of the United States, the Soviet Union, and Great Britain agreed to set up a joint commission to assist the formation of a provisional democratic and unified government in Korea. The news reached Korea through an exclusive news report that solely stressed the possibility of a four-power trusteeship, including China, for a period of up to five years before the creation of a Korean government. The public was outraged since they perceived trusteeship as another form of colonialism. Rightist groups seized the initiative to mobilize public opposition and strengthen their weak popular base.

The leftists also initially opposed the agreement, but later changed their position and supported it, arguing that the newspaper report was biased and that the trusteeship was not only different from colonialism but was also a necessary step toward the creation of a unified government. The difference between the Right and Left was clear: the leftists supported the Moscow Agreement in *totality*, focusing on the creation of a unified government in the Korean peninsula, while the rightists opposed the *trusteeship*, which they perceived as an extension of rule by foreign powers. The Moscow Agreement created a deep chasm between rightists and leftists, and represented a significant shift in the country's political topography in that public support for the leftist groups declined dramatically after it.[19]

Eventually, two political groups—one at each ideological extreme—remained at the center of South Korean politics. On the extreme left was the South Korean Labor Party, led by Park Heon-yeong; at the opposite end of the spectrum, Rhee Syng-man and the Korean Democratic Party formed a strong coalition based on their interest in maintaining the political and economic status quo.[20] Although moderate leaders were greatly respected by the public, they failed to create political infrastructure and popular support bases such as newspapers, schools, patrons, and organized loyalty, and they could not survive the violent political upheaval.[21] For instance, Yeo Un-hyeong and Kim Gu were assassinated by extremists, and many moderate socialists such as Kim Weon-bong fled to the North.

The US occupation forces operated within this bipolar political context. Between 1945 and 1948, the US military government pursued three major policies: first, suppressing grassroots state-building efforts, reviving the colonial state apparatus and filling it with former colonial officials; second, banning the Communist Party and suppressing progressive social movements; and third, favoring rightist groups in the course of pursuing important socioeconomic policies such as the redistribution of vested land and industries.[22]

The US military government declared grassroots state-building efforts illegal and dissolved the local councils that had been created across the country under the Korean People's Republic.[23] This was a big shock to the South Korean population, since the interim authority and the local councils, known as people's committees, "had come far closer to legitimacy than any other groups" and had control in most rural areas.[24] The military government retained the three most hated institutions of the colonial state—the police, the military, and the judicial system—and staffed them with former colonial officials, mainly for the purpose of administrative expediency. During the colonial period, the public saw the police as the most visible and oppressive agency in the country, and Koreans in the colonial police had been viewed as traitors. Nevertheless, the military government reemployed 85 percent of the former colonial policemen, which proved to be a grave mistake. In addition, the privileged colonial elite filled most positions in the administration, including the key posts.[25]

Second, the anti-Communist policy of the US military government became official in May 1946 when the US authority smashed counterfeiting rings in which sixteen Communists had allegedly been involved. Three days later, publication of all leftist newspapers was suspended, and arrest warrants were issued for Communist Party officials, including the leader, Park Heon-yeong. The hostility between the Communist Party and occupation forces climaxed as Park ordered a "new strategy" in 1946, which is summarized by the motto "offense by way of self-defense."

The US military government had two main socioeconomic resources: the vested properties of the Japanese and US foreign aid.[26] The military government, which already controlled foreign aid, eventually gained control of the vested properties, which constituted 80 percent of real estate and industrial property.[27] The key posts administering these economic resources were held by the rightist groups, who used them to bolster their political influence. The military government ignored popular demands for revolutionary land reform for some time, and the belated land reform was a huge disappointment, as only a quarter of all arable land was redistributed. The failure of land reform resulted in part from pressure from the rightist landlord class in the Korean Democratic Party but also from simple incompetence and poor planning.[28]

The military government's rice policy was another cause of nationwide frustration. The US forces first abolished the Japanese-style rationing system, and this caused the price of rice to skyrocket. Within three months, the military government had reinstated the previous rice collection and distribution policy, which again met with strong resistance from the public.

In general, the military government's policies empowered the rightist political forces and suppressed the leftist groups. Even in 1946, Bertram Sarafan, an officer who served in the military government, pointed out that the military government had "adopted a position of 'neutrality' but it was no secret that it favored the right and was anxious for the parties of the right to acquire strong popular support."[29] These policies had two major consequences that created the preconditions for the Jeju 4.3 events: first, the failure of the implementation of the Moscow Agreement, and, second, nationwide popular uprisings.

In line with the Moscow Agreement, US-USSR joint commission meetings took place in March and May 1946 to discuss the process for creating a unified Korean government. The US and Soviet occupation forces, however, were unable to reach an agreement on selecting political parties and civil society organizations to be invited to the conference. In a growing global confrontation, both the United States and the Soviet Union wanted the new state in the Korean peninsula to follow its own model.[30] For instance, of the twenty parties and organizations that the US military government proposed, only three were leftist groups; and the opposite was the case for the Soviets. The talks reached a deadlock in May 1946, and in June Rhee Syng-man became the first South Korea politician to publicly raise the possibility of creating a separate government. On the failure of the joint commission, the United States transferred the Korean issue to the UN, and, as a result, UN-monitored elections were scheduled to be held on 10 May 1948. The obstruction of the UN election process, which would provide justification for the creation of separate government in the South, was one of the key goals of the Communist insurgents in Jeju.

Nationwide protests against the major policies of the military government occurred in 1946 with the September strike and the October protest. The September strike started, when railroad workers demanded increased wages, and soon spread to other sectors of industry such as printing and electricity. Similarly, the October protest started with a food demonstration by a couple hundred citizens in Daegu, but it soon escalated into a popular uprising in the southern provinces.

Both events were uprisings of people who were deeply dissatisfied with the military government's socioeconomic policies.[31] At the same time, people's frustration increased with the government's policy of giving important positions to former collaborators and reappointing former police officers. Not only former policemen in the South but also those who fled from the North, with a clear record of collaboration, had been accepted into the police force.[32] It was no coincidence that, in many parts of the country, former police officers were major targets of the violence. The military government suppressed these uprisings, using the police, the military, and rightist youth groups, and, in consequence, they successfully quashed the popular uprisings. Furthermore, the occupation forces, firmly believing that these uprisings were subversive acts based on Communist ideology, began a crackdown on all leftist organizations and social movements. Although Jeju did not participate in the uprisings, the widespread uprising and an increased antagonism against the military government certainly left a deep imprint on the islanders.

Furthermore, starting in 1947, the international environment made the occupation forces strengthen their support for anti-Communist and rightist political groups in South Korea. The US foreign policy of containment was finally institutionalized as the Truman Doctrine in March 1947, and the Marshall Plan was declared in June 1947. Moreover, by the end of the year, the prospect of a civil war between the Kuomintang government and the Chinese Communist Party went against the desires of the United States. At the same time, the US burden for funding the Greek-Turkey aid program increased as Great Britain withdrew from the plan. This made it extremely difficult for President Truman to ask Congress for money for an extension of the US military in South Korea. The United States made the decision to withdraw from South Korea, and a strong anti-Communist government in place in South Korea was a critical prerequisite for the withdrawal. All these domestic and international contexts pushed the occupation forces to create a bulwark against Communism in South Korea.[33]

The Jeju 4.3 Events

Jeju is the largest island in South Korea, located in the southernmost part of the country. It is a volcanic island dominated by Mt. Halla, which is the highest mountain (6,398 ft.) in South Korea. Due to its location and the presence of Mt. Halla, Jeju was considered a secluded, isolated, and mysterious island. For a long time, Jeju had been a place where government officials exiled from Seoul were sent. Jeju is equidistant from Japan and China and is considered a place of strategic importance in Northeast Asia. During the Second World War, both Japan and the Allied Forces saw Jeju as an important location for ensuring victory in the war. During colonial rule, Japan fortified the entire island and built three military air bases there, and the United States also considered building a naval base on the island in the 1950s. With the beginning of the Pacific War in 1941, the Japanese turned Mt. Halla into "a labyrinth of fortifications in preparation for an American attack."[34]

With the launch of a passenger boat service between Jeju and Osaka, Japan, in 1918, people from Jeju were able to work, trade, and study in Japan. Naturally, Japanese culture and products were easily imported to the island because of its location. Many Koreans returned from Japan after liberation, and Jeju recorded the highest rate of population mobility of all South Korean provinces. The estimated population of Jeju before 1945 was 220,000, but it reached 280,000 after 1946. Many returnees had received higher education in Japan, and this created a strong desire for education infrastructure in Jeju. Schools and local newspapers were founded earlier in Jeju than in other provinces. Furthermore, returnees had a higher level of national or class consciousness because many had experienced discrimination during their time in Japan. Within this social and cultural context, members of the local elite actively participated in the nationwide state-building effort. The Jeju People's Committee, chaired by Oh Dae-jin, was set up on 10 September 1945, with one hundred representatives representing every town and county.

In contrast to the situation in Seoul, the Jeju local council remained in place for around a year, representing the local population and working with the local branch of the US military government, especially in maintaining public order.[35] However, as with provinces on the mainland, frustration with the major policies of the occupation forces grew over time. A couple of factors exacerbated the situation in Jeju. First, despite opposition from the local elites and the public, Jeju Island, which had long been a subordinate administrative unit of South Jeolla Province, acquired independent provincial status in August 1946. As a result, three key changes occurred that stirred complaints from local residents: the amount of tax the new province needed to collect increased; the local administration and police numbers expanded significantly; and regimental forces of the army were stationed there. By 1948 the local police numbered five hundred, five times the number in 1945, and an additional four hundred army troops had arrived on the island. Second, Jeju's economy was deteriorating, mainly because the trading relationship with Japan that had sustained the local economy had been severed. Overseas workers had to return home, and their remittances discontinued.[36] Then there was a widespread cholera epidemic on the island in the summer of 1946. In addition, staple crops such as barley, millet, and sweet potato failed that year.

The underlying political and socioeconomic tension erupted on 1 March 1947 when leftist groups organized a rally to commemorate the twenty-eighth anniversary of the 3.1 Independence Movement of 1919.[37] As a precaution, one hundred police reinforcements arrived from the mainland in late February. A ceremony that the local authorities had authorized began at 11a.m., attended by a crowd of around twenty-five thousand. At around 2 p.m., an unauthorized street demonstration was initiated. After about forty-five minutes, when demonstrators had already passed the city center where the police station was located, a six-year-old child among the spectators was hit by a mounted policeman, who then rode off. Enraged spectators pursued the policeman, who was retreating to the police station. The police opened fire on the pursuers, severely injuring eight people and killing six, including a fifteen-year-old student and a twenty-one-year-old mother nursing a baby.

The local police were quick to justify the shootings as necessary self-defense. However, public sentiment had already turned against the police, and even Governor Park Gyeong-hun admitted that the demonstrators had already passed the police station and the victims had all been spectators. In response, the local branch of the Communist Party organized a general strike; the result was an unprecedented province-wide strike in Jeju that began on 10 March 1947. Not only factory and office workers, teachers, and students in the private sector, but many in the public sector, including workers in provincial administration offices and most county and township offices, actively participated in the strike. Notably, even police officers participated in the strike, and, as a result, sixty-six officers were dismissed from the force. In all, around forty thousand local people from 166 organizations participated in the strike, which gives some indication of the provincial consensus surrounding the unjustifiable police shootings.

Figure 5. Policeman guarding the Jeju Police Station (May 1948) (US National Archives and Records Administration)

There were several subsequent small-scale conflicts between the police reinforcements and rightist youth groups, on the one hand, and the people of Jeju, on the other, such as those in Udo and Jungmun in March, Jongdal in June, and Bukchon in August.[38] Hostility toward the police forces from the mainland was certainly ignited by the shooting incident in March, but traditional enmity between the islanders and mainlanders fuelled the discontent. The proportion of mainlanders on the local police force had increased rapidly, and the shooting incident itself had involved police from the mainland. Traditionally, islanders distanced themselves from mainlanders;[39] the police from the mainland, in turn, had a negative stereotype of the islanders as unruly people, since six rebellions took place on the island during the nineteenth century.[40] To make matters worse, a new extreme rightist governor, Yu Hae-jin, took office in April 1947, and two local rightist youth groups—the Korean National Youth Association and the Northwest Youth Association—were formed with the governor's support.[41]

Against this background, several leaders of the local Communist Party planned an armed protest against the police and rightist youth groups. At 2 a.m. on 3 April 1948, around 320 leftist insurgents, armed with twenty-seven rifles, three pistols, twenty-five grenades, and seven smoke shells, but mostly with swords, clubs, and bamboo spears, attacked police substations and the offices and residences of rightist political leaders. In the leaflets they handed out to the police and local citizens, the leftist forces made it clear that they would resist if the police and rightist groups continued to suppress leftist actions; they opposed separate elections and government in South Korea; and they resisted "cannibalistic" US imperialism.[42] As a result, four policemen were killed, six were injured, and four remained unaccounted for; eight civilians were killed and nineteen injured; two insurgents were killed and one was captured.

There were two facets to the initial response to the armed uprising: a hard-line policy of prompt suppression and a conciliatory policy of appeasement. The police, who were the key target of the insurgency, advocated

Figure 6. Confiscated weapons from the insurgents, including bamboo swords and axes (May 1948) (US National Archives and Records Administration)

a hard-line policy, whereas the military were in favor of appeasement. (Initially, the insurgents only attacked the local police and made a clear distinction between the police and the military. Thus, the military remained neutral and tried to avoid becoming involved.[43]) The occupation authorities dispatched two hundred police reinforcements within a week, blockading the island. Importantly, the director of the Korean National Police, Cho Byeong-ok, asked the president of the national Northwest Youth Association, Mun Bong-je, to send around five hundred "committed anti-Communist" members to Jeju. At the same time, at the request of the US occupation authorities, Colonel Kim Ik-ryeol, commander of the 9th Regiment in charge of Jeju, met with the leader of the insurgent forces, Kim Dal-sam, and reached a peace accord on 28 April 1948.

Despite this, a critical incident occurred three days later in Ora village. After the funeral of the wife of one of its members, around thirty rightist youth group members set the houses of the local leftists on fire in retaliation. About three hours later, around twenty leftist insurgents counterattacked. Both the police and military arrived to investigate the incident, but they reached different conclusions. The police concluded that the insurgents initiated the attack, while the military reported that the rightist youth group members had triggered it. The US occupation forces adopted the former view, declared the incident a serious breach of the peace accord by the Communist insurgents, and ordered the prompt suppression of the insurgency. Interestingly, the whole incident itself was filmed from the air by a US aircraft and made into the propaganda film, *May Day on Cheju-Do*. The film was edited in such a way as to justify the subsequent hard-line policy by showing insurgents initiating the attack on the village.[44]

Colonel Kim Ik-ryeol, who had led the peace talks with the insurgents, was replaced by hardliner Colonel Park Jin-gyeong on 6 May 1948, and, with the elections approaching, the leftist attacks became more frequent. The insurgents attacked the local election administration committees, burning voting lists and ballot boxes. In addition, election officials, who were usually members of the rightist groups, became the targets of assassination. As a result, the elections in two of the three electorates in Jeju were declared invalid, and it was not until 10 May 1949 that new elections could be held.

Mainly due to the failure of the election, the military launched a full-scale counterinsurgency operation in June and July 1948, "sweeping through the mountains from west to east."[45] Colonel Park employed a three-phase counterinsurgency strategy: first, to create strategic villages with fortresses and train local militia around the coastline; second, to conduct massive sweeps of the interior of the island by burning all mountain villages and relocating residents to refugee camps; and finally, to remove suspected Communist insurgents and their supporters from refugee camps.

Figure 7. Captured insurgents (May 1948) (US National Archives and Records Administration)

Colonel Park's indiscriminate and swift counterinsurgency operation began in mid-May, and, in several battles, hundreds of Communist guerrillas were arrested. However, the arms seized were insignificant, which indicates that "battles" against "Communist guerrillas" were, for the most part, military operations against residents of the mountain villages. For example, over a six-week period, the military and police indiscriminately arrested four thousand suspects, of whom only five hundred were subsequently detained. They used torture widely in the course of the interrogations of refugees and detainees, which occasionally led to false testimonies and often to death. The sweeping arrests caused many young people in the mountain villages to flee their homes; in an ironic twist, most of them joined the insurgents. In addition, Colonel Park himself was assassinated by his subordinates, who opposed the cruel and indiscriminate military operations.

The fighting intensified after the creation of the separate South Korean government in August 1948 when the insecure government, backed by US military forces, decided to quickly end the war. Both domestic and international political situations pushed the government and the US military advisers toward a hard-line policy. First, after the split with the South,

Figure 8. Detainees waiting for interrogation (November 1948) (US National Archives and Records Administration)

in September 1948 a Soviet-influenced Communist government was established in the North under the leadership of Kim Il-sung. In the course of this, the Communist Party in the South organized the "underground election" to elect representatives who would participate in the Haeju Conference and support the creation of the Democratic People's Republic of Korea. Six representatives from Jeju, including the leader of the insurgent forces, Kim Dal-sam, successfully escaped blockaded Jeju and participated in the conference. Kim expressed his full support for the government in the North. Thus, for Rhee Syng-man, the first president of South Korea, the Communist insurgency in Jeju meant that he faced confrontations with Communists on two fronts—both North and South.

To make matters worse, a watershed event that "threatened the foundations of the fledgling republic" broke out in Yeosu, a port city on the mainland, on 19 October 1948.[46] The 14th Regiment in Yeosu in South Jeolla Province, which was scheduled to be dispatched as reinforcements to Jeju, staged a revolt, "refusing to murder the people of Cheju-do [*sic*] fighting against imperialist policy."[47] Around two thousand members of the armed forces under the leadership of Sergeant Ji Chang-su revolted and quickly took two cities, Yeosu and Suncheon, and the surrounding areas. The military revolt quickly turned into a popular uprising as the local Communist cells and leftists joined the insurgent troops. The revolt within the military was a major embarrassment and shock to both the nascent South Korean government and the US military.[48] The government suppression was extremely harsh, and, in the course of operations, the military arrested and detained all those suspected of being Communist insurgents or their supporters and executed them on the spot. Scholars and a local research organization estimate that around ten thousand civilians were killed, and, in all individual cases, they attribute responsibility for 95 percent of the deaths to the military.[49] The revolt had a major impact on counterinsurgency operations in Jeju by pressing the Rhee government and the US military advisers to promptly suppress the insurgents.

On 11 October 1948, various counterinsurgency forces—the army, navy, and police—were reorganized under the newly instituted Jeju Defense Headquarters in preparation for a full-scale counterinsurgency operation. On 17 October, the commander of the headquarters, Major Song Yo-chan, issued a decree stating that anyone who was captured without a permit within a five-kilometer radius of the coastline would be executed. This was an extreme measure because many villagers in Jeju lived not only near the coastline but also at the foot of Mt. Halla, within the five-kilometer radius. Major Song reinforced the military by organizing civilian and student defense forces and incorporating an additional one thousand rightist youth group members as makeshift police or military forces. President Rhee proclaimed martial law in Jeju Province on 17 November 1948, and a full-fledged counterinsurgency operation began. The military razed mountain villages in order to destroy the hideouts and potential supply lines of the insurgents. Residents of the mountain villages were forced to abandon their houses, livestock, and farms, and they relocated to the coastal villages. The military forcibly relocated around eighty to ninety thousand residents of mountain villages, around one-third of the total population of Jeju.

The military operation relocating villagers and destroying food-supply and recruitment bases in the mountain villages was completed by the end of the year. This operation brought most of the population under government control and isolated the insurgency groups.[50] A full-scale operation against the insurgents began the next year, and between January and

Figure 9. Residents relocating from mountain villages to refugee camps in coastal areas (US National Archives and Records Administration)

March 1949 the military encircled Mt. Halla, defeating the main insurgency forces. Cornered insurgents made several attacks in January, but none of them were successful, and, in turn, the attacks seriously weakened the remaining forces. This was also the period when the mass killing of civilians was most concentrated. According to the report of the Jeju Commission, almost 80 percent of the deaths of children and elderly took place in this period.[51]

By March the military had almost destroyed the main forces of the insurgents, and only five hundred insurgents were left near Mt. Halla. Simultaneously, the military started an amnesty program and induced voluntary surrender. In April President Rhee himself visited the island and demonstrated the restoration of government control and a successful suppression of the insurgents. Consequently, new elections took place on 10 May 1949, exactly a year after the original date, while the leader of the insurgents, Lee Deok-gu, was killed by the police.

However, sporadic guerrilla warfare continued until the Korean War broke out on 25 June 1950 and the Communist insurgency and counterinsurgency in Jeju entered a new phase. During the Korean War, Jeju did not once come under the control of the North Korean military. The remaining insurgents resumed their attack in the hope that the People's Liberation Army from the North would make it to Jeju. However, after the successful Incheon landing operation led by General Douglas MacArthur, the North Korean army retreated. By 1952 the number of remaining insurgents had declined to just sixty-eight, and only five remained when the authorities officially lifted the restrictions on Mt. Halla on 21 September 1954.

Three Key Debates

The Jeju 4.3 events have been variously labeled as a democratic movement, a popular uprising, massacres, riots, rebellion, revolt, an anti-American struggle, a unification movement, and simply 4.3, which gives some indication of the ideologically controversial and polemic nature of the events themselves.[52] In this section, I introduce three key debates regarding the characteristics and definition of the Jeju 4.3 events. Since these debates reappear in the course of the transitional justice movement in the 1980s and 1990s, I will leave the details for that later chapter but will here introduce the big picture.

The first relates to the characteristics of the armed uprising that started on 3 April 1948. Before 1987 the Jeju 4.3 events were mostly understood and referred to as a "Communist rebellion" (*gongsan pokdong*) in all public records, including government documents, mass media, and textbooks. By defining the key events as a Communist rebellion, civilian massacres and human rights abuses were easily justified as collateral to and a necessary part of the effort to prevent communization. However, since democratization in 1987, scholars and activists have begun proposing alternative definitions such as "popular uprising" (*minjung hangjaeng*) or "democratic movement" (*minjuhwa-undong*).[53] These scholars commonly agree that the armed uprising was, first, widely supported by the general public and, second, an inevitable response to the oppression and misrule of the US military government and the incompetent Korean government. There are also moderate and more cautious scholars and activists who refer to the "events" (*sageon*) or "4.3" (*sa-sam*) without expressly defining its characteristics.

There is also debate regarding the starting date of the Jeju 4.3 events. Before 1987 the orthodox view was that it started on 3 April 1948 when the Communist guerrillas launched an attack. With democratization, however, a revisionist view emerged arguing that it started on 1 March 1947 when dissatisfaction with the US military government exploded in a demonstration and the local police, under the control of the US military, opened fire, severely injuring eight and killing six. This incident led to a general strike in Jeju, followed by a series of confrontations that resulted in the government and local police drastically losing the support of the residents. According to this perspective, an armed uprising on 3 April 1948 was one of several instances of public resistance to the US military government, which originally started on 1 March 1947.

The debate on the starting date of the process is closely related to a third debate about responsibility for civilian massacres. The traditional argument is that the Communist guerrillas were mainly responsible for the disruptions, including the massacres and human rights violations.[54] In contrast, others now argue that since the armed protest was merely a response to oppression and misrule, the US military government and the nascent Korean government were responsible for the massacres and abuses.[55] A few scholars further argue that the United States, not the US military government, is responsible, since the United States had direct rule over South Korea at this time.[56]

Part I

The Establishment of a Truth Commission

2

Suppressed yet Stubborn Truths

> The hallmark of factual truth is that its opposite is neither error nor illusion nor opinion, not one of which reflects upon personal truthfulness, but the deliberate falsehood, or lie. . . . All these lies, whether their authors know it or not, harbor an element of violence; organized lying always tends to destroy whatever it has decided to negate, although only totalitarian governments have consciously adopted lying as the first step to murder. . . . That facts are not secure in the hands of power is obvious, but the point here is that power, by its nature, can never produce a substitute for the secure stability of factual reality, which, because it is past, has grown into a dimension beyond our reach.
>
> Hannah Arendt, *"Truth and Politics"*

The period between 1954 and democratization in 1987 marks the first phase of the movement to find truth and restore justice. It was the darkest time for advocacy. The Rhee Syng-man regime, which was responsible for the massacres, remained in power for twelve years and suppressed any hint of a local attempt to bring up past atrocities. A short period of democracy followed after the fall of the regime in 1960, but the new democratic government could not last long, and in 1961 it was overthrown by a military coup led by General Park Chung-hee. Park's military government was even harsher in clamping down on victims and activists, and the dictatorship lasted for eighteen years until Park was assassinated by one of his trusted subordinates. A brief moment of hope, known as the Seoul Spring, followed, but another anti-Communist regime came to power, following the successful coup by General Chun Doo-hwan. Through all these years, the victims' calls for truth and justice had been systematically suppressed, and victims and their family members remained fearful, submissive, and passive. At the same time, the general public accepted the government's official narrative, perceiving the Jeju 4.3 events as a Communist rebellion and the victims as Communists and their supporters.

Nevertheless, even under conditions of harsh repression and overt menace, the truth was resilient, and it was impossible for the government to totally cover up all traces of the atrocities. At every opportunity, at least one person brought up the dark and unresolved history of state violence. In most cases, it was not the victims themselves but those who sympathized with them or who were inspired by a sense of justice, truth, and historical awareness that opened up the new path. It was the power of individuals and visionaries pursuing ideals such as justice, truth, and compassion that made a difference. The facts proved to be much more enduring than the government-fabricated version. It was university students, journalists, and writers who were especially important in the early advocacy process. During the early 1960s, students and a local newspaper spearheaded the movement, and in the late 1970s writers of literature broke the twenty years of total silence and opened up a new phase of advocacy. This chapter is the story of these individuals.

Total Suppression, 1954–1960

By means of an illegal constitutional amendment in 1954 that allowed for a lifelong presidency, Rhee was able to serve three terms as president of South Korea, about twelve years, engaging in an ultra anti-Communist policy, suppressing basic civil and political rights, censoring opposition, and gagging any criticism of the regime. The National Security Law, which was enacted in 1948, provided a convenient tool for punishing political opponents by charging them with pro-Communist sympathies.[1] Communism was the main enemy of the state, and deterring both internal and external Communist threats was the number one policy priority for Rhee. The Korean War ended in an armistice in 1953, and Rhee further strengthened his anti-Communist stance by changing to it a "defeating Communism" (*myeolgong*) policy rather than a simple "anti-Communist" (*bangong*) policy. He vehemently opposed the US-led armistice talks and campaigned for the total defeat of North Korea.[2] With citizens terrified by their war experience and fearful of further civilian massacres committed by the government, a perfect environment was in place for enforcing the political legitimacy of Rhee's regime.

Ordinary citizens were deprived of their civil and political rights, and prominent opponents, such as Cho Bong-am of the Progress Party, were found guilty of espionage on fabricated charges and executed. "Communists," which including anyone with a slight hint of socialism, were purged from the police, the military, congress, and public administration, and many were executed. The demand by victims to bring up the past abuse of state power was completely suppressed, with the government claiming that those killed had either been Communists or aligned with the Communists. Any activities or "disgraceful" complaints against the military or police, who were fighting against Communists on the front line, were regarded as acts benefiting the enemy. Democratic ideas and values were easily trumped by security and anti-Communist imperatives, and unfortunately this precedent had a lasting impact on South Korean politics. Anti-Communism became a tempting and easily available political tool to suppress popular demands for democracy.

In April 1960, however, Rhee's dictatorship was overturned after a student-led demonstration. The movement was sparked by election fraud in the voting for prime minister in March, and it soon escalated when the body of a student protestor was found with a tear gas grenade embedded in his head. Not only students but also ordinary citizens participated in the protest against the Rhee dictatorship, and Rhee finally stepped down, fled the country, and lived the rest of his life in exile in Hawaii. The twelve-year-old dictatorship came to an end, and people were eager for a meaningful democracy to take its place. The series of political events that took place in April 1960 is known as the 4.19 Revolution.

Before studying the initial attempts in 1960, we first have to ask why and how it was possible for the victims to remain in silence for over a decade. We can find answers to this question in both the government policy and the victims' attitude. Of course, it was not the first time when victims embarked on collective action. The first attempt came after seven hundred villagers in Geochang, South Gyeongsang Province, were killed by the 9th Regiment of the ROK Army in 1951.[3] Despite Rhee's strong objection, a special commission composed of lawmakers and ministers was set up, and a special military court was instituted. Although three officers were convicted of murder and cover-up, all of them were soon pardoned and later held high positions under Rhee's regime. On the other side of the coin, families of victims could not even collect the remains of the dead for three long years and were kept under surveillance and threatened. Victims finally collected the remains of the dead and buried them in a common burial ground because it was impossible to separate the remains of individual victims. However, the burial ground was under constant threat from the authorities. In one incident, unidentified soldiers damaged a monument with a chisel, and the governor openly asked for the removal of the cemetery. Because of the Geochang case, which set the example, victims of other much more severe massacres nationwide remained silent during the Rhee regime.

Even before the outbreak of the Korean War, the Rhee regime relied on the fear of Communism to deal with political crises. In 1948 the congress set up a special court to investigate and punish pro-Japanese collaborators. The court consisted of sixteen judges who had the authority to sentence former collaborators to death for crimes of treason. Within four months, the court investigated 682 cases, indicted 221, and convicted 14 collaborators. Rhee, whose domestic political support came exclusively from the colonial elites, criticized the court and refused to remove identified collaborators from his administration. Rhee and his supporters accused court members of being Communists who threatened national security by instigating social dissension out of hatred and vengeance. Judges were threatened with assassination, and the police, with the tacit consent of Rhee, raided the courthouse, injuring many and destroying documents. The court gradually withered and was eventually dissolved. The failure of the court shows how, under Rhee, even the most agreed-on national agenda can easily be thwarted by anti-Communist ideology.[4]

Victims in this repressive environment could not even imagine addressing the deaths of their family members. Kim Jong-min, a reporter who closely followed the victims, provides two explanations for the silence.[5] First, a very strong self-restraint mechanism was at work because the dead were associated with Communism, which was a strict social taboo at the time. As mentioned, the search for Communists and resident spies was a frequent political topic under the Rhee dictatorship, and victims censored their own speech and collective actions. Rhee's ultra anti-Communist regime was founded on the basis of mass killings, which instilled and diffused terror throughout South Korean society.[6] Second, there was a sense of defeatism—or nihilism—among the victims, as they knew that the perpetrators were still in power and that little could therefore be done. Experiences in Geochang certainly left a deep and long-lasting imprint on victims nationwide.

Initial Attempts, 1960

The first initiative to break out of this passivity occurred when South Korea experienced its first democratic transition from dictatorship to an ephemeral democracy. It is a particularly difficult period to research because there is little documentation available, and many witnesses died without leaving any records.[7] Following the 4.19 Revolution, the Second Republic was created, which adopted a parliamentary system in order to minimize the exploitation of presidential power. The new government protected basic civil and political rights and promoted human rights; it decentralized political power through strengthening the self-governing functions of local governments and councils.[8] There followed a period of revolutionary change, and, as is often the case, it was also a time of some confusion and disorder. It was during this time that the family members of victims started to organize and began to raise their voices nationwide. A core concern for victims was to restore the honor of the dead by clearing victims of false accusations of being Communists.[9]

Since it had only been a decade since the events took place, most of the family members were still alive, and they actively participated in the process. Victims and their families were no longer afraid of the government because they firmly believed that it was the right thing to do and that "a new era had come."[10] Political elites also firmly believed that the new government should address people's grievances. For example, in Busan, victims met with the prime minister through the good offices of district congressmen and received large amounts of condolence money to be used for memorial services.[11] Eventually, the 4th National Assembly took the initiative and resolved to investigate the civilian massacres that had occurred under the Rhee regime, and the Congressional Special Committee for Investigation of Civilian Deaths (Congressional Committee) was set up in May 1960.[12]

With the decision, the suppressed memories of the Jeju 4.3 events started to slowly float to the surface in Jeju. Students at Jeju National University were the first to have the courage to publicly investigate the massacres. Lee Mun-gyo, a sophomore and law major, and six other students created the Student Association for Investigating the Truth of the Jeju 4.3 Events (4.3 Jinsang Gyumyeong Dongjihoe) on 26 May 1960 and began to investigate the mass killings through on-the-spot investigations. The students published a statement in the most important local newspaper, the *Jeju Sinbo* (Jeju newspaper), which was the first recorded public call for transitional justice since the end of the events in 1954. The statement contended, "The time has come for us to appease the souls of the millions murdered by barbaric guns and swords by testifying to their innocence." Students proposed that "after the truth is established, those who were responsible for the murders and the arson attacks should be punished." Immediately, the students' action attracted the suspicions of the police, security, and counterespionage agents. Lee recalled both threats and conciliatory overtures being made by the local police through contact with his parents and professors.

The students' efforts were derived purely from a "strong sense of justice," according to Lee. When I asked why he started the movement despite the possible dangers, Lee, who now is his seventies, answered:

> Why? I was a student. Students have courage. They don't calculate. Students take action when they believe it is the right thing to do so. In addition, I studied law as an undergraduate, and law, in a nutshell, is about the pursuit of justice. Justice was and still is really important to me. I was not scared. I was young. I was not scared of the police, military, or counterespionage agents because I did the right thing.[13]

The students traveled around Jeju on foot at their own expense and stayed with their relatives. They met with village elders and collected information about any mass killings. Lee recollected that they were able to fill "five university notebooks" with information, but these were later burned by Lee's mother as a precaution after Lee was arrested. The investigation was not an easy process; about half of the elders refused to talk. They turned away from students "as soon as the word '4.3' [*sasam*] was uttered."[14] The student movement was the first organized effort to address the civilian massacres in Jeju. Students who brought an end to the corrupt and resilient Rhee Syng-man dictatorship also took the initiative to correct the past wrongs. After that time, students continued to play a key role, not only in South Korean politics in general, but also in advocacy for the Jeju Commission. Students have been at the center of advocacy despite the obvious danger under the military governments.

Inspired by the students' activism, on 2 June 1960, the *Jeju Sinbo* and its owner, Shin Du-bang, who himself had been a victim of illegal detention and torture, started to investigate the massacres systematically. The newspaper conducted the first province-wide investigation and distributed application forms to the victims to report the details, such as personal information about the victim, the date and place of the killing, the perpetrator, if known, and the whereabouts of the body. The newspaper reported that 1,259 applications were received, and 1,457 victims were identified.[15] Of the 1,457 who had been murdered, 588 (40%) of the killings were carried out by the military, 439 (30%) by the police, and 430 (30%) by unidentified perpetrators. Although this number constitutes only 5 percent of the total number of people killed, it was a representative sample since it showed that most of those who died were victims of state violence.[16]

Amid this excitement and hope, investigators from the Congressional Committee—Congressmen Choi Cheon, Cho Il-jae, and Park Sang-gil—arrived and spent two days on the investigation. Time and resources, however, were insufficient to carry out a full-scale investigation that could lead to substantial conclusions. The investigators spent most of their time listening to reports of past investigations carried out by the students and the *Jeju Sinbo*. Only one public hearing was held, in which seven victims and witnesses testified. Creating a huge disappointment, investigators decided not to report on the Jeju case at their congressional plenary session.[17] In consequence, all there was to show for their two-day investigation was eighteen pages of stenographic records. The ostensible reason for not reporting was "insufficient evidence and lack of preparation." Nevertheless, more convincing reasons may be found in the innate limitations of the congress and the lack of political will among the elites.

First, members of the 4th National Assembly were elected under the Rhee dictatorship in 1958, and many of its members were allies of Rhee. The public constantly demanded the dissolution of the assembly after the 4.19 Revolution, and it did in fact dissolve itself on 28 July 1960, a month after the investigation. Thus, although the members of the congress created the committee in response to strong public demand, the committee members' hands were really tied. The chair of the committee, Choi Cheon, made a statement before launching the nationwide investigation that summarizes the limitations of the committee:

> A full-scale investigation of the massacre nationwide in a week is very difficult, and I do not believe that the 4th National Assembly can complete the investigation. Maybe a more complete investigation will be possible in the 5th National Assembly. . . . The current Congressional Committee's aim is to make a policy recommendation to the next government to punish those whose criminal acts are supported by evidence and to make reparations to the family members of the civilian victims.[18]

Choi had been chief of the Jeju police during the Jeju 4.3 events, and if the massacres had been thoroughly investigated, Choi himself would not have been completely free of responsibility. The lack of commitment is clearly shown in Choi's concluding remark after spending four hours listening to the painful story of the massacres:

> We [investigators] reached the conclusion that, in principle, the government should make reparations to civilian victims. However, the Jeju 4.3 events are not a matter of concern here because in our criminal law, aiding and abetting a murder has a ten-year statute of limitations. The 4.3 events happened over ten years ago. . . . I am letting you know this for your own information. . . . Also, Jeju was under a strong Communist influence at the time. I remember making an order based on my judgment that, if not controlled, a huge rebellion would start from Jeju. . . . We have to think hard about how to distinguish civilians from those who were not civilians.[19]

Here, Choi argues that the Jeju 4.3 events are beyond the statute of limitations in criminal law. However, even in South Korean criminal law, the statute of limitations for murder, not aiding and abetting a murder, is fifteen years, which had not yet elapsed when he made this remark. His selective understanding and interpretation of the law clearly reveal his lack of will to bring perpetrators to justice.

Despite the failure of the Congressional Committee, students and the local newspaper continued their advocacy for the victims by pressuring the congress. Students organized a rally calling for a thorough investigation and punishment of the perpetrators. In addition, journalists and victims initiated criminal trials based on the evidence collected through the province-wide investigation. Shin Du-bang took the initial step by filing a complaint against Lieutenant Kim Byeong-chae and policeman Lee Yun-do for murdering ten innocent civilians. Shin wrote in the *Jeju Sinbo* why he filed the complaints:

> Even under martial law, there is no precedent in history for killing ten members of one household, from a sixty-seven-year-old senior to a ten-day-old child, in one place at one time. It is never justifiable to kill such people with bamboo spears and swords. There is no such punishment in world history. These tragic deaths in one family were reported by one of the applications our newspaper received. Surviving members of the family have kept their silence for over ten years because of the fear instilled in them by the former regime. I have no political motive, and I do not want my acts to cause any social dissent. I act on behalf of the family members only because my heart was broken when I read their application and I truly wanted to know whether these people had deserved such a death by bamboo spears and swords in the twentieth century.[20]

This is reminiscent of the motivation of the university students: a sense of justice, an emotional response to the plight of the victims, and a drive to pursue the truth. Shin filed the complaint because he had been deeply moved by the family's story and wanted to know whether the dead had deserved to die in such a brutal manner. In addition, it was not the victims but other brave figures who first took action. Although Shin was a victim himself, he did not file a complaint based on his own case but on behalf of others. Shin wanted his complaint to serve as a "model case," and unsurprisingly, a second complaint was soon filed.[21]

All these attempts to bring the Jeju 4.3 events to light came to an abrupt end with the military coup by Park Chung-hee on 16 May 1961. The initial advocacy lasted for about thirteen months, and the advocacy lost its momentum with the failure of the Congressional Committee. Nevertheless, I do not see the failure of the committee as the failure of the local transitional justice movement in the 1960s. This brief initial period of advocacy has great significance in the overall advocacy process. The embryonic form of the advocacy that took shape after the democratic transition in 1987 was fully conceived during this initial period. The early activities of students, local media, and victims reached their full potential and final form after democratization. These early actors were key figures in securing the establishment of the first truth commission in South Korea. Without their contributions, later achievements would have been more difficult and much slower.

Another Period of Total Suppression, 1961–1978

The fledgling democracy of the Second Republic lasted only a year as people's discontent grew as they experienced economic decline and social disorder as a result of political instability. In May 1961, a group of military elites headed by General Park Chung-hee staged a coup and took over the government. Park suffered serious challenges to his legitimacy due to his "illegal usurpation of power and extralegal exercise of authority."[22] Challenges to his authority came from both outside and inside. On the one hand, the United States was seriously concerned with Park's previous involvement in Communist activities. On the other, the elites and the public questioned Park's intentions because he overturned the new democratic government created after the successful popular uprising against the Rhee dictatorship. Park overcame the opposition by legitimizing his rule with the assertion of the need for a strong anti-Communist policy, national security, and economic growth. This transitional period in justice advocacy is marked by seventeen years of absolute silence and total suppression.

Following in the footsteps of Rhee, Park treated any attempt to investigate and provide redress for the civilian massacres committed by the military and police as Communist acts.[23] Park further enacted the Anti-Communism Law of 1961, which was more draconian than the existing National Security Law and made any criticism or challenge to the regime an act of Communism. The logic was simple: any criticism of Park's government, which was officially still at war with the North, would cause social dissension in the South and thus endanger national security by benefiting the North. Many of those who had led the early justice movement nationwide were arrested and sentenced to long prison terms, or even death, in the Revolutionary Court.[24]

The president of the national victims' association—Roh Hyeon-seop—and many local leaders were arrested two days after the coup.[25] In many places, any evidence of the massacres, such as common burial grounds, monuments, or written documents, was destroyed by the local and military police. In Daegu, for instance, a massacre ground discovered by the victims after the 4.19 Revolution was buried deep underwater through the construction of a dam immediately after the coup. Police destroyed stone monuments and dug up and burned the remains of the dead that were in a common burial ground.[26] However, faced with the new anti-Communist and military government, victims and their family members could not utter a word about these inhumane acts.

Similar measures were taken by the Jeju local police and military in Daejung, one of the counties in Jeju where 132 villagers had been killed during the Korean War. Immediately after the killings, the military had proclaimed the murder site a restricted area and refused to allow the remains of the dead to be buried. The murder site was "fenced in, locked tightly, and guarded by soldiers for six years and eight months."[27] Although the victims' families demanded the bodies, it took six years before they were handed over. In 1959 family members formed an organization, created a common burial ground, and built a stone monument in memory of the tragic deaths of their relatives. Because the 132 villagers had been killed at a local ammunition depot and secretly buried, it was difficult to separate and identify their remains. The descendants decided to create a common burial ground and name their group the Association of One Hundred Ancestors but One Descendent (Baekjo Ilson Yujokhoe), reflecting the fact that their parents had been one hundred or more individuals who had become one through brutal and barbaric state violence, which had led them all to become the descendants of the one ancestor.

A month after the coup, local police Chief Kang Gyu-ha and his subordinates, armed with hammers, shovels, and gasoline, tore down and destroyed the stone monument. The police further attempted to dig up and destroy the remains of the dead, but they faced vehement resistance from the families. For a long time, the families "almost lived—ate and slept—at the burial ground to protect the remains of the dead."[28] Exactly identical incidents occurred on the same day, 15 June 1961, on the mainland in Geochang and Milyang, and this provides undeniable evidence that the order came from the central government. Ironically, Park's efforts to erase the past atrocities left further evidence of state violence. After democratization in 1987, victims by chance found the pieces of the shattered monument near the mass grave. They decided to erect a new monument to commemorate not only the original massacre of 1950 but also the second atrocity of 1961.

Figure 10. Display of the broken monuments stating "Remains of a Monument Torn Down by the Park Regime" (2005) (Photo by author)

It was not something Park Chung-hee and his subordinates could have envisaged when they tore down the original monument in the 1960s; it manifests the stubborn durability of the facts, even under coercion and repression.

A day after the coup, the police arrested two university students, Lee Mun-gyo and Park Gyeong-gu, on the charge of assisting the Communist North by stirring up social unrest using the Jeju 4.3 events. Both the police and counterespionage agents interrogated and tortured Lee for two months before he was transferred to a detention center in Seoul. Lee spent six months in detention on suspicion of being a Communist; he was released when authorities decided to suspend the indictment due to a lack of evidence.[29] Lee had been nicknamed a "watermelon Communist" by government agents because of his tenacious denial of being a Communist despite the torture he had endured. Lee insisted that he had led the movement purely because of his desire to pursue truth and justice. Since the interrogators were unable to find any evidence despite their strong suspicions, they dubbed him a watermelon Communist, implying that he was a

Communist at heart (red on the inside) in a perfect disguise (green on the outside).[30] The police also arrested Shin Du-bang, owner of the *Jeju Sinbo*, on the charge of inciting students to engage in social dissent. Since students and the local newspaper were the two key actors, the authority tried hard to link the two groups and eventually succeeded in convicting Shin.[31]

Due to harsh repression and a few exemplary cases like those of Lee and Shin, all attempts to bring truth and justice were again completely stifled. Park's draconian measures made those who had been terrified under the previous Rhee dictatorship even more reluctant to speak or act. Three factors helped to sustain the total silence for seventeen years. First, the Park military regime kept a constant eye on victims and activists. The military police paid regular visits to Lee to "check on his well-being."[32] The local police constantly followed victims and often arrested and tortured them if any suspicious acts were detected. Ko Jeong-ha, the leader of the Association of One Hundred Ancestors but One Descendent, was followed by police almost all the time. Ko held an annual memorial service for his deceased father at the murder site, and every year, the local police arrested him the next day. Ko was labeled as a resident spy, and this made heroes out of the local policemen who captured the same spy *annually*.[33] Yang Bong-cheon, who organized victims in Uigui in the 1970s, also testified that whenever he met with others, the police visited his office the next day to check on the details.[34]

Second, victims' participation in organized action drastically decreased, and they often denied being victims of the Jeju 4.3 events.[35] Victims were shocked by the reinstatement of the anti-Communist dictatorship and strictly censored themselves so as not to provoke the military. Victims were also unable to speak out due to the stigma associated with being Communists or reds (*ppalgaengi*). Victims simply feared the word "red," and one even testified, "It [the reds stigma] haunted me throughout my sixty years."[36] The most common complaints psychiatrists in the 1950s and 1960s heard from their patients were: "Someone falsely accuses me of being a red!" and "'Reds' follow me everywhere."[37]

Finally, the public turned a blind eye to the plight of the victims. The public passively accepted the government's account of the Jeju 4.3 events, partly due to fear and partly because of an inability to contemplate the gravity of the situation. The elites were mostly responsible for unquestioningly accepting the dominant discourse and blindly moving forward.

A good example can be found in history professors Lee Hyeon-hee and Shin Jae-hong, who wrote a history textbook that portrayed the Jeju 4.3 events as a Communist rebellion instigated by the North. When tenacious reporters questioned the source of this view, Lee replied, "At the time I was writing this, there were no new historical documents so I had to use the previous and available ones."[38] In addition, Shin admitted, "I have not really studied the Jeju 4.3 events. My major field is Korean history under Japanese colonialism, not contemporary history. I wrote both chapters only for expediency. . . . I mostly used existing textbooks and government materials."[39] This is a clear example of a highly educated person who lost the ability to think through both the immediate and long-term consequences of his simple act. A similar example can be found in a group of successful people whose parents had been victims of state violence. For fear of losing their jobs, a majority of them made every effort to deny and hide having been victimized by the Jeju 4.3 events.[40]

Sowing Seeds, 1978–1987

For almost seventeen years, between 1961 and 1978, there was *absolutely no* public mention of seeking the truth of the Jeju 4.3 events or restoring the honor of the dead.[41] An important breakthrough came in 1978 when Hyun Gi-yeong published his short story "Aunt Suni" in a prominent literary magazine. In the following year, Hyun published a book of short stories he had written on the theme of the Jeju 4.3 events.[42] It was the first time that the Jeju 4.3 events were publicly addressed under Park's dictatorship. Almost all activists testified that this was the key moment in the history of the advocacy movement. They described Hyun's short story as a "hole in the dam" for the movement.[43] In Hyun's "Aunt Suni" the main character tells his story in a monologue as he flies from Seoul back to Jeju for his grandfather's memorial service. The story is really two stories—that of the dead (the narrator's grandfather and many other villagers in Bukchon, whose descendants are having a memorial service on the same day) and that of the living (Aunt Suni). The short story begins with the news that Suni, a distant relative of the narrator, has committed suicide in her sweet potato field by poisoning herself. On the same day, the narrator also learns that the military summoned all the villages to the elementary school and killed three hundred of them, including his grandfather, on nearby farms during the Jeju 4.3 events. The two stories are linked through the medium of the murder site. The massacre occurred at Aunt Suni's farm, and she lost consciousness when the military opened fire; when she revived, she found out her two daughters were dead. Since that time, Suni had lived alone, working on her farm, now and then harvesting the remains of the dead and picking up empty bullet shells. Suni lived a miserable life, suffering from nervous prostration and hallucinations and finally committed suicide. The narrator ends his story saying, "Aunt Suni's death is not a recent one but a thirty-year-old death. Although she lived on after the massacre, Suni was killed in her sweet potato field with her two daughters thirty years ago."[44] This suggests that there is only one tragic story of the Jeju 4.3 events—a story of the dead.[45]

Hyun's short story, which was based on the massacre that occurred in Bukchon, marked a critical turning point. Surprisingly, the short story was greeted with acclaim by readers and critics nationwide. Hyun himself was astonished by the unexpected attention his work received, and he became nervous about the popularity as he was concerned that he would be arrested for writing about "such a provocative and radical topic."[46] He admitted to being so afraid that he had sworn to himself, "I will never again write on the Jeju 4.3 events, if only, through the grace of God, this time passes without trouble."[47] Hyun, nevertheless, was arrested by the intelligence agents and was severely beaten for three days and locked up for another twenty days or so until his bruises could disappear. Hyun described his three days of torture as follows:

> I was like a dog in an interrogation room in the basement of the building. It still makes me extremely nervous when I think about the brutal and inhumane beating and whipping that left my whole body covered in ink-colored bruises. Although the pain and bruises disappeared in about two weeks, I still suffer from the mental scars that have haunted me ever since.[48]

Hyun was released, but was arrested again a few months later and locked up for five days and tortured. In both cases, Hyun was released without charges, but his book was soon banned.

Hyun's short story, however, sparked the second round of advocacy, providing further evidence of the persistence and potential of the truth, even in the face of severe suppression. Through "Aunt Suni," lost and suppressed memories were slowly rediscovered, and activists started to realize how important it was to uncover the facts of the Jeju 4.3 events. Hyun's courageous act inspired others who sympathized with his cause to act together, and Hyun himself was encouraged by them. Students, activists, writers, and intellectuals became involved in regular underground study groups, and the first secret memorial service was held in April 1979 at Pastor Lee Jong-weon's house. It also was a period of recruitment and training: most of those who later became key activists were university students at this time and first encountered the Jeju 4.3 events in "Aunt Suni."[49] Intellectuals found "Aunt Suni" both "shocking and shameful," shocking because of the severity of the atrocities and shameful because nothing had been done.[50]

Concurrently, the support for Park's regime slowly declined after a constitutional amendment was passed in 1969 allowing him to run for a third term.[51] After a close win against Kim Dae-jung, Park staged a self-coup in 1972 by dissolving the legislative and judiciary branches and creating an extremely powerful presidency, which allowed the president to be elected indirectly in secret. Students, intellectuals, workers, and churches started to vocally oppose Park's rule. At the same time, the international political and economic environment was unfavorable to Park: two oil crises slowed down the economy, which was the key source of legitimacy for Park's repressive rule; détente in the 1970s threatened Park's emphasis on anti-Communism; and the US president, Jimmy Carter, with his focus on democracy and human rights, seriously challenged Park's dictatorship. The protests started in Busan and Masan and were on the brink of exploding into a national uprising. However, all these movement suddenly stopped when Park was assassinated by his close subordinate in October 1979.

The brief moment of democracy known as the Seoul Spring was followed by another military coup, staged by a clique of army officers led by General Chun Doo-hwan in December 1979. Chun was elected president and pursued anti-Communist, development-oriented, and authoritarian policies. The most violent challenge to yet another military rule occurred in May 1980 in Gwangju in South Jeolla Province. Student demonstrations against the martial law imposed by Chun on 17 May 1980 soon turned into a massive student-worker-citizen uprising, and the military opened fire on the civilians. Popular desire for democracy was blamed on just a few troublemakers sympathetic to the Communist North and was suppressed with brute force, leaving 5,060 victims, including 154 deaths, 70 disappearances, 3,028 injuries, and 1,628 arrests, tortures, and detentions.[52] Under the Chun regime, numerous national and local media outlets were closed down and merged into a small number of outlets for more convenient media control. Many reporters and journalists, especially those opposing continued military rule, lost their positions. At the same time, there was a nationwide sweeping arrest of gangsters and ex-convicts in the name of "the purification of society." Disappearances of students, activists, and dissidents continued.

Chun's authoritarian regime certainly was not a favorable environment for victims and activists. Students, intellectuals, and activists, however, continued studying the Jeju 4.3 events, reading "Aunt Suni." In addition, Merrill published "The Cheju-Do Rebellion" in the *Journal of Korean Studies* in 1980 and provided the first detailed analysis of the Jeju 4.3 events using US government documents.[53] Merrill's article was circulated among students and activists and also provided important background information. At the same time, both journalists and victims embarked on important initiatives during this period. Local journalists, who were silenced by the military and authoritarian regimes, slowly started to disclose the civilian sacrifices during the Jeju 4.3 events. For example, conservative journalists Kang Yong-sam and Lee Gyeong-su, although viewing the Jeju 4.3 events as a Communist rebellion, shifted one step back and reluctantly admitted that there were massacres and human rights abuses of unarmed civilians, though they saw them as mainly committed by the Communist guerrillas and, in only a few inevitable cases, by the police and military.[54] Similarly, Park Seo-dong, editor of *Gwangwang Jeju* (Travel Jeju), started a series of special reports, titled, "4.3: Our Everlasting Pain," investigating almost exclusively the atrocities committed by Communist insurgents. Although these efforts contributed somewhat to revealing the civilian massacres, they strengthened the traditional anti-Communist view by stressing the atrocities committed by the leftist guerrillas, which made up 12 percent of total deaths.

In addition, a small number of victims in Uigui openly made a common burial ground and raised their stone monument in 1983, which marked the first public action taken by victims since 1961. This actually started in 1964 when a few villagers under the leadership of Yang Bong-cheon secretly purchased a mass murder site. Yang, whose father and a brother were buried under the site, and others had secretly taken care of the murder site by creating a fence and covering the site with turf beginning in 1976. Despite objections and obstructions, Yang finally raised a monument inscribed with the words, "A Monument to the Illustrious Memory of the Righteous [*Hyeonui Hapjangmyo*]." When I asked how he was able to do this without fear under the repressive regime, Yang replied:

> My father and my brother were killed during the Jeju 4.3 events at the hands of the military, for sure. I was the only one who survived. I thought someone should do something about it; someone should appease the innocent souls. I had a vision that the Jeju 4.3 events and the mass killings of the innocent civilians would become a historically significant issue in the future. That is why I voluntarily started this. Anyone should have done anything. . . . Of course, there were objections from people. I consistently persuaded them. I persuaded them by assuring them that I will take all the responsibility if things turn ugly. If someone should be beaten and arrested, I will be beaten and arrested.[55]

In his remarks, I found another motivation for his courageous act under repression. It was Yang's consciousness of history, a sense of duty as a survivor, and the firm belief in innocent deaths that made his courageous act possible.

After ruling for seven years, Chun tried to pave the way for a long-term seizure of power by amending the constitution to favor his reelection and obstruct the united opposition party. The constitutional amendment and the death of a university student from drowning during torture, however, united civil society against Chun. Prodemocracy demonstrations initiated by students and opposition leaders spread to the general public, including workers, farmers, churches, and the urban middle class. Students, journalists, and local activists in Jeju who had been involved in the transitional justice advocacy for the Jeju 4.3 events fought hard against Chun in 1987. Due to public pressure, Roh Tae-woo, Chun's proclaimed successor, agreed to have direct presidential elections on 29 June 1987, and this marked the official democratic transition in South Korea.

However, in December 1987 Roh Tae-woo was elected president with 36.6 percent of the total votes, mainly because opposition blocs were not able to agree on a candidate in the presidential election. The opposing power was split between Kim Young-sam (28%) and Kim Dae-jung (27%), who had strong regional platforms in two historically antagonistic southern provinces—South Gyeongsang and South Jeolla. The Roh administration was in a transitional period from authoritarianism to democracy. Certainly the arrival of institutional democracy, which allowed the free, fair, and direct election of the president and other key state offices, was an important change. Despite the formal transition to democracy, however, South Korean society did not change much under President Roh. The police, military, and intelligence agencies were as powerful and obtrusive as during the Chun regime, and incumbent politicians and public officials maintained their positions. Despite this unfavorable political environment, however, students, journalists, and local activists were now ready to open a new chapter in the advocacy campaign.

Lessons Learned

What lessons can we draw from the ups and downs of the transitional period of justice advocacy between 1954 and 1987? The failure of the Congressional Committee in 1960 provides three lessons about the danger of a premature measure. First, if the commissioning body, whether it's the congress or the president or prime minister, has limited tenure remaining, it is highly likely that the truth commission's work will be ineffective and may remain incomplete. Although a truth commission is an independent body, the life and effectiveness of such a commission is closely linked to the body that commissions the investigation. Second, if those who were involved, directly or indirectly, in the past abuses are members of the commissioning body, such a commission is less likely to accomplish its task. Moreover, if a truth commission is established immediately after transition from autocracy, there is a high probability that perpetrators will still exert influence over the commission's activities. In the worst case scenario, those responsible could also be inside the commission itself. Third, once an investigatory commission has been established and disbanded without any substantial results, there is a danger that this failed experience will undermine future efforts. A failed attempt can allow perpetrators to falsely claim that the matter has already been investigated. In other words, past investigations, even if incomplete, can be used as an excuse not to pursue a full-scale and thorough investigation in the future. At the same time, a failed attempt can give the general public the mistaken impression that a full investigation has been carried out and that there is actually not much to be revealed.

On the bright side, the fact that "Aunt Suni" ignited the second phase of the advocacy teaches us about the critical role of culture and story in bringing to light hidden and suppressed past atrocities. Cultural activism brought the forgotten discourses and lost memories back to life. The advocacy almost died out under Park's military dictatorship, and it was a courageous attempt of one writer, Hyun Gi-yeong, and his short story that resuscitated the movement. It was only after reading "Aunt Suni" that concerned individuals started to gather together and act. New generations then started to learn about the Jeju 4.3 events and the terrible pain and suffering of the islanders and decided to devote themselves to finding the truth and restoring justice. Although Hyun did not intend or even foresee this enormous impact, his short story had huge repercussions that finally healed the depressed and shattered hearts of living victims and family members of the dead. It was the relative distance of the cultural sector from governmental suppression and surveillance that provided the conditions that made such a breakthrough possible. Since the political and social realms were completely suppressed and under strict surveillance before the transition to democracy, culture was the only public sphere in which activists had leverage. Because of this relative autonomy, the cultural sphere played a decisive role in leading the advocacy movement over the next twelve years.

3

From Oblivion to Social Attention

> Truthfulness has never been counted among the political virtues, because it has little indeed to contribute to that change of the world and of circumstances which is among the most legitimate political activities. Only where a community has embarked upon organized lying on principle, and not only with respect to particulars, can truthfulness as such, unsupported by the distorting forces of power and interest, become a political factor of the first order. Where everybody lies about everything of importance, the truthteller, whether he knows it or not, has begun to act; he, too, has engaged himself in political business, for, in the unlikely event that he survives, he has made a start toward changing the world.
>
> Hannah Arendt, *"Truth and Politics"*

South Korea, after democratization, had as its first president Roh Tae-woo from 1988 to 1993. Soon after Chun Doo-hwan stepped down, a nationwide focus was given to the 1980 Gwangju massacre for which Chun and Roh bore responsibility. Roh quickly set up a presidential commission to promote "national unity" and "reconciliation." The commission acknowledged that the Gwangju uprising was a prodemocracy movement but opposed any punishments for perpetrators or truth seeking in order not to disrupt "national unity." In response to the creation of the commission, lawmakers set up special hearing sessions in June 1988 and held seventeen hearings, summoning sixty-seven individuals including Chun. It was the first time in South Korean history that a former president was brought into a public hearing and questioned. Despite the sensation, however, the congressional commission suffered innate limitations, partly due to the lack of power to force reluctant perpetrators to come forward and testify and partly due to the lack of political will of Roh and his ruling party. The cases were not transferred to the special court for further prosecution, as the general public expected; Chun simply retired to a hermitage in the Baekdam Temple in Gangweon Province under Roh's protection.

As can be seen from this critical evidence, the overall political environment had not changed that much from the previous Chun regime. Citizens, who had high expectations for the democratic regime, experienced a huge disappointment and saw the period as even more "dark and depressing."[1] Students, activists, and citizens had actively participated in prodemocracy demonstrations against Chun in "hope for a new society but ended up seeing an old society again."[2] Concurrently, Roh pursued various neoliberal economic reforms: fiscal austerity, wage freezes, currency devaluation, and privatization of state enterprises, which increased tension among labor, management, and the state.[3] The demand for freedom, justice, and equality soon spilled over to various sectors—mass media, education, and even public offices. In response, the Roh administration continued the practice of controlling how politically sensitive issues were managed. Thus, the general atmosphere was not amenable to revelations of facts about the Jeju 4.3 events, and the level of repression remained almost constant.[4]

Nevertheless, a mass and public movement started at the local level around three core projects: (1) annual memorial services on every April 3rd including a month-long art festival, (2) special media coverage by local newspapers and television media, and (3) research activities led by volunteers at the Jeju 4.3 Research Institute. The power and resources that had been accumulating underground after the publication of "Aunt Suni" now came to the surface. Local students and intellectuals, social movement activists, and journalists were at the center of these core activities. Although the first victims' association was created in 1988, victims were not the prime movers of the advocacy. In conjunction with these three activities, four changes occurred at the local, national, and international level that facilitated the advocacy process. At the local level, victims and elders started to address the abuses and the material losses caused by the state violence. In addition, national events such as the appearance of the Jeju 4.3 events in a popular TV drama series and the congressional hearings on the Gwangju massacre also helped to facilitate the movement. At the same time, activists and intellectuals started to translate novels and memoirs of the Jeju 4.3 events written in Japan during the military and authoritarian regimes. These efforts reached a climax with the excavation of the Darangshi cave and the discovery of the skeletal remains of eleven civilians killed by the military during the counterinsurgency campaign in December 1948. The discovery and the subsequent advocacy process certainly was a textbook example, not only of effective collaboration among civil society groups, but also of effective government suppression and political maneuvering.

Continuing Suppression and Surveillance

During the Roh regime the level of state repression and social stigmatization remained as high as under the previous Chun regime.[5] The authority closely monitored students, victims, and activists using the local police and intelligence agency and thwarted any attempts to bring up the Jeju 4.3 events and civilian massacres. For instance, Song Yeong-ran, president of the local student association, was arrested immediately after she put posters around the Jeju National University campus demanding government investigation of the massacres. In addition, a public memorial service in 1991 ended up as a violent street rally and led to the indiscriminate arrest of four hundred student and activist protesters in one day.[6] Furthermore, whenever victims or activists had a gathering of more than three persons, local policemen or intelligence agents were present and closely monitored the activities.[7]

In addition, publications were also strictly censored, similar to the case of "Aunt Suni" in the previous regimes. In 1987 Lee San-ha published an epic poem entitled *Mt. Halla* (Hallasan), which made the Jeju 4.3 events and state violence a popular talking point among students and activists around the country. As a result, Lee was arrested on charges of violating the National Security Law, and his poem was banned. Similarly, Kim Myeong-sik published an important edited book titled *The Jeju People's Movement* (Jeju Minjung Hangjaeng) in 1987, which, for the first time, introduced the 1963 memoir of Kim Bong-hyeon, a former Communist Party member, and Kim Min-ju, a former Communist insurgent, written in Japanese.[8] The authors documented the process of the armed uprising in detail, based on extensive interviews with people who had taken refuge in Japan. Similar to the situation for Lee, Kim also was arrested on the charge of violation of the National Security Law and sentenced to prison. Although Lee and Kim were not subjected to torture and beating, unlike Hyun Gi-yeong, their convictions betrayed the arrival of a new democratic era.

Finally, all attempts to find the facts and restore justice, even when made by a respected member of the National Assembly, were dismissed without consideration or even without much justification. Immediately after democratization, congressmen who represented the popular demands of the islanders urged the government to undertake a reinvestigation.[9] In a delayed response to the congressmen, the minister of internal affairs, Ahn Eung-mo, two years later dismissed their request and stated, "Jeju 4.3 events and crimes committed in the course of the events are already legally concluded and the government investigation at this time is not desirable."[10] Here, Ahn was repeating the previous excuse used by the chair of the Congressional Committee in 1960 that the statute of limitations for the murder in case of the Jeju 4.3 events had already expired. The minister represented the popular and dominant view of the Jeju 4.3 events among high-level public officials.

On the other hand, social stigmatization of the Jeju 4.3 events and the victims continued in various forms. In 1988 the first victims' association, the Anti-Communist Association for the Civilian Victims' Families of the Jeju 4.3 Events, was created. As the word, "Anti-Communist" in the name manifests, it was victims of the leftist guerrillas who launched the association. The chair of the association, Song Weon-hwa, lost his father to the insurgents, and he himself was injured. The victims of state violence, however, either refrained from joining the association or joined but "simply kept silent and followed the anti-Communist leadership."[11] Similar to the anti-Communist investigation by conservative journalists in the 1980s, anti-Communist victims' associations had more of a negative effect than a positive one. Even though it was the first victims' association, it simultaneously strengthened the orthodox anti-Communist view of the Jeju 4.3 events and helped to sustain the social stigma associated with victims of state violence.[12] Some speculated that the anti-Communist victims' association was "a government-patronized one, which was established in order to counterattack the transitional justice advocacy."[13]

The other example of stigmatization can be clearly seen in an incident that occurred at the Korean Broadcasting System (KBS) in 1990. The station announced that a three-part documentary on contemporary history, in which the Jeju 4.3 events were the first theme, would be aired, but the broad of directors decided not to release the series at the very last minute.

Reporters and labor unions vehemently protested the decision, but the decision has not been revoked.

As we have seen in a series of examples, the Jeju 4.3 events were still portrayed as a Communist rebellion, and the majority of victims were viewed as Communists. Institutional democratization did not necessarily change the forty-year-old dominant perspective. Moreover, since the new administration was headed by the remnants of the previous regime, the change was very slow. The South Korean democratization is understood as a negotiated or "pact" transition in which old and new elites arrange a compromise. Samuel P. Huntington has argued that under this circumstance accountability is less likely and that the demand for truth and justice will decrease over time.[14] Huntington's prediction, however, is not entirely correct in the South Korean case in that key breakthroughs were made in the period of negotiated transition. In addition, contrary to his prediction, the demand for justice did not subside but increased over time. Huntington was right in predicting the difficulties of the advocacy under a negotiated transition, but he underestimated the power of civil society to correct past wrongs.

Three Early Projects

Annual Memorial Services

With democratization, various nongovernmental organizations were created in Jeju to focus on labor, human rights, national unification, the environment, farmers, women, social justice, culture, political reform, and transitional justice issues. The first two years were a period of laying the groundwork through establishing institutional foundations. The mainstay of these organizations were those students and activists who secretly studied the Jeju 4.3 events. Every social movement organization in Jeju attached great importance to the Jeju 4.3 events; the initial uprising against the misrule of the US occupation forces and the resistance against the separate election in the South was a model for the later democratization movement. Moreover, it was almost impossible for local NGOs to be effective in Jeju without fully understanding the deep impact of the Jeju 4.3 events on every corner of Jeju society.

In April 1988, only four months after Roh was elected president, students and activists secretly planned the first public memorial service to appease the ghosts of victims and to commemorate the fortieth anniversary of the uprising of 3 April 1948 against the US military government. The local police, however, detected the plan, arrested leaders, and frustrated the action. Thus, instead of a province-wide memorial service, only two small gatherings took place: one at Jeju National University and the other in Tokyo. Despite the police interference, the Jeju Student Association carried out the original plan to have an open and public memorial service. On 3 April 1988, students held a memorial service on campus and took to the streets demanding a government investigation. This marked the first public commemoration and political rally, which became a yearly tradition.

On the same day, around five hundred Korean Japanese originally from Jeju created an organization, the Association of People Remembering Jeju 4.3, and held a public memorial service in Tokyo.[15] It was the first memorial service held outside Jeju, and it also became an annual event in Japan. Interestingly, this small gathering in Tokyo had a lasting impact on the trajectory of the advocacy because students who participated in the memorial services become key leaders of the later movement. For example, Kang Chang-il served as a director of the Jeju 4.3 Research Institute and is currently a congressman representing Jeju Province, and Kim Myeong-sik published important books on the Jeju 4.3 events and participated in the establishment of the Jeju 4.3 Research Institute.

In the following year, the authority permitted the first public memorial service organized by local NGOs, including the Jeju 4.3 Research Institute, the Jeju Student Association, and the Jeju Cultural Movement Association. Despite the authority's unenthusiastic permission, it was a rocky path. Leaders were constantly shadowed and exposed to frequent unexpected visits by intelligence agents.[16] The police arrested leaders with absurd charges in order to frustrate and complicate plans. Hyun Gi-yeong, author of "Aunt Suni," was scheduled to deliver a lecture, but he could not come because the police detained him for a few days in Seoul. Similarly, Ahn Sa-in, who was scheduled to lead the traditional ritual ceremony, could not come as he was forcibly locked in his hotel room in Busan. Oh Seung-guk, president of the Jeju Literary Society, was arrested because one of the poems publicly displayed contained "the first name" of the insurgent leader Lee Deok-gu.[17] Despite the obstacles, activists managed to host the first province-wide ceremony, which marked the "manifestation of civil society power."[18] In other words, prior to 1989, the movement was mainly led by a few individuals, but with this memorial service the movement truly became a mass movement.[19] Kang Deok-hwan, a reporter who closely followed the earlier movement, stated: "The year 1989, with the first April memorial service, was the first year of mass public movement."[20]

Since 1989 a public memorial service has been held every April 3rd in Jeju. Memorial services have been more than a mere one-day ceremonial event. Delegates from every NGO in Jeju have participated in creating a temporary body called the Preparation Committee for the April Memorial Service every year and spend at least two months together preparing the memorial service. The Jeju 4.3 Research Institute and the Jeju Cultural Movement Association have played a leading role as they focus most exclusively on the Jeju 4.3 events.[21] Activists from various NGOs gather to discuss the Jeju 4.3 events and share effective advocacy strategies. This network of local NGOs that led to a sharing of human resources, expertise, information, tactics, and strategies was one of the important keys to the success of advocacy during the next ten years. Annual collaboration helped to form "a common identity among activists," which facilitated effective communication and burden sharing among the various NGOs.[22]

Memorial services were also accompanied by art festivals, which made the Jeju 4.3 events and massacres known to the general public. The art festival lasted about a month before the memorial service and comprised an art exhibit, traditional plays, a literature night, testimony hearings, a film and documentary exhibition, musical concerts, and a ceremony of traditional ritual. As we have seen in the case of "Aunt Suni," art and literature have long played a significant role in the advocacy. Through public display and performance, the arts enhanced public awareness and disseminated "alternative memories or discourses" to the official narratives of the Jeju 4.3 events as a Communist rebellion[23] Alternative messages or beliefs, which cannot easily be communicated in words, can be "subtly expressed in the form of art and culture in the public sphere."[24] It was the role of the arts that drew the Jeju 4.3 events near to the public, and this role became even more significant when activists tried to influence a national audience.

Media

Local media also played a key role in discovering, recreating, and popularizing an alternative discourse of the Jeju 4.3 events. The local newspaper was particularly effective in opening the tightly sealed mouths of the victims, who were still afraid of state repression and social stigma. It all started when sixteen reporters for the *Jeju Sinmun* (Jeju daily) planned a serial report on the Jeju 4.3 events, titled "Testimonies of 4.3," and set up a 4.3 reporting team headed by Yang Jo-hoon in March 1988. The original plan was to collect news materials for a month and publish in April, following a routine for news coverage.[25] However, after the preliminary investigation, the reporters decided to postpone publication for one year because the breadth and depth of the Jeju 4.3 events were beyond imagination. Many of Yang's close friends, colleagues, and family members tried to dissuade him from unearthing the past, warning that his entire career could go astray.[26] Yang struggle for a couple of weeks but made up his mind after a mysterious experience:

> For about a month, I suffered nightmares and was haunted by the ghosts who tried to choke me almost every night. One night in my dream, I had a mysterious experience of the rumbling of the earth. So terrified, I shouted, "I will do it!" and then I fell off from my bed. Since then, I have had no more nightmares, and I have peace in my mind. I firmly believe that it was a supernatural experience in which the ghosts of the 4.3 victims were involved.[27]

Immediately after the first report was published on 3 April 1989, the police and intelligence agency started to "pressure the board of directors claiming that the reportage disturbs social stability by raking up already concluded history."[28] The managing editor, Song Sang-il, had to submit a written note to the broad of directors that he would resign if anything went wrong because of the report. In addition, after every publication of the report, police visited the village and asked witnesses whether the information published in the newspaper was exactly consistent with what they had testified. If any minor misinformation was found, the police were prepared to investigate the newspaper and reporters; intelligence agents were ready to incite witnesses to sue the newspaper on the charge of libel, which was a popular strategy to frustrate the opposition.[29] Ironically, obstruction and interference ultimately resulted in more objective, reliable, and fact-based reportage. Yang and his team adopted stringent fact-checking measures and strictly follow the procedures:

> Only 10 percent of materials that we collected were able to be published because we had to go through a very strict cross-checking process before writing reports. What we have published in the newspaper was only the tip of the iceberg. The other 90 percent of facts and testimonies buttressed what we published. This is one strong reason why the authorities could not easily interfere with our reports. Our reportage was firmly and strictly fact based.[30]

The experience of meticulous fact checking and cross-checking continued later when Yang Jo-hoon and Kim Jong-min led the team of experts under the Jeju Commission. This practice led to the establishment of the objectivity of the commission's report, which further contributed to the effectiveness of the commission.

Governmental repression, however irksome, was not the most difficult obstacle, Yang recollects. Victims' tightly sealed mouths as the result of the "red complex" was the most difficult impediment to ascertaining the facts:

> It was difficult to find witnesses who actually were alive and had seen the massacres. It was even more difficult to find those who were willing to testify. No one was willing to testify. People would not let us take our shoes off in front of their houses; oftentimes, elders were ready to talk, but their spouses dissuaded them. In many cases, we had elderly witnesses who were willing to testify to anything except their own stories.[31]

Occasionally, witnesses reversed their testimonies after the release of the report. One witness from Donggwang village testified that residents, including his parents, were killed by the military. As soon as the report was out the witness and other victims were immediately cut-off from a government subsidy they received. What the witness did not know was that he and other victims were falsely registered as victims of Communist guerillas and thus had been receiving a government subsidy on that basis.

However, the series of special reports suddenly halted in January 1990 after only fifty-seven reports. A conflict between workers who were trying to create a labor union and management ended with closing down of the newspaper in January 1990.[32] As a result, 110 reporters and staff inevitably lost their jobs, and the 4.3 reporting team was also dissolved. Journalists successfully launched a new newspaper, the *Jemin Ilbo* (Jemin daily), by soliciting contributions from citizens and journalists nationwide. This much-respected local newspaper began to publish a biweekly report on the Jeju 4.3 events starting in its first issue on 30 June 1990, under the series title "4.3 Speaks." Reporters who were now with the *Jemin Ilbo* wanted to convey two important messages with the new title. First, they used "4.3" without labels such as "uprising" or "rebellion" in order to show their neutrality. A few reporters strongly demanded that Jeju 4.3 events be defined as a democratic uprising, but Yang objected to the idea because he believed that the definition of the Jeju 4.3 events should come after the facts were established.[33] Second, reporters made an intentional grammar error by using the "4.3" as a subject and not as an object in the sentence, suggesting it is not reporters but the facts of the Jeju 4.3 events themselves that reveal the truth.[34] The *Jemin Ilbo* published 456 reports over nine years, based on interviews with three thousand witnesses. This extensive reportage played an indispensable role in the advocacy process by discovering the truth. Reporters discovered critical facts, documents, and testimonies, and made the Jeju 4.3 events an important social issue. Both Yang Jo-hoon and Kim Jong-min, two key reporters, later worked for the Jeju Commission and transmitted their expertise and knowledge. The majority of new facts established in the commission's report came from their earlier investigation. The coverage was also effective in inducing victims to participate.[35]

The local broadcast company, the Jeju Munhwa Broadcasting Cooperation (MBC), also played a role in making the Jeju 4.3 events known to the public. The news director, Lee Mun-gyo, who was a student leader in the 1960s, made a documentary that was aired on 2 April 1989 titled, *The Sorrow of Contemporary Korean History*: *The Jeju 4.3 Events* (4.3 Gihoek: Hyeondaesa-eui Keun Sangcheo).[36] The Jeju MBC aired special programs every year and became "the major producer of the TV image of the Jeju 4.3 events."[37] With these efforts, victims and the public slowly started to see the possibility of a long-time taboo being broken. The level of testimonies, openness, and welcome gradually increased with the news reports and media images. The media exposure and victims' engagement had an escalating effect: the news reports became more and more accurate as the testimonies increased, and in turn victims became bolder and bolder since what they had been afraid to talk about was now out in the public.[38] However, this process was not without obstacles. Conservative media watered down the *Jemin Ilbo*'s reports either by publishing objections or carrying stories about the abuses committed by Communist guerillas.

Research

The role of researchers in the advocacy process was crucial since almost a half a century had passed and the consecutive anti-Communist regimes systematically destroyed the evidence. A few intellectuals and journalists in Seoul set up the Research Group for the Issues in Jeju Society in 1987.[39] This was a group composed of members of the elite originally from Jeju—professors (Jung Yun-hyeong), journalists (Ko Hee-beom), and writers (Kim Myeong-sik, Hyun Gi-yeong). Unlike others who forgot the Jeju 4.3 events after having successful careers, these intellectuals believed in "the historical significance" of the events.[40] The first project they took on was hosting a conference in Seoul on 3 April 1988; they were also invited to the conference in Jeju three months later, and they filled the Jeju Young Men's Christian Association (YMCA) auditorium to overflowing.[41] Even the national newspapers covered these conferences and demanded a governmental investigation.[42]

After the success of these conferences, the Research Group proposed creating a research institute specializing in the Jeju 4.3 events. At the same time, in Jeju, local historians (Moon Mu-byeong), teachers (Kim Chang-hu, Lee Seok-mun), and activists (Yang Seong-ja) had been secretly collecting testimonies about the Jeju 4.3 events.[43] In May 1989, with one year of preparation, the Jeju 4.3 Research Institute was created on the foundation of material resources and expertise of two devoted groups: people in Seoul who contributed the seed money and those in Jeju who did most of groundwork.[44] The Research Institute was the idea of the Research Group in Seoul, but it was local activists who maintained and nurtured the organization. In the early years, it was difficult to pay for personnel (there was only one paid staff member), office supplies, publishing costs, and rent. Every December, which was when the annual rent in Jeju was due, the office was "virtually empty because everyone had to visit his friends for contributions."[45] If volunteers—teachers and ordinary citizens working in private and public sectors—had not devoted their time and energy, the success of the Research Institute would have been unlikely.[46]

The first report of the Jeju 4.3 Research Institute, *Now I Speak* (Ijesa Malhaemsuda), was published in 1989. Since there were virtually no written records known at this time, activists heavily relied on the testimonies of victims. Researchers encountered the exactly same obstacles with the witnesses—silence:

> It took a year to finish *Now I Speak*, which was a two-volume report based on testimonies. It was extremely difficult to collect testimonies from victims, so we first went to the elders in the village. But still, we had to spend long hours chatting on other issues such as weather, agriculture, economy, politics and so on in order to get a few sentences on the Jeju 4.3 events.[47]

The main goal of the Research Institute was to find information and disseminate this information through newsletters, articles, and reports. Anything that was remotely related to the Jeju 4.3 events was collected, translated, and published. In the course of research, highly significant but rare documents, such as copies of the *Jeju Sinbo* from January 1947 to April 1948, a US military documentary film, posters and fliers used during the 4.3 events, were collected. The Research Institute then conducted history classes, organized annual conferences, and led annual field trips to the historic places and mass murder sites. Finally, the Research Institute took a leading role in the transitional justice advocacy, as we have already seen in the case of the annual memorial service. With these research and advocacy activities, "it became almost impossible to discuss the advocacy history without considering the role of the 4.3 Research Institute."[48]

Other Facilitators

Three core activities—memorial services, media coverage, and research—were closely connected and had a synergistic effect. The memorial services, art festivals, and research activities led by activists were significantly covered in the local newspaper, and reporters depended on researchers for information. The discovery of copies of the *Jeju Sinbo* (1947–48) is a clear example. The Research Institute first obtained the newspaper, and it significantly helped reporters to fill in details in their special biweekly reports about the Jeju 4.3 events. In turn, reporters' detailed analysis of the pre-1948 period provided important background information about conditions before the outbreak of the armed uprising and helped researchers define the characteristics of the Jeju 4.3 events. Moreover, there were four other factors that facilitated the early advocacy process.

First, with democratization, victims started to investigate civilian massacres at the community level in Jeju. The first attempt was made at Gasi village in 1988 when elders launched an investigation that revealed that 374 residents were killed and 12 were missing after a military operation in the village in 1948. Elders reported this record in the village newsletter—*Gaseureum*—in order to "pass the exact history to the descendants."[49] Elders in Tosan and Josu villages made a similar effort and collected information of the dead and recorded it as a village history.[50] Victims in Bukchon, the village that was the model for the setting of "Aunt Suni," petitioned for a government investigation, and individuals, mainly writers such as Oh Seong-chan and Han Lim-hwa, privately interviewed victims and published their interviews.[51] Descendants of victims of mass murder in Weondong village filed a lawsuit claiming lost lands of their murdered parents, which mysteriously had been transferred to a different person during the military regimes. The court finally ruled in favor of the family, and the properties were restored to them.[52]

Second, despite the limitations of the congressional hearing on the Gwangju massacres, the process of the truth-seeking effort and the sensation that having former president Chun on the witness stand had a significant impact on Jeju. The hearing continued for six months, and every session was nationally televised. Not only perpetrators but also victims and their families were invited to testify about deaths, losses, and damages. Victims in Jeju certainly sympathized with Gwangju victims who had experienced similar state violence and who had been falsely accused of being Communists. Nevertheless, the number of those killed in Gwangju was only one hundredth as many as those killed in Jeju, and the years of stigmatization and discrimination was one sixth as long. Reporters who were interviewing victims in Jeju at this time sensed the change in victims' attitude: "Victims and witnesses started to open up their mouths after watching the testimonies of Gwangju victims."[53] One reporter noticed that victims often opened their first sentence by saying, "The Gwangju hearing is a huge issue nowadays, but Gwangju is nothing, absolutely nothing, compared to what happened in Jeju."[54]

Third, the Jeju 4.3 events, which had long been taboo to mention, were addressed for the first time in the popular television historical drama series *Eyes of Dawn* (*Yeomyeong-eui Nundongja*) in 1992. Many interviewees have told me that the screening of these episodes was considered highly sensational. It was sensational in three respects. First, the television series in question was a particularly popular one that constantly had an audience rating of 50 percent or more. Second, the Jeju 4.3 events were the main theme of the drama across four episodes, which screened over a two-week period. Third, the Jeju 4.3 events were not portrayed in these episodes from the dominant anti-Communist perspective; rather, the screenwriter had tried to treat both ideological perspectives fairly. In other words, the episodes touched on the Jeju 4.3 events not only as a Communist rebellion but also in terms of human rights abuses and a democratic uprising, through the eyes of the characters. Some of the lines delivered by Jeju residents in the drama included: "We are facing either starving to death or being beaten to death. Even the meekest of creatures will retaliate if pushed too far"; "Why do the members of the rightist youth group use violence against us? The police are protecting and using these groups and there is an American at the top"; and "Will the government treat three hundred thousand Jeju residents as enemies simply to destroy a few Communists?" These words reflected a perspective that had not previously been aired in public arenas such as politics, education, or the media.

What made this change possible? One answer lies in the screenwriter, Song Ji-na, who had spent about four years in high school in Jeju. In an interview with a local newspaper, Song explained that she had a desire to tackle the issue as a screenwriter, but it was difficult to create a standalone drama. Song, and later the show's producer, admitted that the flow of the drama had actually been compromised by the inclusion of the Jeju 4.3 events. Nevertheless, both screenwriter and producer had decided to sacrifice the artistic values of the drama in order to reveal this historic injustice.[55] This came through clearly in Song's interview:

> People criticized me for raking up the tragic past. However, I thought that it was my duty as a screenwriter to address a past history of injustice, if it really existed. I believe the only way to prevent historical wrongs from repeating themselves over and over again in the future is through the investigation and thorough study of what went wrong in the past.[56]

However, Song's will and desire were not the only contributing factors. Song has acknowledged that these episodes of the drama would not have been possible if not for the efforts of journalists from the *Jemin Ilbo*, who provided the factual details on which the episodes were based. Thus, the programs were a collaborative effort between the local media and one courageous screenwriter.

Finally, the winds of change were blowing in from across the borders, especially from Korean Japanese who were originally from Jeju.[57] Korean communities in Japan provided a refuge for people fleeing Jeju during the Jeju 4.3 events, and they served as a repository of written records, memories, and alternative discourses. This was crucial, because the South Korean government systematically destroyed any evidence of the Jeju 4.3 events. Thus, records, memories, and narratives created and maintained in Japan played an important role in the early phase of advocacy. For example, in 1957, Kim Seok-beom, a Korean Japanese writer, published a novel, *The Death of a Crow*, based on the Jeju 4.3 events and also wrote *A Volcanic Island*, which was serialized in a major Japanese newspaper over twenty years. Kim wrote constantly on the theme of the Jeju 4.3 events, and his work was read widely, not only by Korean Japanese but also by the Japanese public. In 1963 another important book, *A History of the Jeju People's 4.3 Armed Struggle* by Kim Bong-hyeon and Kim Min-ju, was published in Japan. All these books were translated immediately after democratization and became popular and served as key historical records.[58]

Excavation of the Darangshi Cave, 1992

An epoch-making event occurred on 2 April 1992 when local and national media broke the news about the discovery of the remains of eleven civilians in the Darangshi cave. Since Jeju is a volcanic island, natural caves are abundant, and local residents used these caves as places of refuge during the conflict. Members of the 4.3 Research Institute (Kim Gi-sam, Kim Dong-man, Kim Eun-hee, and two others) first discovered the cave on 22 December 1991 during a research trip to find destroyed villages.[59] The researchers planned a trip in hopes of finding some evidence of massacres because it was rumored that the remains of bodies were still left in some caves.[60] Thus, the discovery was not a coincidence but a result of activists' ardent desire to find evidence. Researchers went near the cave with an eyewitness, Moon Eun-cheol, who was at the scene during the "counterinsurgency operation." However, despite his confidence, Moon was confused and could not find the cave for about an hour. Everyone was tired and taking a break when Kim Dong-man spotted a small entrance to the cave.[61] Kim Dong-man and Kim Gi-sam caught a glimpse of the remains in the cave, but they kept it secret from Moon lest the information be leaked. The research team was extremely cautious not to make the find public until they could obtain full information and could go back to the cave two days later, where they found eleven skeletal remains.[62]

After three months of deliberation, members of the Research Institute headed by professor Ko Chang-hoon decided to break the news on 3 April 1992. In the meantime, activists in Seoul and Jeju planned to excavate the cave and undertake other follow-up measures. Ko was excited by the anticipation that the truth would be revealed and justice restored. On the other hand, he had mixed feelings because he and his research team could get in big trouble.[63] Ko had sleepless nights and was able to sleep only with the help of alcohol.[64] His diary shows his distress:

> I struggled hard after knowing that the research team had discovered the cave. Four questions kept haunting me every moment. First, do the skeletal remains we found in the cave really belong to the victims of the Jeju 4.3 events? Second, will it be possible to have an objective inspection of the scene without interference from the authorities? Third, will it be possible for us to find witnesses? Finally, after almost four decades, will it be possible to find the family members or relatives of the victims?[65]

Kim Eun-hee, who was at the scene of the discovery, also testified that members were "excited to find evidence but also terrified not knowing what would happen next."[66]

Concurrently, researchers started to work with local activists and journalists in order to overcome the government's interference and obstruction. The Research Institute made one more investigation of its own on 22 March 1992 and then invited reporters from the *Jemin Ilbo* to visit the cave a week later. The collaboration of the two groups again had a synergistic effect and solved one of the four questions Ko worried about. Reporters already had a report covering the surrounding villages and had a list of witnesses who testified to the military operation near the cave. Chae Jeong-ok, who also took refuge near the cave, was invited and gave an accurate testimony of the massacre. Another question was solved: the remains were from 1948, and it was certain that the victims were unarmed civilians murdered in an indiscriminate operation. Researchers and local journalists again realized the gravity of their findings and decided to undertake a full-scale investigation. On 1 April 1992, the final investigation was conducted with experts including a doctor (Chun Sin-gweon), a lawyer (Choi Byeong-mo), a historian (Lee Cheong-gyu), and reporters from national media—the *Donga Ilbo*, the *Hankyoreh*, and the MBC.

Expert investigation and testimonies revealed that nineteen civilians from Jongdal and Hado villages who took the refuge in the cave were all killed on 18 December 1948 in the course of a full-scale sweeping operation. Oh Ji-bong, who participated in the military operation, and Chae Jeong-ok, who took refuge in the cave, gave consistent testimonies. Chae lived with the families in the cave but narrowly escape death because he was hiding in another cave at the time of the massacre. The military first found several people outside the cave and killed them on the spot and then ordered those in the cave to come out. However, villagers inside saw those outside shot to death and refused to come out; the military threw in a few grenades and eventually set a fire with dried grass and suffocated everyone in the cave.[67] The dead comprised three who were under ten years old, three who were over fifty, and four women and nine men between twenty and forty-nine.[68] The victims were unarmed civilians, primarily a couple with their children and their parents.[69]

The revelations made the headlines in every newspaper and television in Jeju, and the national news media also gave it significant coverage. This was the first time that the Jeju 4.3 events were ever covered in depth by national media since the occurrence of the events in 1948. The remains of the dead that included children, women, and old people provided sufficient evidence of indiscriminate killing. This was the first evidence of the massacre that was vividly presented to the general public. The fifty-year-old events, which had been almost forgotten, now came back to life though the bones of the bodies in the cave. Most of all, the authorities—mainly the police and intelligence agency—were dumbfound by the news. The police had no idea about the cave until professor Ko informed the local police chief a couple of hours before the news out of "courtesy."[70]

It really "put 2,500 Jeju local police to shame," the chief of Jeju police said in a private conversation with Ko.[71]

As expected, the police reaction was rapid: they immediately investigated the cave and then interviewed those who were involved in the counterinsurgency operation. They hurriedly announced that the cave was a hiding place for Communist guerillas who committed suicide when they were discovered by the military.[72] However, police information turned out to be false when their key witness (Moon Eun-cheol, who also accompanied the research team but could not find the cave) gave inconsistent testimony.[73] The evidence—the remains of children and elderly and the absence of any arms—also did not back up the official interpretation. The next steps for both activists and the police were clear. Even though the first round was a complete defeat for the authorities, they had a relative advantage over activists in the second round. Activists wanted to find and organize the families of victims to hold a public funeral ceremony and to create a common burial ground with a stone monument to commemorate the dead.[74] Local NGOs, politicians, and religious leaders formed the preparation committee for the funeral on 21 April, and the families and relatives of victims decided to have a common burial ground.

However, the police had their own plan: they wanted the process to be over as quickly as possible, with no public funeral and with discussion about the cave stopped immediately. As a first step, the police sealed the entrance of the cave with cement and declared the place a restricted area. Then, they set up a separate funeral committee composed of four state officials, two elders, and two victims' family members, and decided to cremate the remains and sprinkle the ashes in the ocean. One reporter wrote that everything went so quickly, just like it was pushed by an "invisible hand."[75] In the course, a couple of bereft family members, such as Ko Gwang-eon whose father was murdered, objected to the idea and asked for "one piece of the bones" so that he could have a tomb of his deceased father, but his request was denied.[76] After cremation, he again asked for "one eleventh of the ashes," but again the police rejected it.[77] They even staked out inside one of victims' houses lest "activists try to come and persuade them."[78] Mysterious interference continued on the day of the funeral. Without notice, the funeral process, which started with collecting the remains of the dead from the cave, shifted one hour ahead of the original schedule. Not only the local media, activists, and politicians but also families of victims could not come in time. The ashes of the dead were sprinkled in the nearby water, and the funeral processes concluded as the authorities desired.

In response to the manipulative interference of the police, activists organized a province-wide rally to commemorate the death of the victims. Nevertheless, the police again forestalled the civil society's attempt, and only a limited campus gathering was allowed instead of the original plan. Professor Ko kept a record of the threat made by the local police chief:

> Would you please stop acting on the Darangshi cave? Haven't you already achieved a lot from discovering the cave? Wasn't the discovery much more effective than writing one hundred books and organizing one hundred rallies? Please don't go any further this time . . . please. . . . I really have to arrest you if you insist on acting on this. . . . And, you will suffer . . . and suffer a lot . . . a lot. I guarantee it. . . . Please retract the rally and commemoration.[79]

Interestingly, in his threat, the police chief revealed the significance of the Darangshi cave. The event and its coverage actually had a more significant impact than "one hundred books and one hundred rallies." It was certainly the most epochal event since Hyun Gi-yeong's "Aunt Suni" in 1978.

The Darangshi cave brought the advocacy to "another level."[80] It transformed the advocacy from mainly students, activists, and journalists to the general public by revealing evidence of real brutal and gruesome state violence. Since the Jeju 4.3 events and massacres had been taboo, there had been no clear evidence to "show the Jeju 4.3 events," and the Darangshi cave "revealed the reality of the Jeju 4.3 events."[81] These revelations especially affected two groups of people who played a significant role in the next phases of the advocacy, that is, the victims and the local public. Victims who had already started to act together and openly after the democratization became even more courageous, since the cave demonstrated exactly the same state violence they had been subjected to. On the other hand, ordinary citizens in Jeju did not know about and had not been interested in the forty-year-old events. With the news, however, once forgotten history became an important contemporary social issue in Jeju, and the public started to express their anger at the unjustified abuse of the state's power. Activists now secured critical allies for the advocacy, and the victims' participation and the local public support become the basis for three key activities in the next phase: the united memorial service, a province-wide investigation, and the petition movement.

In addition, the Darangshi cave revelations not only affected victims and the public but also had a deep impact on researchers, activists, and journalists themselves. Although researchers had been passionately searching for concrete evidence of massacres, the discovery of the cave, when it actually happened, came as quite a shock to them. The discovery and the following intervention by the authorities changed activists in two ways. First, the cave and the subsequent truths revealed by the investigation consolidated activists' belief that the tragedy of the Jeju 4.3 events was mainly caused by the abuse of state power. This, in consequence, strengthened their commitment to the transitional justice advocacy movement and thus empowered activists and their organizational platforms. Second, activists themselves experienced a dimension of state violence when the police prevented a proper funeral process. Activists were frustrated because a similar abuse of state power was still ongoing under "the democratic regime" in the form of surveillance and suppression. These two reactions created the momentum for the next phase of the advocacy. Activists, who were now even more confident in their cause and who had secured strong support from victims and the local public, began to work with the local government to make a change.

The Resilience of Truth

The advocacy between 1987 and 1992 has many parallels with that of previous years under the authoritarian system. First, it was students who first acted immediately after the democratization in 1987 as students did in 1960 after the fall of the Rhee Syng-man dictatorship. Students were the first ones to hold a public memorial service in Jeju, have a street rally, and organize the local conference in 1988. Second, as Shin Du-bang and the *Jeju Sinbo* had been one of two pillars of the advocacy in 1960, reporters of the *Jemin Ilbo* and their special report, "4.3 Speaks," were indispensable elements of the post-1987 advocacy. Third, the cultural sector continued to create the images and narratives that contributed to melting down frozen hearts and minds of victims and communicating with the general public. Fine arts and literature remained an integral part of the movement, but the new pop culture including songs, plays, documentary films, and TV drama series were also now part of it. Finally, a few courageous victims who were always one step ahead of others also took the lead in this phase. Pioneers privately investigated the massacres in their villages, came first to testify for the newspaper or researchers, and filed a lawsuit to get their parents' property back.

There also was a new and meaningful change. Most of all, the discovery of the Darangshi cave was a victory with its indisputable evidence that tipped the scale in favor of activists. For over forty years, previous regimes had been systematically destroying evidence and intimidating victims to shut their mouths. Under these conditions, even the testimonies of victims were sometimes ineffective since the public had been educated to accept the government's perspective and not to be deceived by "Communist agitation." The whole society had been built on the ground of forced oblivion and distorted understanding. Concrete and indisputable evidence of the remains of eleven civilians was the most effective way to defeat the endless objections and threats to the advocacy. The Darangshi cave opened a new chapter in the advocacy because activists became acutely aware of the importance of evidence. In the next two phases of advocacy, critical evidence reappeared and helped activists make a breakthrough.

However, the Darangshi cave also left another important lesson. There is a stark similarity in the government reaction to the transitional justice advocacy in 1961 and that of 1992. The military regime tore down and destroyed the stone monument in 1961. Likewise, the authorities in 1992 wanted to minimize the impact of the Darangshi cave. They made the funeral process be rapid, private, and quiet; the remains of the dead were cremated and sprinkled in the ocean; and the entrance of the cave was sealed and buried. What the authority did not know is that as they tried harder and harder to efface the facts, the brutality of the state power was revealed more and more openly. Another layer of state violence was added on top of the original atrocity. The Park Chung-hee regime, after the coup in 1961, attempted to completely erase all the traces by destroying the burial grounds, shattering stone monuments, and digging up and burning the remains of the dead. Ironically, the result was that the victims fought harder and harder not to forget what the authorities did to them and even built a memorial out of the broken pieces of the stone monument. Facts become more and more resilient as the authorities destroyed them more and more completely.

Exactly the same thing happened with the Darangshi cave. Frustrated by the government's reaction, activists, mainly artists, made the Darangshi cave into a symbol of the Jeju 4.3 events and also of government suppression. The cave now revealed not only the initial atrocity in 1948 but also the government suppression afterward. As Kim Dong-man explained to me:

> The Darangshi cave symbolized the status of the Jeju 4.3 events and civilian massacres. Forty-year-old corpses were still lying in the cold Darangshi cave unattended.... This represented the status of the transitional justice advocacy in 1992, which was still being suppressed. The corpses in the Darangshi cave became a critical symbol showing that the Jeju 4.3 events had not yet been resolved and should be resolved soon.[82]

Moreover, due to this symbolic significance, a replica of the Darangshi cave is now located at the very center of the Jeju 4.3 Peace Memorial Park. In contrast to the hopes of the authorities in 1992, the Darangshi cave survived in the hearts and minds of activists. Furthermore, now it will live in the museum indefinitely, embodying not only the original murder of 1948 but also the attempted murder of the truth in 1992.

4

The Struggle of the Periphery

With the arrival of a fledgling institutional democracy in 1987, civil society required substantial changes to consolidate it. One of the key needs was the decentralization of state power, which had been concentrated in the president under the dictatorial and authoritarian regimes. First, the opposition party and civil society demanded separation of legislative, administrative, and judicial authority. A few demanded adoption of the parliamentary system in order to minimize the exploitation of presidential power, as the Second Republic did after the fall of the Rhee dictatorship. Another need was to transfer some state power to local governments, reinstituting a regional self-governing system, which had been abolished with the military coup of 1961. The Roh administration revived the local councils in December 1991, but the new era of self-governing was not complete because Roh refused to give up executive power and indefinitely postponed local elections.

The end of the Cold War also brought a significant reduction in antagonism toward former Communist bloc countries, and President Roh, in part due to the lack of a domestic source of legitimacy, focused on foreign affairs. Roh established diplomatic relations with former Communist states such as Hungary, Mongolia, China, and the Soviet Union (called "northern diplomacy"); significantly improved military, social, and cultural relations with North Korea; and joined the UN at the same time as North Korea in 1990. In April 1991, Soviet president Mikhail Gorbachev visited Jeju and had a summit conference with Roh. China People's Republic president Jiang Zemin also visited Jeju in 1995. The mood of reconciliation in the Korean peninsula was especially meaningful for activists and victims in Jeju whose activities had been suppressed on the pretext of fighting Communism.

The inauguration of President Kim Young-sam in 1993 ended thirty years of presidents from the military. However, the Kim administration had vestiges of the past regime since Kim gained his power by merging his party with the ruling party of the old authoritarian regime. As if struggling to overcome a birth defect, Kim made drastic reforms in the early years of his presidency. He dissolved the elite military clique known as Hanahoe, adopted the real-name system for financial transactions, and started a strong anticorruption drive. Kim disclosed his own property and pressured high-level state officials and politicians to be transparent about their political funds. At the same time, Kim supported prosecution of former presidents Chun Doo-hwan and Roh Tae-woo, who along with fourteen other generals, were arrested and sentenced to death (Chun) and life imprisonment (Roh).

Human rights lawyers and activists first filed several lawsuits against Chun, Roh, and their subordinates charging them with murder and other offences. However, after intensive investigation, the Seoul district prosecutorial office acknowledged the crime of general murder in the course of suppressing Gwangju protestors but decided not to prosecute the case, claiming that acts of the military coup and the hard-line suppression of protestors were highly political decisions that did not fall under its legal jurisdiction. Both elites and the public vehemently protested the decision, and, at the same time, information about Roh's hidden assets was disclosed. President Kim, who was initially against the criminal prosecutions, supported the special law, which removed the statute of limitations and provided an opportunity for retrial of those who had been convicted in relation to the Gwangju protest.

With all these reforms and prosecutions, activists and victims in Jeju expected a significant change. However, despite expectations, the advocacy only advanced within Jeju itself—a periphery in South Korean politics. Although a few attempts were made to push the issue onto the national agenda, the attempts were frustrated by a lack of political will and public interest in the center. To make matters worse, President Kim made a drastic change in his policy and suppressed civil society by the end of his tenure. Two political issues explain his sudden turn. First, North Korea's announcement to withdraw from the Nuclear Nonproliferation Treaty in 1993 provoked the conservative and military elements of society. In addition, the death of North Korean president Kim Il-sung in 1994 sharply divided South Korean society around the issue of condolence. Second, Kim pushed for a retrogressive revision of the Labor Law, which would have allowed for massive layoffs and the labor dispatch system, but he had to withdraw his policy due to a month-long nationwide strike. As society became more ideologically divided, the Kim administration tilted toward the right.

Activists in Jeju worked with these ups and downs of the Kim administration. Between 1993 and 1997, activists, journalists, students, and intellectuals continued their part in the advocacy. In addition, two new actors became important. Victims who had been relatively inactive under the Roh administration started to raise their voices. And the Jeju local council, created in December 1991, began to play a leading role in the advocacy process. The local council was at the center of the advocacy because it conducted the first official investigation, mediating ideologically opposed social groups to achieve a united memorial service, and leading the province-wide petition movement. Civil society and activist groups effectively supported the major activities of the local council. However, the success also caused backfire from the anti-Communist community, especially during the latter half of the Kim administration. The authorities closely monitored activists and even arrested them on the charge of violating the National Security Law. At the society level, barriers were still high and prejudice against the Jeju 4.3 events was resilient, as can clearly be seen in the case of the history textbook debates in 1994.

Official Investigation by the Local Council

With the reinstitution of the Jeju local council in December 1991, the Jeju 4.3 events came up in the very first meeting when council member Yang Geum-seok questioned the governor's view on possible ways to find the truth, restore the honor of the victims, and reconcile the divided local society.[1] Governor Woo Geun-min replied:

> We are in a new political era of the regional self-governing system, and recently the local council had also been summoned. Thus, I personally think that it may be possible for the Jeju local government to support the activities of harmony and reconciliation if the local council or any other reliable civil society organizations can lead those activities.[2]

Here, Governor Woo delivered a mixed message. First, it is his *personal* opinion, not an official position as governor. Second, it *may be possible* for the local government to *support* civil society or local council activities, meaning that his government will not actively pursue this. Finally, the government can only support those activities aimed at "harmony and reconciliation," meaning not other measures such as investigation or reparations. The governor's statement clearly demonstrates the limitations of the new era: there was a newly created local council, but the local government was still headed by a governor appointed by the president.

In contrast, council members, who represented each city and county, were more sensitive to people's voices. The demands of local citizens were more effectively channeled through council members, and the local demand peaked with the discovery of the Darangshi cave. The Special Committee on 4.3 was created by the local council within this political setting. A consensus was formed by council members on 2 April 1992, the day that the newspapers released the story on the Darangshi cave. After a year-long preparation, the Special Committee was launched on 20 March 1993. Following the tradition of the *Jemin Ilbo*, the committee was named the "Special Committee on 4.3" without labeling the events in order to show the council's neutral position.[3] The creation of the committee marked a significant event, since the government, as a legislative branch of local government, was now involved. The Jeju 4.3 events, which had never been a political issue, became a contemporary issue. The long-time taboo was now broken at a local level, at least in its appearance, because a government body was now willing to address the issue.

The Special Committee was composed of seven council members, headed by Kim Yeong-hun.[4] The committee set its aims as "first, to find the historical facts of the Jeju 4.3 events and civilian massacres, and to take appropriate follow-up measures and eventually achieve unity among Jeju residents."[5] The goal clearly reveals that council members knew that their activities should not be considered the final stop but that further measures such as a national investigation or reparations program should follow. The committee decided on a three-step action plan: (1) investigation, (2) defining the characteristic of the Jeju 4.3 events, and (3) taking reconciliatory measures.[6] The committee first set up an advisory broad with twenty members including journalists, scholars, activists, and victims. The advisory board was an important body since it served as an arena where local leaders with diverse backgrounds could meet and communicate with one another.[7] It also served as a channel where the expertise, strategies, and human resources of civil society could be transferred to the local council.

Yet, the creation of the Special Committee was not a smooth process. Chairperson Kim remembered that the political situation in 1993 was not favorable at all. A few council members accused Kim of politically using the painful past and obtrusively interfering with victims who had made their peace with the past. Kim also received menacing calls, and, in an extreme case, a right-wing activist threatened him saying, "I will someday cut the throats of all the committee members with an axe."[8] Due to constant threats and the difficulties of the task, most council members were reluctant to be Special Committee members. Although council members unanimously agreed to set up the Special Committee, they did not themselves want to be involved in it.[9] The situation dramatically changed when seven members from the first term were all reelected in a landslide with the strong support of victims and activists.[10] In the second term, it was not difficult to recruit members, and many volunteered for the committee.[11]

The first task of the committee was to investigate the facts. The most important fact to investigate was to ascertain the number of victims, which had been estimated as being from fifteen thousand to sixty-five thousand.[12] Although there had been small-scale investigations such as those in 1960, a province-wide investigation had not yet been conducted. Thus, the number of victims was always a controversial issue, the anti-Communist element of society claiming that fewer than eight thousand had been killed.[13] A second important fact to ascertain was the composition of the perpetrators. Though almost all local people knew that the military and police were responsible for most of deaths, no one could point to an exact percentage. An investigation by the *Jeju Sinbo* in 1960 revealed that 80 percent of killings were committed by the state, but the sample was too small—only 5 percent of the total victims—to be persuasive. It was imperative to find out the exact number of victims and the composition of the perpetuators by conducting a full-scale investigation.

The local council set up an office, and seventeen investigators, corresponding to each constituency in Jeju, were appointed to conduct additional on-the-spot and archival investigation. Based on a year-long investigation, the council published its first report in May 1995 and announced a list of 14,125 victims. The follow-up investigation continued, and the council published its revised report in February 1997 with an additional 379 victims. The investigation continued and ended with the establishment of the Jeju Commission in 2000. Of the 14,504 victims, 12,243 were reported victims and 2,598 were identified ones.[14] Reported victims were those whose names were listed in application forms, and identified victims were those who were found by the investigators based on testimonies. Among 12,243 reported victims, 78 percent were males, 21 percent female, and 1 percent unidentified; 9,987 (81.6%) were killed and 2,256 (18.4%) disappeared. In addition, 84 percent of individual cases were attributed to state agents (police, military, or rightist youth group members) and 11.1 percent to the insurgents. The council also found out that about 11 percent of victims were civilians under ten (5.52%) or over sixty (5.77%).[15]

The council's investigation, which resulted in a 585-page report, was a landmark. The investigation was conducted, for the first time, by a branch of the government. It also differed from previous investigations—for example, the investigation by the *Jeju Sinbo* or the Congressional Committee in 1960—in the length of the investigation and the completeness of the report. In addition, the total number victims became available based on a province-wide empirical inspection. Activists and victims now had a specific number to use in their advocacy: it was now no longer *approximately* fifteen thousand or thirty thousand but "at least 14,504." Finally, it also provided the first analysis of the characteristic of the Jeju 4.3 events.

Among 14,504 victims, 82 percent were dead and 12 were disappeared; 84 percent were killed by state agents and 11 percent by the insurgents. These figures undermined the traditional understanding of the Jeju 4.3 events as a Communist rebellion in which civilians were sacrificed by the insurgents. Human rights abuses and state violence was now understood with a clear number of victims and clear percentage of perpetrators.

This report became a stepping stone for the first national truth commission in South Korea by helping activists and victims obtain official and reliable evidence of state violence. In the course of the advocacy, activists encountered many in Seoul claiming that fewer than one thousand were dead and most of them killed by the insurgents. The report was manifest evidence against their argument and other unfounded claims.[16] The report was widely distributed nationwide, and scholars, politicians, and reporters used it as the most important primary source of information. Furthermore, the provincial report helped the Jeju Commission by laying down the groundwork for the national investigation.[17] A year-long investigation and continued revisions demonstrated that the investigation by a national commission was not an easy process. Certainly, the local council made a "great accomplishment that even the central government could not easily make."[18]

United Memorial Service

Activists and students held the first memorial service in 1989 and made it annual with an art festival, but, after 1991, the Anti-Communist Association for Civilian Victims' Families of the Jeju 4.3 Events started to hold their own ceremony. This separate ceremony was not welcomed by civil society groups because former police or conservative journalists led the association. For example, the organization's president, Song Weon-hwa, was a former policeman, and its secretary-general, Park Seo-dong, was an editor of *Gwangwang Jeju*, a magazine with a strong anti-Communist tone. Park, whose mother was brutally murdered by the insurgents, was not hesitant in divulging his deep aversion to students and activists, "who neither experienced nor knew anything about Communists or the Jeju 4.3 events."[19] Others in the association had a similar antagonism against "outsiders" and believed that activists were Communists who were "politically using the Jeju 4.3 events."[20] Anti-Communist victims thus rejected a memorial service lead by activists and further objected to the idea of remembering the 3rd of April, which was the date of the armed uprising. Thus, commemorating their family members along with alleged Communist insurgents was "absolutely intolerable."[21] Certainly, 12 percent of the victims—1,800 if we estimate the total number of victims at 15,000—were killed by the insurgents, and this is not a small number. For instance, the well-known Chilean truth commission reported there were 3,428 victims of the insurgents, and the Presidential Truth Commission on Suspicious Deaths in South Korea investigated 85 cases. But the problem was that anti-Communist victims were privileged minorities. The victims whose family members were killed by the state were hesitant to speak up against state leaders. These victims had a vivid memory of past state violence and also were discriminated against under the anti-Communist regimes in employment, promotion, state examinations, and international travel. (This discriminatory system was known as the guilt-by-association system or the involvement system. It was traditionally used to punish grave violations such as treason or rebellion. It had been abolished in 1894 but revived under Japanese colonial rule, and since then it had officially existed under the military and authoritarian regimes until democratic transition in 1987.)

Therefore, there was a deep divide between the families of those who were murdered by insurgents and those murdered by the state. One victim whose father was killed by the police testified that anti-Communist victims were exchanging whispers when he made an objection to the leadership and the word "the red" was heard.[22] The association dropped "anti-Communist" from its name so that it became the Association for Civilian Victims' Families of the Jeju 4.3 Events in 1990, but it still maintained its constitution, which clearly stated, "The association shall be disbanded if the constitution is amended." (When the Jeju Commission was created in 2000, the majority of victims created a separate association, the Association for the Families of the Disappeared, and later effectively merged with the anti-Communist association.)

The anti-Communist association started to have its own ceremony, claiming that they had an exclusive right to mourn because, unlike activists and students, they were direct descendants of those murdered. Separate services were a manifest sign of the conflict between the two understandings of the Jeju 4.3 events—one as a Communist rebellion and the other as a popular uprising.[23] Accordingly, activists and students commemorated in order to seek the truth and restore the honor of the dead while anti-Communist victims sought "healing" and "reconciliation," code words for doing nothing.[24] Anti-Communist scholars and journalists have often used "healing" and "reconciliation" to oppose criminal prosecutions, investigation, or reparations. Addressing the past atrocities has also been pejoratively referred to as "backward looking" measures compared to "healing" and "reconciliation," which are more "forward looking." Due to these differences, there was hostility between activists and anti-Communist victims: the former viewed the latter as agents of the government and the latter saw the former as Communists.

The difference is also revealed in the titles of their memorial services. Activists and students called their memorial service "cherishment" (*chumoje*) meaning cherishing the memory of the deceased, while anti-Communist victims called theirs "appeasement" (*yuiryeongje*) meaning appeasing the souls of the deceased. These names represent the profound difference between the two groups. For anti-Communist victims, the memorial service was only for the dead, and the sole purpose of the service was to appease the souls of the innocent victims. On the other hand, for activists, the memorial service was for both the dead and the living. They not only wanted to appease the dead but also wanted their contemporaries to remember those who resisted the oppressive rule of the US military government as well as innocent victims of that government.

With the creation of the provincial Special Committee in February 1993, activists and victims in a meeting between Park Seo-dong, secretary-general of the victims' association, and Kim Dong-man, secretary-general of the Jeju 4.3 Research Institute, agreed to have the first united ceremony.[25] However, the victims' association refused to endorse Park's agreement and denounced Park for exceeding his commission. The local council then stepped in to mediate between the two parties and organized a meeting in March 1993.[26] However, the need for negotiation demonstrated a deep chasm between the two groups, and it ended in failure.

In addition to the enormous differences in viewpoint, there were three other reasons why the first mediation attempt failed.[27] First, the initial discussion between Kim and Park started in February and the official meeting was held in late March, a week before the scheduled ceremony. Time was pressing, and it was extremely difficult to discuss and coordinate different positions. Second, the governor's secret support for the victims' association was a major impediment to the negotiation process. A reporter later discovered that during the negotiation, the victims' association had already secured the local government's fund for their ceremony and that they had no intention of sharing it with activist groups.[28] The favoritism of the governor and mayors was explicit when they "participated in the memorial service of the victims' association but did not even send a flower to the activists' memorial service."[29] Third, since the negotiation process moved rapidly, the local media did not have enough time to draw public attention to the possibility of a united memorial service.

The next year, two of the three obstacles—a lack of time and public attention—were effectively overcome. The negotiation had already begun a year earlier, and local media actively followed the negotiation process. Two major impediments still remained—a deep chasm between the two parties and the one-sided support of the governor. Nevertheless, it was not entirely impossible to overcome the ideological divide since the two parties had already reached an agreement in the previous year on two core principles: both parties agreed that victims are ideologically neither left nor right, and both agreed to avoid using ideology-laden labels such as "uprising" or "rebellion." The final hurdle, the governor's partiality, was effectively overcome by a strategic move of the local council, which had authority to review the budget of the provincial government. The governor tenaciously tried to support only the victims' association, but his attempt was blocked by the local council, which strategically threatened to disapprove the next year's budget if the governor kept insisting on his stand.[30]

The leaders of the victims' association and representatives of the activist groups met again with the mediation of the local council and agreed to have the first united memorial service. Both parties agreed to name the ceremony the 46th Appeasement Service of the Victims of Jeju 4.3 (Je 46-jugi Jeju 4.3 Huisaengja Yuiryeongje). The title shows the compromise between the two parties: activists made a concession to victims by using "appeasement" (*yuiryeong*) rather than "cherishment" (*chumo*) in the title, but they insisted on having "46th" (46-*jugi*) and "4.3" in order to remind that the popular uprising started on 3 April 1948.[31] The victims' association also agreed to include those who involuntarily participated or supported the insurgents. On the top of these concessions, both parties adopted the local council's suggestion to leave "Jeju 4.3" without any descriptive label. A joint committee was set up to administer the memorial service, and three representatives from each party served on the executive committee.

The first united memorial service was successfully held on 3 April 1994 at Tapdong Plaza in Jeju with five thousand participants. It was another key moment in the advocacy because ideologically divided groups, for the first time, gathered together to have a memorial service. It was an initial step toward reconciliation and also showed the possibility of activists and the victims' association, no matter how different they are in their ideology, having "one voice."[32] However, immediately after the ceremony, the victims' association complained that activists and the local council violated agreements in two aspects. First, according to the rules of a traditional memorial service, ten thousand mortuary tablets inscribed with the names of the dead were placed on the altar. During the ceremony, a few victims found a tablet with the name of the insurgent leader Lee Deok-gu. Enraged victims accused the activist groups of violating the agreement of neutrality, and the president of the association resigned in protest. On the contrary, activists addressed the possibility of conspiracy by the dissenting members of the victims' association because the tablet was written using Chinese characters. (Both activists and victims prepared the mortuary tablets separately. It turned out that activists happened to use Korean characters, and victims used Chinese characters.) It still is an unsolved mystery and shows that the leaders' compromise was not fully welcomed by every member.[33] Second, victims complained that the speeches made by the president of the local council, Jang Jeong-eon, and chair of the Special Committee, Kim Yeong-hun, were ideologically biased. For example, victims carefully examined Jang's address made a fuss over his description of the Jeju 4.3 events as "distorted history."[34] In addition, victims even complained that students prepared the banners of elegy without consulting the victims' association.

The united memorial service left a significant change in activists and victims, the public, and the local council. First, in the course of confrontation, anti-Communist hardliners dropped out of the association, blaming the current victims' association of having "fallen under the subversive conspiracy of the reds."[35] In parallel, students, the most radical wing of the activist groups withdrew from the alliance, accusing the leaders of the social movement of working too closely with victims who adamantly refused to see the Jeju 4.3 events as a popular uprising.[36] In consequence, the united memorial service and the subsequent conflicts made both ideologically polarized groups more moderate (as the extremists had dropped out) and created a pool of moderates who could later work together. Second, with the united ceremony, the public also started to see the Jeju 4.3 events separated from ideology.[37] The advocacy for truth and justice became the foremost issue in the whole province. Public support grew, from the discovery of the Darangshi cave and the creation of the Special Committee in 1993, and then with the united memorial service in 1994. The success of the united memorial service empowered the local council as a new leader and mediator in the advocacy. It was the first visible success of the local council since its institution in 1993, and the increased popularity and credibility helped the council's other projects such as the investigation.

The Petition Movement

At the same time as the memorial was organized, activists and politicians also searched for a way to bring the Jeju 4.3 events into national politics. Students and the local council nearly simultaneously started a petition movement in July 1993, which took the form of submitting signed petitions to the National Assembly entreating lawmakers to include the Jeju 4.3 events on the agenda. The right to petition was a citizens' privilege guaranteed in the constitution, and victims of other massacres nationwide had submitted petitions to urge lawmakers to act on their behalf. Both students and politicians saw the petition as the most effective way to bring the issue into national politics, but the source of inspiration was different.

Students were one step ahead in the petition movement. Students, after withdrawing from their alliance with activist groups who strategically abandoned the "popular uprising" lexicon, worked closely with the national student association.[38] By refusing to concede, students were left as a "reservoir of the popular uprising narratives."[39] The Jeju National University set up an independent body to focus on the Jeju 4.3 events and published a report and disseminated it nationwide.[40] Faced with this national project, student leaders realized the importance of bringing the issue into national politics and started to collect signatures from students, victims, and citizens.[41] On 28 October 1993, students submitted their petition with

17,925 signatories, which marked another pioneering move initiated by students.[42]

On the same day, Jeju council members also submitted a signed petition to the National Assembly.[43] Unlike the students, who were inspired to start a national campaign, council members were reminded of the importance of petitions from a two-day visit to Taiwan.[44] Taiwan's so-called 2.28 events and transitional justice experience had an important impact on them.[45] The 2.28 events occurred under Chiang Kai-shek's regime in 1947 when Taiwan was a remote island of China inhabited by the aboriginal people before the arrival of Chiang. The crisis started when Chinese state agents beat an old shopkeeper in a cigarette kiosk. Some people fought back and resisted, and the police opened fire and killed one student. The local Taiwanese were outraged and vehemently protested against the Chiang regime. The government brutally suppressed the protest, arguing that it had been instigated, planned, and supported by Communists on the mainland. However, in the course of investigation, no evidence was found supporting the government's allegation of the Chinese Communist Party's involvement. It simply was a protest against the unfair treatment of aboriginals, not a Communist rebellion.

As with the Jeju 4.3 events, the counterinsurgency strategies in Taiwan were extremely brutal and resulted in the deaths of approximately twenty thousand civilians. However, the Chiang regime declared martial law in Taiwan, and the truth was suppressed for more than forty years under two generations of Chiang regime (Chiang Kai-shek and his son Chiang Ching-kuo). With Taiwan's democratic transition in 1987, victims and activists demanded that the truth be revealed, paving the way for reparations. In 1991 the Lee Teng-hui government started an investigation and announced that eighteen thousand to twenty-eight thousand people had been killed and declared that the Kuomintang government was responsible. In 1995 President Lee made an official apology to the victims and made reparations to four thousand remaining victims up to 6 million Taiwan dollars ($230,000). In 2000 the progressive Chen Sui-bian government further investigated the events and declared that Chiang Kai-shek himself had been responsible for issuing the order to kill civilians and made 28 February a national memorial day to commemorate the 2.28 events and civilian victims.

Why did the council seek advice from Taiwan? Primarily because activists and journalists, who first encountered the Taiwanese case, found many stark similarities between the Taiwan and Jeju cases. First, both events occurred in 1948 in the midst of the restructuring of the global order, later known as the Cold War; second, it was an unjustifiable police shooting that triggered the armed protest; third, systemic and province-wide massacres of over twenty thousand civilians were committed by the military and police in the name of counterinsurgency; fourth, both events occurred on an island at the periphery that traditionally suffered discrimination from the political center; fifth, both events were advertised as a rebellion instigated by the Communists who were the enemy of the state; and finally, the truth had been totally suppressed and victims had been silenced under consecutive anti-Communist regimes until 1987.

However, despite the striking similarities, Taiwan was far more advanced than Jeju in seeking truth and restoring justice. By the time the council members paid a visit, Taiwan had already enacted special laws to create a truth commission to investigate the 2.28 events, conducted a year-long investigation, and published a two-volume report with ten volumes of archives.[46] Thus, both the similarity of the event itself and the contrast in the government measures afterward stimulated council members to actively pursue the petition movement.

Based on these two petitions in 1993, Congressman Byun Jeong-il introduced a resolution that would create a special investigatory committee within the National Assembly. It had seventy-four signatures from congress members in 1994. But the 14th National Assembly, after three years of procrastination, decided to pass the issue on to the next assembly with the flimsy excuse of "a lack of time." It was not the first time that a local attempt was frustrated in Seoul with the exact same excuse. In the 4th National Assembly in 1960, the Congressional Committee's activity was terminated with the dissolution of the assembly. However, it was not an entirely fruitless effort. Local media such as the *Jemin Ilbo* and the Jeju MBC closely followed the review process between 1993 and 1996, and it had three unintended consequences.

First, frequent and continued news coverage helped draw local attention to the Jeju 4.3 events and "induced a political atmosphere where local people felt that finding the truth and restoring justice was the single most important issue in Jeju."[47] For example, during the congressional campaign in 1996, most candidates in Jeju announced that the Jeju 4.3 events were their top priority.[48] Changes in public attitudes also affected public officials in the local government. In March 1996, Governor Shin Gu-beom pledged support for a prompt and appropriate investigation into the truth and to restore the honor of victims and further sent an official request to the prime minister demanding a specific policy. The Jeju 4.3 events now officially became "*the* issue of Jeju as a whole."[49] It really was an unexpected consequence of the petition movement that procrastination in the center had caused.

Second, in the course of the petition movement, a piece of important documentary evidence was discovered by Congressman Hyun Gyeong-dae. Interestingly, Hyun had been known for his lukewarm attitude concerning the Jeju 4.3 events, but with the change of political mood in Jeju, local media started to criticize his attitude and Hyun was pressured to impress his constituency.[50] Prior to submitting the petition, council members visited the National Assembly to press congress members representing Jeju to act on behalf of the petition. At their visit, council members referred to the prior investigation of the congress in 1960, and Hyun then discovered the investigation report, minutes, and victims' application forms in the congressional archive. Although the existence of these documents was known, the details of the committee's activities and victims' information were open to the public for the first time. For a month, local newspapers carried the special report on the released documents, which garnered further public attention.

Third, activists and victims realized how difficult it was to bring the Jeju 4.3 events into national politics. Three years of pending action, silence, and final dismissal helped victims and activists realize the barriers that existed at the political center. This barrier was composed of two elements. One was simple ignorance and indifference to the Jeju 4.3 events, which occurred fifty years earlier on a remote and peripheral island. For instance, one congressman was skeptical when the local council members submitted the petition and said, "Why are you even sweating and bothering the National Assembly for events in which fewer than one hundred people died?"[51] Others even asked, "What on earth are the Jeju 4.3 events?"[52] The other barrier was the still strong anti-Communist belief that the Jeju 4.3 events were a Communist rebellion and that people who were killed were armed guerrillas and their supporters. Activists and politicians learned how high the national barrier was through experience, and they started to plan an effective strategy to overcome the barrier.

In November 1996, the local council submitted another petition to the newly formed 15th National Assembly. This time, activists and politicians moved quickly in order to avoid the feeble excuse of a lack of time. A month later, three congressmen representing Jeju quickly proposed another resolution, which won the support of 154 congress members, urging the creation of a special investigatory committee within the National Assembly. This constituted a majority since the assembly was composed of 299 representatives. This number alone evoked optimism, and all major local newspapers and media made it their headline.[53] Many newspapers cautiously predicted that the Special Committee at a national level would be possible in the following year.[54] However, the process was much more tedious than most people had expected. Few expected that the resolution would be pending for another three years, which again proved the resilient nature of the barrier.

Yet Another Barrier, Suppression, and Backfire

Three key activities during the Kim Young-sam administration—an investigation, a united memorial service, and the petition movement—certainly helped to advance the movement in Jeju. However, as the fate of the petitions clearly demonstrates, the barrier in the National Assembly was still high. In addition, three other events that occurred during the Kim administration also indicate the social barrier, the continued state suppression, and the backfire from anti-Communist elements.

The first issue came in March 1994 around the revision of history textbooks for middle school and high school students. Under the authoritarian regimes, the Jeju 4.3 events had been referred to as "the Jeju 4.3 rebellion" instigated by the Communists. A more neutral term, "the Jeju 4.3 events," was used after democratization, but it was still explained as a Communist rebellion. Activists and intellectuals hoped for a change, since many historical facts had been discovered by the efforts of local journalists, researchers, and intellectuals. Seo Jung-seok, a professor of modern and contemporary history at Sungkyunkwan University and a member of the textbook revision committee, cautiously suggested renaming the Jeju 4.3 events "the Jeju 4.3 uprising."[55] Immediately, right-wing politicians, journalists, and intellectuals vehemently protested against his suggestion. Professor Seo soon fell under a barrage of attacks from the anti-Communists, who had been vociferous since North Korea's announcement it would withdraw from the Nuclear Nonproliferation Treaty. Even Kim Jong-pil, a leader of the ruling party, openly criticized the textbook revision committee, arguing, "There should not be a distortion in history textbooks."[56] The Ministry of Education quickly announced that it was the professor's personal view and that the committee would go through a proper review process so that it reflects "the perspective that most scholars can agree on."[57] The committee adhered to the ministry's directive throughout the review process and no change, except an added sentence on the civilian victims, was made in the final draft. The debates around the textbook revision, and especially the heated objections to professor Seo's remark, revealed that the social barrier, which is mainly composed of prejudice and ignorance, was still high outside Jeju.

The second challenge came in 1997 when documentary film director Kim Dong-man and director of the Sarangbang Group for Human Rights (Ingweon Undong Sarangbang) Seo Jun-sik were arrested on the charge of violating the National Security Law. The arrests were made after the Kim administration made a turn to the right after the Labor Law issue. As the strike and demonstrations increased, the police searched the offices of labor unions and student associations and noticed two documentary films on the Jeju 4.3 events. Kim Dong-man made the film *The Unquenchable Shout: The Jeju 4.3 Uprising* in 1995 to publicize the Jeju 4.3 events nationwide, and the film had been distributed to university campuses by the local student association. In 1997 Cho Seong-bong made a similar film, *The Red Hunt,* which focused on the civilian massacres and the government's responsibility. Seo Jun-sik, the head of a human rights NGO, screened the film at the Human Rights Film Festival. Immediately, the police announced that these films were illegal since they "benefited the enemy North" and arrested and indicted both Kim and Seo.[58]

The third challenge came in October 1997 when Rhee In-su, adopted son of Rhee Syng-man, filed a lawsuit against the *Hankyoreh* requesting a correction for a newspaper article on Rhee Syng-man. On 1 April 1997, the *Jemin Ilbo* and the *Hankyoreh* reported that the martial law declared by President Rhee during the Jeju 4.3 events was illegal and unconstitutional. The 4.3 reporting team of the *Jemin Ilbo* were the first to question the legitimacy of the martial law because diverse documents had different starting dates for the martial law. Reporters investigated and found an official document of the martial law signed by President Rhee and his ministers on 17 November 1948. Here, the date was an issue because the Martial Law Act, which gave the president authority to declare martial law, was not enacted until 24 November 1949.[59] Activists and victims pressed the government to investigate. In response, the Office of Legislation hastily responded by claiming that Japanese martial law was in force in Korea during the colonial period and that in 1948 Japanese law was still in effect in South Korea. However, a legal scholar found that martial law had never been declared during the Japanese occupation, which made the government's interpretation questionable.[60] In the midst of the debate, Rhee In-su filed his lawsuit, but he eventually lost the case. Although the lawsuit ended favorably for the newspaper, the civil lawsuit and the possibility of future lawsuits put a great burden on journalists and intellectuals. As expected, it was the beginning of a string of lawsuits against the advocates.

The Primacy of Local Activism

With the first non-military president, Kim Young-sam, the advocacy considerably advanced. Certainly, the most critical change was the advent of the Jeju local council, which kept a neutral position between the Left and the Right and gained credibility for the movement as an official and representative body of government. The existence of the local council was the result of democratic consolidation, which allowed for the decentralization of political power. The transition to democracy and maturing consolidation provided the most open and favorable environment for the advocacy. However, if we look into the process more closely, we can see the primary importance of the local actors.

Democratization and the decentralization of power was itself the result of a long and painful struggle for democracy by social movement activists across the country, including those in Jeju. In other words, the fact that favorable space opened up with democratization is not something that should be taken as a matter of course; rather, it was the result of persistent local activism. The core members of the advocacy networks—students, activists, and journalists—were all heavily involved in the democratization movement. Therefore, democracy was not an exogenously given structure but a condition made possible by the local advocacy. In addition, without the full support of local activists, the local council would not have been able to make such an important contribution. Every major project was carried out by local activist groups. The information, expertise, and personnel supplied by the local advocacy networks were a key element in the work of the local council.

Furthermore, if we look even closer, we find that local activism was an indispensable element in both publicizing and capitalizing on the Taiwanese case, which heavily affected the local council. The Taiwanese case was initially brought to awareness by a reporter at the *Jemin Ilbo*, Kim Jong-min, who saw considerable parallels between the 2.28 events and the Jeju case in terms of their characteristics, timing and location, perpetrators, number of victims, and aftermath.[61] Interestingly, the publicity given to the Taiwanese case in South Korea was not triggered by or related to a particular event in Taiwan, such as the establishment of the commission or the presidential apology. Rather, it was publicized by a concerned local journalist who had been involved in the Korean advocacy movement and was eager to achieve a breakthrough. It was made possible by the keen eyes of Kim, which had been sharply focused on the Jeju 4.3 events as he collected data and interviewed witnesses for his weekly newspaper reports. Even though the Taiwanese case did not receive extensive coverage in other national newspapers, one local journalist read an international news article and saw the potential of the Taiwanese case to inspire and guide the advocacy in Jeju. This single international news report could easily have been overlooked among the thousands of other news stories that appeared that day.

Furthermore, after the local community became aware of the Taiwanese case, local activists engaged in information politics in order to maximize the impact of the Taiwanese case. Kim made the significant move of asking prominent intellectual Lee Yeong-hee, a student of contemporary Chinese history, to analyze the 2.28 events, and then he published a series of articles comparing the Taiwanese case to the Jeju 4.3 events.[62] Simple information on the experience of a neighboring country would not have been a significant factor in itself, but it became useful once it had been strategically studied, understood, and reinterpreted by local activists. Because of their efforts, the Taiwanese case was no longer an event that had simply occurred in a neighboring country but an event that was highly relevant to Jeju. In sum, the Taiwanese experience had a significant impact on the local council because the local activists and journalists actively sought to use it to their benefit.

With the advancement of the advocacy in Jeju, activists and victims started to see the possibility that the Jeju 4.3 events could be addressed at the center in Seoul. For five years, activists not only saw the obstacles and barriers that existed in the center but they also started to see and find ways to overcome the barriers of ignorance and prejudice. In addition, the prosecution of two former South Korean presidents during the Kim Young-sam administration gave hope to activists and victims that the facts could be found and justice could be done for the Jeju case sometime in the future. At the same time, Kim Dae-jung, who retired from politics immediately after his defeat in the 1992 presidential election, decided to run for president in the 1997 election. A new hope grew among victims and activists with the prospect of Kim Dae-jung, who had consistently pledged himself to finding the truth and restoring of the honor of victims of the Jeju 4.3 events, becoming the next president. Activists envisioned mobilizing the accumulated power and resources of the advocacy movement in the year 1998, which was symbolic because it was a "half century" since the outbreak of the Jeju 4.3 events.

Part II

The Process of the Jeju Commission

5

The Establishment of the Jeju Commission

In 1998 President Kim Dae-jung, whose political constituency was based in North and South Jeolla and Jeju Provinces and who had pledged several times to enact a special law for investigating the civilian massacre in Jeju, was inaugurated. Kim made his first public pledge in November 1987 when he visited Jeju during his presidential campaign immediately after democratization:

> People in Jeju have suffered the tragedy of the Jeju 4.3 events. I will be with you in your regrets, pain, and hope. The military and authoritarian governments also falsely accused me of being a Communist, and I myself am a victim. If I am in power, I will investigate the truth of the Jeju 4.3 events, in which people have been falsely accused of being Communists, and will restore the honor of the victims.[1]

In later statements in 1992, Kim further promised to enact a special law to investigate civilian massacres during the Jeju 4.3 events and to restore the honor of victims by clearing them of false accusations of being Communists. One reporter who closely traced Kim's commitments counted at least twelve public pledges made within an eleven-year period after democratization.[2]

Professor Ko Chang-hoon of the Jeju National University was mainly responsible for drafting Kim Dae-jung's Jeju address in 1987 and for the decision to include the Jeju 4.3 events and civilian massacres in the statement.[3] According to Ko, Lee Mun-yeong, a professor at Korea University and a long-time supporter of Kim Dae-jung, sent Ko a note a few days before Kim's arrival in Jeju asking him to draft a campaign address that would stand out from those of the other candidates, Roh Tae-woo and Kim Young-sam. Ko, who had been studying the Jeju 4.3 events, firmly believed that the issue of civilian massacres should be included in Kim's address.[4] When Kim delivered his address, it caused a sensation, not only among people in Jeju but also in Seoul. Thus, Kim's first pledge was the result of the research of one local intellectual. Even though it was Kim himself who promised to deliver truth and reparations for the victims, the cumulative efforts and research of local researcher were an indispensable precondition for his pledge.

Kim Dae-jung's appearance was even more sensational and controversial because Kim retired from politics after being defeated by Kim Young-sam in the 1992 presidential election. Since Kim Dae-jung was the only major political figure who had been consistently promising truth, justice, and reparations, his decision to retire from politics was a huge disappointment for victims in Jeju.[5] However, a new hope grew as he returned to politics by creating his own party, the National Congress for New Politics in 1998. Although Kim Dae-jung was criticized for going back on his word about retirement, proponents of transitional justice in Jeju welcomed his return as they believed that a settlement could only come into being with Kim Dae-jung in office. Not only people in Jeju but also victims of state violence during the Korean War and under the authoritarian regimes had a similar desire and hope for Kim.

Moreover, victims and activists became even more optimistic because of an important development under the Kim Young-sam administration. President Kim Young-sam had his constituency in Gyeongsang Province and promised to investigate and make reparations to the victims of the Geochang massacre who were murdered by the South Korean 9th

Regiment in 1951 during the Korean War. In 1996 the special law on the Geochang massacre was enacted, and a special commission was set up in 1997 to investigate the massacre and identify civilian victims. The commission acknowledged the responsibility of the military and identified 548 victims and 785 family members.[6] The title of the law was the Special Law on Restoration of the Honor of Victims of the Geochang Event and Others. The law was designed not only to address the Geochang massacre but also other similar cases by including the words "and others." Nevertheless, the special law had never been applied beyond the Geochang case for two reasons. First, victims were still hesitant to go public because the political elites of the authoritarian regimes were still powerful under the Kim Young-sam administration because his ruling party was created as a result of a political compromise with the old elites. Second, due to antagonistic regional politics between Gyeongsang and Jeolla Provinces, victims in Jeju were more attached to Kim Dae-jung than to Kim Young-sam. Victims in Jeju expected that Kim Dae-jung would enact a special law for Jeju as Kim Young-sam had done for Geochang.

In addition, activists were eager to make the best use of the symbolic "fiftieth anniversary of the outbreak of the Jeju 4.3 events." In Korean, fifty years are often referred to as "half a century" (*bansegi*), which oftentimes is associated with word "division [of the Korean peninsula]" (*bundan*). When these two terms were used together—"half a century after the division of the Korean peninsula" (*bundan bansegi*) it had a connotation that something needed to be done about the grave problem of Korean bifurcation. By intentionally using the concept of "half a century" in their advocacy, activists wanted to evoke public awareness that something substantial had to be done about the Jeju case also.

The year 1998 was also a half a century since the creation of the separate government in South Korea in 1948. Internationally, the whole world was celebrating the fiftieth anniversary of the Universal Declaration of Human Rights. Activists wanted to contrast the dark and unresolved history of the Jeju 4.3 events with the glorious and exuberant story of the foundation of the republic and the birth of the global human rights principle.[7] In addition, activists adopted the notion of the jubilee, which came from the Christian tradition. Activists understood the jubilee as "a year of forgiveness and reconciliation," which was extended from the biblical concept of setting slaves free, restoring property, and remitting debt.[8] Although the notion was initially foreign to most activists and victims, it resonated well with other ideas such as human rights and peace.

In order to maximize the effectiveness of the advocacy, elite groups in Seoul created the Pan National Committee for the 50th Anniversary of the Jeju 4.3 Events (Pan National Committee) in April 1997.[9] Many prominent progressive leaders—scholars, activists, religious leaders, journalists, and lawyers—participated.[10] Concurrently, local activists, artists, and researchers created a national organization called the 50th Anniversary Commemoration Committee for the Jeju 4.3 Events through the Cultural and Academic Projects (Commemoration Committee) in February 1998 to organize a special arts festival and international conferences.[11] The Commemoration Committee later became the Provincial Solidarity for the Investigation of the Truth and Restoration of Honor for the Jeju 4.3 Events (Provincial Solidarity). The advocacy proceeded based on these two centers—one in Seoul and the other in Jeju. The two centers of activism worked closely with a division of labor between them. The former worked with prominent political figures such as congress members and presidential staff in Seoul while the latter focused on publicity and mobilization of the public in Jeju. The interaction of these two associations became more effective and powerful in 1999 when both groups pushed for the enactment of the special law.

Commemoration Projects in 1998

From the onset, the situation under President Kim Dae-jung looked promising. The ruling party set up the Special Committee on the Jeju 4.3 Events and hosted public hearings in Jeju (7 May 1998) and Seoul (28 September 1998).[12] With these changes, the national news media started to cover the Jeju 4.3 events as a current issue. Previously, news media in Seoul covered the Jeju 4.3 events as a historic issue or as personal stories.[13] In addition, newspapers sporadically released sensational news items such as the discovery of the Darangshi cave, the controversies around textbook revision, or the illegality of Rhee Syng-man's martial law of 1948. But with the inauguration of Kim Dae-jung, the Jeju 4.3 events truly became a controversial but relevant current political issue. However, progress in 1998 was limited to advancement *within* the ruling party. It fell short of the expectations of activists and victims, who started to realize that the resolute political will of Kim Dae-jung alone would not be enough to lead to success. Many activists had naively believed that the special law would be naturally and smoothly legislated after President Kim's inauguration. The creation of a special committee within the ruling party and two public hearings also raised expectations. Nevertheless, Kim Dae-jung spent his first year as president rebuilding the economy in the aftermath of the 1997 Asian financial crisis. Economic recovery was his primary goal, and he was successful in avoiding state bankruptcy. By the end of 1998, activists learned the lesson that "politicians, even Kim Dae-jung, must be consistently pressed in order to act."[14]

In 1998 activists focused on organizing cultural and academic projects to help increase public awareness and participation. Three projects were particularly important. First, a local ritual known as *gut*, a traditional shamanic way to cure illness by exorcising evil spirits, proved to be a sensational success. Traditionally, *gut* was also used to appease spirits by calling them, communicating with them, and guiding them to heaven. Cultural activists believed that a province-wide exorcism could appease the souls of the dead and communicate between the dead and the living.[15] Despite a strong storm on the chosen day, the province-wide *gut* was crowded with 1,200 participants, including approximately 700 victims and their family members. The exorcism lasted about eleven hours, but victims and their family members would not leave but kept crying. In a newspaper interview, a victim testified, "Fifty years of distress and rancor seemed to have gone away."[16] One participant of the ceremony sympathized with the victims, saying, "I think I know why victims and their families are participating in *gut* for over eleven hours in spite of severe weather."[17]

Second, cultural activists erected a tower, *bangsatap*, which fishermen traditionally built in order to ward off evil spirits and misfortune and to give them well-being in their unpredictable and fragile work at sea. The tower was built in the middle of Jeju, as a wish for the enactment of a special law and to ward off objections from the conservative and anti-Communist members of society.[18] Victims and activists laid down one stone for each individual victim one at a time, and an official report of the local council, which had a list of 14,125 victims, was kept underneath the tower, as a symbol. The tower was significant because it was the first visible symbol of the Jeju 4.3 events and the transitional justice movement. The activists celebrated the passage of the law in December 1999 around the tower.

Third, activists hosted three academic conferences. The one hosted by the Jeju 4.3 Research Institute was the largest and most influential.[19] Between 21 and 25 August 1998, the Research Institute hosted the 2nd International Conference on Peace and Human Rights in the 21st Century East Asia. (The first conference was held in 1997 in Taipei and commemorated the fiftieth anniversary of the 2.28 events.) This conference involved six hundred activists and scholars from Taiwan, Japan, and South Korea, as well as internationally prominent activists, including 1996 Nobel peace laureate José Ramos-Horta from East Timor; Fazel Randera, a commissioner of the South African Truth and Reconciliation Commission; and a former Japanese senator, Den Hideo. Organizers of the conference admitted that a conference of this scale and internationally prominent persons was "absolutely beyond the ability of the Research Institute but did it anyway in order to draw national and international attention."[20]

It was a watershed event that framed the Jeju 4.3 events as a case of massive human rights violations: the Jeju 4.3 events, which had been defined as either a Communist rebellion or a prodemocracy uprising, were now reframed as human rights violations. This change was timely and important because human rights discourse started to be widely adopted in South Korean society with the inauguration of Kim Dae-jung, who was known for his life-long fight for democracy and human rights. Moreover, activists intentionally pressed President Kim by inviting Senator Den Hideo, who had led an international campaign for Kim during the Park Chung-hee dictatorship. Senator Den came to prominence in 1973, when he led an international campaign to rescue Kim Dae-jung after Kim was kidnapped by the Korean secret service in Tokyo and almost drowned in the Pacific Ocean. Activists firmly believed that Senator Den was someone who could exert maximum influence over Kim and remind him of his past promises, and the meeting between the two helped to publicize the Jeju 4.3 events.[21]

The cultural and research sectors of the advocacy movement led the commemoration project of 1998 and paved the way for the enactment movement in 1999. The cultural and research sectors again played a key role, which was possible for two reasons. First, the cultural and research realms in the advocacy were the most advanced areas and had enough potential and resources to lead the project.[22] The fiftieth anniversary projects were possible because of the expertise and know-how of these sectors, which had been accumulating over ten years of activism. Second, it was also possible because visual art, songs, poems, literature, plays, and traditional exorcism were easily accessible to the victims and the general public. With this momentum, activists pursued further political projects by creating Provincial Solidarity.[23] Unlike the transitory Commemoration Committee in 1998, Provincial Solidarity was created as a permanent body of local NGOs aiming to pass a special law under the slogan "The events of twentieth century must be redressed before the turn of twenty-first century."[24]

The Enactment Movement of 1999

In 1999 the focus of activism was no longer on the creation of a special committee *within* the National Assembly but on enacting a binding special law that guaranteed the institutionalization of a national investigatory committee and possible reparations. The Jeju local council, which led the petition movement beginning in 1993, again took the initiative in the enactment movement in 1999. As council members themselves, they knew the fragility of a resolution or a temporary committee without any binding force. The council members made visits to the National Assembly and the offices of major political parties. In each visit, local council members and activists stressed that the special law was a pledge made by President Kim and reminded politicians that there was no visible policy or action so far other than establishing a small committee within the ruling party. The words "president's pledge," "promise," and "the will of the president" had been frequently used to push congress members and party members to act.[25] Eventually, floor leaders of both the ruling and opposition party promised to establish a special committee and enact a special law by the end of the year.

Simultaneously, activists in Seoul and Jeju carried out a public awareness campaign by organizing a weekly rally at the city centers, which proved to be highly effective way to "push politicians forward, especially whenever there is a deadlock in the National Assembly."[26] Thus, the advocacy existed at two levels: lobbying elites and congress members and publicizing the Jeju 4.3 events and civilian massacres.[27] The two levels of activism closely interacted with and strengthened each other. For example, there were several occasions when activists encountered a deadlock in their activism at the elite level. Yang Dong-yun, president of Provincial Solidarity, later said that activists in Seoul often contacted him to organize a political rally or to pay a visit to Seoul to press the movement on.[28] These large-scale rallies in turn empowered activists in Seoul and strengthened their hand in negotiations with politicians and congress members.

Although both floor leaders of the ruling and the opposition party promised to enact the special law, it was never a smooth process. Despite the verbal promises, there was no visible advancement, and leaders were hesitant to move forward, claiming that more prudence was needed in addressing such an ideologically controversial issue as the Jeju 4.3 events. President Kim Dae-jung visited Jeju on 12 June 1999 and promised to give 3 billion won ($2.6 million) to the local government to purchase land for a memorial park. However, this caused heated debate in Jeju because many activists believed a government investigation should come before securing a memorial site.[29]

One congresswoman in the ruling party—Choo Mi-ae—played a critical role in making the ruling party fulfill its commitment. Congresswoman Choo was not from Jeju but encountered the Jeju 4.3 events for the first time when serving as a vice-chair of the ruling party's committee and participating in the memorial service in 1998. Yang Jo-hoon, who closely worked with Choo, later said that Choo was shocked when she first learned about the Jeju 4.3 events in 1997. She admitted, "I took pride in being an intellectual myself, but I did not know what the Jeju 4.3 events were at that time."[30] Choo became the center of attention after she successfully chaired the first public hearing on the Jeju 4.3 events organized by the ruling party. People in Jeju were impressed by her ability to lead a discussion on a highly controversial topic in a very difficult debate that included loud voices and showers of abuse, mostly by anti-Communist victims and activists.[31]

Amid the debate about the enactment of a special law, Choo released an official government court file containing a two hundred–page list of 1,650 persons who were court-martialed during the 4.3 events. Both Park Chan-sik, a senior researcher, and Kang Chang-il, the director of the Jeju 4.3 Research Institute at the time, told me that it was the Research Institute that first found out that the list was in the National Archives in Daejon, but they *strategically* gave Choo the opportunity to find the list because they believed it would be more dramatic and effective for her to announce the list.[32] However, Choo, denied Park and Kang's claim that any information was passed to her by the Jeju 4.3 Research Institute.[33] However, Choo admitted that she started to search the National Archives when she was inspired by Lee Do-yeong, a victim, researcher, and activist, who sent her a critical document on the status of the victims' family members prepared by the local police.[34] Activists and researchers in Jeju had ceaselessly asked for the release of the government document for over a decade, but the National Archives was hesitant to release it until a congress member officially asked for it.[35]

The document contained detailed personal information including name, age, address, occupation, charges, sentence, and a location of the prison, along with a five-to-twenty–page description of each of the military trials between December 1948 and July 1949.[36] Previously, evidence of the Jeju 4.3 events entirely relied on newspapers, interviews, and US military documentation. Although the report of the Congressional Committee in 1960 was released in the middle of the petition movement in 1995, it was first time any document from the executive branch, which was mainly responsible for the massacres, was released. All major national newspapers, including the one highly critical of the transitional justice advocacy, carried the news report, and local papers made it their headlines.[37] Choo also released a document of the Jeju police, which contained a detailed list of fifty-two persons in Dosun village who were killed during the Jeju 4.3 events.

The release of these two documents was important in three ways. First, it provided undeniable evidence of the execution of a large number of people in a short period of time without due process, which indicated the abuse of state power. The documents provided evidence that most people were executed within a month after initial trials and showed that, at some point, 132 prisoners were executed in one day. Since these documents were made by government officials, this provided indisputable evidence of mass killing in the name of the law. This evidence was beyond dispute and an indispensable element in advancing the advocacy movement. Concrete and indisputable evidence was the most effective way to defeat the endless objections and threats to the advocacy.

Second, the list was meaningful to the families of victims who wanted to know whether their family members were killed or disappeared. Listed victims were those who had been regarded as disappeared by family members. The documents provided personal information and the place where they were executed, which was important information for family members. One activist told me that "families now finally could have a memorial service because they now knew for sure that their husbands and fathers were dead."[38] People in Jeju were highly respectful of their ancestors, and they often kept the tombs in the middle of the fields where they worked every day. Family members of the disappeared now could either build an empty tomb and have a memorial service or visit the prison where the execution was carried out and have annual memorial service there.

Third, the timing of the release was critical for the enactment of a special law, since many right-wing and conservative congress members had objected to creating a special law because they claimed there was insufficient evidence.[39] In previous regimes right-wing and conservative congress members had objected to any legal action in regard to the Jeju 4.3 events and civilian massacres because it was a "Communist rebellion." It was simple enough to argue that the conflict started as a Communist rebellion against the free, legitimate, and democratic government and that the civilian loss of life was the collateral damage of legitimate counterinsurgency operations. However, since President Kim Dae-jung's inauguration, not many right-wing congress members relied on this logic any more. In discussions of the Jeju 4.3 events, language representing this viewpoint—"reds," Communists, or rebellions—was seldom used. The basis of objection had veered toward "insufficient evidence," "a historic event that should not be judged from the current political viewpoint," or "a task for historians, not politicians."[40] But, with the release of the documents, these objections became less valid.

Two Separate Bills

After the release of the documents, activism both in Seoul and Jeju noticeably accelerated. In addition, the last regular session of the 15th National Assembly was approaching, and activists and victims knew that there was no guarantee that the same promises and efforts would be made by congress members in the 16th National Assembly. The first move ironically came from members of the opposition party (Grand National Party) who had their constituency in Jeju. In October 1999, Congressmen Byun

Jeong-il, Yang Jeong-gyu, and Hyun Gyeong-dae announced the draft of the bill. The limitation, however, was that it was the action not of the opposition party itself but of three *individual* congress members. Activists criticized the move since the bill lacked any party platform or concrete action plan. Provincial Solidarity even stated that the bill was merely a "calculated political gesture aimed at the upcoming election."[41] It was not the first time that a bill was proposed by congress members shortly before the next congressional election. Congressman Byun at the very end of the 14th National Assembly had hurriedly proposed an unsuccessful resolution, and activists criticized it as "a mere political tool for the next election."[42]

Despite the criticism, the bill was meaningful because it was the first bill proposing a truth commission, and, within a month, the opposition party agreed on a bill with only a minor change. One striking difference of this bill from the two prior resolutions in 1994 and 1996 was that this bill went beyond proposing a special committee within the National Assembly and proposed the establishment of an independent truth commission (article 3 of the bill). Furthermore, it was the first time that the Jeju 4.3 events were redefined in the political realm as an event other than a Communist rebellion. In article 1 of the opposition's bill, the Jeju 4.3 events were defined, using a cautiously chosen neutral term, as "a disturbance that occurred on 3 April 1948 in Jeju Island with a following process of governmental suppression." By using the word "disturbance" (*soyo*), the authors of the bill wanted to avoid pointing out or even mentioning who were the responsible parties for the atrocity.

Most important, the basic skeleton of a special law was formed with this bill, including the structure of a truth commission, publication of a report, institution of a local administrative committee, building a memorial site, and providing financial and medical support for the victims.[43] The opposition's bill provided a basic frame of reference for the later bill of the ruling party, and arguments were made for and against this initial bill. Thus, despite the criticism, it was a timely and important bill in the trajectory of the enactment of the special law, and the role of Congressman Byun was critical.[44] It is important to recognize the first actions in a political process since they provide a frame of reference against which later actions can be evaluated. It was a rather surprising event because many expected the ruling party would propose a bill first. Nevertheless, it was individual lawmakers from Jeju who first laid down the cornerstone of a special law, and this again shows that the local efforts were more important than those of the committed elites in Seoul. Byun continued to play an important role in the National Assembly. Lim Mun-cheol, who was closely involved in the process, told me, "It would not have been possible if the bill came from Congresswoman Choo alone. It was almost certain that Choo's bill on its own could not move the opposition party."[45]

Within a month, the Pan National Committee announced its version of the bill after critically examining the opposition's bill.[46] This bill was different from the opposition's bill in three aspects. First, the Jeju 4.3 events were defined (in article 2) as "the events that occurred in Jeju from 1 March 1947 to 27 July 1953 when civilians were abused without a good cause during the armed protests and the counterinsurgency operations by the US military government's police and military, the South Korean military and police, and paramilitary organizations." By defining the Jeju 4.3 events as the abuse of state power, activists wanted to go beyond the neutral definition of a "disturbance" of the opposition's bill. In addition, activists continued to frame the Jeju 4.3 events as serious and systemic human rights violations, a concept adopted during the commemoration projects.

Second, there was a difference in the period that the commission was mandated to investigate. The date 3 April 1948 is the day when the Communist insurgents embarked on their armed protest. The opposition party adhered to this date because its members, representing conservative, right-wing, and anti-Communist groups, focused on the fact that the Jeju 4.3 events started as a "Communist rebellion." On the other hand, activists pointed to another date, 1 March 1947, when the police under the US military government opened fired on protestors. Emphasis was given to this date because activists perceived that the shooting incident and subsequent police brutality was a critical precondition for the outbreak of armed protest in April 1948. Local researchers and journalists were the first to discover the significance of the 3.1 shooting incident. In their view, the 1948 armed protest was a reaction to the 1947 shooting incident, the subsequent suppression of the general strike, and police brutality throughout the year. The argument about the date is further related to the issue of responsibility. If the shooting incident was the starting point, then US occupation forces and the US government would have direct responsibility.

The third difference was regarding the nature and scope of financial and medical support to victims. The opposition's bill had an article providing "a financial and medical subsidy" for victims (article 10). The authors of the bill carefully used the term "subsidy" (*bojo*) in order to avoid the word "reparation" (*baesang*). The concept closest to reparations in the opposition's bill was "a restoration of the honor" (*myeongye hoebok*) of victims and their family members. But there was not a single line in their bill as to what "restoration" meant and how "restoration of honor" could be carried out in a concrete manner. One of the authors of the opposition's bill, Congressman Byun later stated:

> It was practically impossible for the government to make reparations to so many victims. In order to pass the law, political reality has also to be considered. . . . I myself, and other congressmen who were working hard on this bill, knew that the conservative members of both the ruling and opposition parties would never allow the bill to pass the National Assembly if the bill would give a penny to the victims in the form of government reparations.[47]

On the contrary, the activists' bill clearly defined the responsible actor as the state and the United States and articulated (article 6) that the state should "make reparations to victims and their family members."

In addition, there were two minor differences between the two bills. First, activists proposed a truth commission, operating under the president (article 9 of the Pan National Committee's bill), which was intended to give more power and resources to the commission. Second, activists defined the family members of victims much more broadly (article 5) than did the opposition party. In addition to the spouses and lineal descendants of victims, activists also included the de facto spouses and siblings of victims. In response to the bill drafted by the Pan National Committee, the opposition party made a radical change to its previous bill. The opposition included the possibility of retrial for those who were falsely convicted during the Jeju 4.3 events (article 14).[48]

Legislation of the 4.3 Special Law

However, the policy direction of the ruling party was still not in support of enacting a special law. Instead, the ruling party's official position was to set up a special committee within the National Assembly first to investigate the Jeju 4.3 events and then to consider enacting a special law, depending on the results of the investigation. Congresswoman Choo told me:

> Since many elites and the general public still remembered the Jeju 4.3 events as a Communist insurgency, President Kim Dae-jung and his aides were still extremely cautious in bringing the Jeju 4.3 events issue forward because the opposition could easily make ideological criticisms against President Kim Dae-jung. As you might know, ideological issues such as the Jeju 4.3 events were President Kim's Achilles' heel.[49]

In addition, conservative members of the ruling party also thought that there was more to lose than gain—especially with the upcoming general election in six months—by bringing up the ideologically still controversial issue of the Jeju 4.3 events. Especially, party leader Park Sang-cheon strongly objected to the idea, and many in the party such as executive Cho Sun-hyeong followed his lead.[50] Despite continuous pressure from activists and victims to change its policy, the ruling party turned a deaf ear to the demand.

On 16 November 1999, partly in reaction to the initiative taken by the opposition party and partly pressed by the demands of activists, the Jeju local committee of the ruling party drafted a bill and proposed it to the ruling party in Seoul. The proposed bill was mainly based on the bill drafted by the Pan National Committee, adopting exactly the same definition and period of the Jeju 4.3 events. Nonetheless, party leaders in Seoul insisted on creating a special committee within the National Assembly first, which was a trick to avoid putting forward a bill. Despite the proposal from the local committee, the ruling party submitted a nonbinding resolution with 101 signatures of congress members to set up a special committee on the very next day. Although the party members in Jeju already knew that the enactment of a special law was the right direction at this point, more time and effort was needed before party leaders in the center would be willing to drop a resolution without teeth.

By 18 November 1999, both a resolution to set up a special committee submitted by the ruling party and a revised bill submitted by the opposition party were on the table. For activists and victims, who had been working more than a decade to see steps taken in the National Assembly, it was an undesirable situation. Oh Yeong-hun, then executive director of

Provincial Solidarity, described the situation as "an emergency for the advocacy" because activists would be in a very bad situation if once again (considering the failed resolution in the mid-1990s) a bill and a resolution from both parties were put on the table but both did not succeed.[51] The failure caused by a lack of consensus between the two parties would give both parties permission not to pursue further measures because each party "already have done its best but did not succeed due to a lack of consensus with the opponent."[52]

The Pan National Committee and related local organizations immediately expressed their objection to the resolution submitted by the ruling party. The dilemma here was that activists and victims were torn between the two parties' political moves. Victims welcomed the opposition party's pursuit of a special law, but most deeply disagreed with its contents and understanding of the Jeju 4.3 events. It was most likely that their decade-long activism would be obstructed by the current bill proposed by the opposition party, since the bill did not portray the Jeju 4.3 events as human rights violations and state violence. The term "disturbance" could in no way capture the abuse of state power and civilian massacres the local population experienced. It was a neutral term that did not pinpoint the perpetrators of the violence, insinuating that both parties caused the commotion and civilians were caught in the middle. However, for victims, this was not right because most of the atrocities they witnessed were carried out by the police and military whose job was to protect them. At the same time, while appreciating President Kim Dae-jung and his ruling party's will to redress the civilian massacres, victims were exhausted by a series of unsuccessful and nonbinding resolutions over the last six years in the National Assembly. Moreover, there was no reason for the ruling party to ponder because the opposition party, which had consistently opposed enacting legislation to address the Jeju 4.3 events, now initiated the bill.

The period between 17 November 1999, when the ruling party initially submitted a resolution, and 2 December 1999, when the ruling party finally decided to submit a bill, was the most strained time in the advocacy. Realizing the graveness of the situation, local council members and thirty-four representatives from various NGOs in Jeju set up a special task force to go to Seoul and protest against the plan of the ruling party. Representatives visited the ruling party and got a verbal agreement to draft a bill from Congressman Lim Chae-jeong, head of the party's policy planning committee. However, on the same day, the congressional steering committee processed the ruling party's resolution and decided to create a special committee. If created, the special committee would only have three to four months to work in before the dissolution of the 15th National Assembly. In addition, since the committee was not a permanent one, there was no guarantee that the 16th National Assembly would reinstitute the committee. The worst scenario seemed near since the bill of the opposition party was scheduled to be reviewed and there was a high chance it would not pass various committees where the ruling party, which opposed the bill, held a majority.

Nevertheless, within a week, the ruling party dramatically changed its policy and decided to submit a bill on 2 December 1999. What made this change possible? Two people close to President Kim Dae-jung—Lim Chae-jeong and Kim Seong-jae—were critical to swerving the policy of the ruling party. As mentioned, Congressman Lim was the head of the policy planning committee in the ruling party; it was an executive position determining the priorities of the party's policies and coordinating policy concerns between the ruling party and the president's office. Secretary Kim was a senior secretary to the president for civil affairs and had worked for a long time with President Kim during the authoritarian period. Both were visited by the representatives from Jeju and were sympathetic to the victims, understood the concerns of activists, and channeled those concerns to President Kim.[53] Yang Dong-yun, who cochaired Provincial Solidarity and participated in the visits, stated, "These two people were critical in the last phase of the advocacy by bridging between the activists and President Kim."[54]

On 6 December 1999, the first step was taken in the National Assembly to review the bills submitted by the ruling party and the opposition party. The bills first had to go through a small screening committee of the Administration and Self-Governing Committee. The coordination within the committee was successful, and a bipartisan bill was created the very next day. The bipartisan bill passed a plenary session of the Administration and Self-Governing Committee and a plenary session of the Legislation and Judiciary Committee with only minor and technical adjustments. However, as the bill went through the process conservative elements of society started to criticize both the ruling and opposition parties and press them to withdraw the bill.

The bills from the ruling and opposition party had to go through a negotiation process. As expected, two points were at the center of the debate—first, the definition and period of the Jeju 4.3 events, and second, issues related to reparations. For the ruling party and activists, the definition of the Jeju 4.3 events was the single most important aspect, one which could not be compromised. The new understanding of the Jeju 4.3 events as human rights violations was achieved through fifty long, painstaking years of research, activism, and local-level investigations. Activists and victims had fought hard to clear themselves from being seen as "the reds," since all those killed, disappeared, or imprisoned had been regarded as Communist insurgents. In addition, families and relatives of victims suffered grave social disadvantages in the guilt-by-association system. Victims and family members lived in shame and disgrace under the false accusation of being Communists. The only way to redress the issue was to redefine the Jeju 4.3 events as, at least, state violence and human rights violations and, at most, a democratic and popular uprising. Therefore, both the definition and period of the Jeju 4.3 events were critical in defining the nature of the armed protests and civilian victims.

The opposition party, on the other hand, rejected any retributive or restorative measures beyond the investigation and objected to including the term "reparations" in the law. In a sense, a simple *investigation* of the Jeju 4.3 events was not a huge threat to the opposition party because an investigation could target either the armed protests or the civilian massacres, but codifying *reparations*, thus acknowledging responsibility under the law, was a different matter. Therefore, activists and victims held fast to their definition, and the opposition party held fast to the principle of no reparations and this provided a window of opportunity for negotiation. For victims and activists, reparations could be a secondary matter compared to the investigation of civilian massacres and redefining the Jeju 4.3 events so that the honor of the dead and disappeared could be restored. In addition, activists were confident that reparations could be achieved through later advocacy once the official investigation revealed the gruesome nature of the state violence. Eventually, victims and activists made "a strategic and provisional concession in order to enact a special law."[55] Reparations were the core element of the advocacy, but they were also something that could be deferred and might—and must—be achieved by future activism.

The bipartisan bill was a compromise between the opposition party, representing conservative and anti-Communist groups, and the ruling party, acting for victims and local activists. The definition of the Jeju 4.3 events was exactly the same as the one proposed by victims and activists. The opposition adopted the broader period of the events, which started in 1 March 1947, and also accepted the emphasis on state violence and mass atrocities. Congressman Byun's effort made this change possible despite strong objections from the opposition party. Byun struggled hard but finally decided to adopt 1 March 1947 as the starting point for investigations and persuaded his colleagues in the opposition party to accept it, arguing that the local understanding of the Jeju 4.3 events is different and "there is a strong local consensus."[56]

The words "reparations" and "compensation" were not included in the compromise bill. An article discussing a financial and medical "subsidy" for victims who were still under medical treatment due to the Jeju 4.3 events was included. The only further measure beyond the investigation of the events was the commemoration project including establishing a memorial park and museum. A few articles were also dropped out of the final bill due to Assembly officials' objection that there was a high chance that the bill will not pass the National Assembly with these options as they were either too progressive or too costly. (For example, the opposition party had a retrial clause in their revised bill to allow an opportunity for victims who were convicted during the Jeju 4.3 events to be retried and the declaration of 3 April as a memorial day. The ruling party's bill had an article that would create a permanent foundation to support further investigation and study of the Jeju 4.3 events and also had a clause that would provide living expenses for the victims.) Although victims and activists retreated on the reparations issues and some other measures, the most important foundation—the redefinition of the Jeju 4.3 events—was successfully laid down. In a way, the opposition party did not fully understand the significance of this definition at the time. The new definition in the special law played a critical role in the subsequent battle against the opponents of truth commission activities.

On 15 December 1999, the bipartisan bill first appeared at the regular session of the National Assembly with an explanation of the bill by Congresswoman Choo. She explained that the purpose of the bill was "to investigate the truth of the Jeju 4.3 events and restore the honor of related victims and families, and thereby promote human rights, democracy, and the unity of the nation" as stated in article 1 of the proposed bill.[57] The bill encountered objections on the next day when Congressman Kim Yong-gap, a renowned conservative politician, made a speech objecting to it and then walked out of the session. However, a consensus had been reached through the negotiation process, and the bill even passed without a vote by virtue of the chairman's authority. On 16 December 1999, at the regular session of the National Assembly, the Special Law for Investigation of the Jeju 4.3 Events and Restoration of the Honor of Victims was finally passed.

Local Activism, Evidence, and Korean Japanese

The commemoration projects in 1998 and the enactment movement in 1999 were the crux of the transitional justice advocacy movement. All the political, social, and cultural power of activists was concentrated on these two projects with the full support of victims and the general public. The cultural and research sectors of the advocacy movement played the most important role by successfully leading the fiftieth anniversary commemoration projects, which was a stepping stone for the enactment movement in 1999. Certainly, the inauguration of President Kim Dae-jung and the support of the ruling party and individual lawmakers such as Congresswoman Choo were indispensable preconditions for success. Nevertheless, constant activism and persistent demands from local civil society was the critical factor in making these politicians to do what they promised to do. Politicians can—either intentionally or unintentionally—forget or fail to follow through with their promises, and quite often their behaviors fall short of expectations. Local activists were able to narrow this gap by pressuring President Kim and the ruling party using a highly effective and tight network of activists in Jeju and Seoul.

In addition, the process of enactment proved that release of critical evidence in a timely manner was a key determinant for the successful passage of the Special Law. If it were not for the release of the list of court-martialed victims by Congresswomen Choo, the enactment process would not have been possible in the 15th National Assembly. It was the power of consecutive critical and concrete evidence—the Darangshi cave in 1992, release of the congressional report, official minutes, and victims' applications of 1960 in 1996, and finally, the release of the list of court-martialed victims in 1999—that facilitated the enactment of the Special Law. When the events were over fifty years old and previous regimes had been systematically destroying evidence and intimidating victims and witnesses to shut their mouths, it was extremely difficult to find evidence. Under these conditions, even the testimonies of victims and witnesses were sometimes ineffective, since the public has been taught to accept the government's perspective and not be deceived by "Communist agitation." In other words, South Korean society itself had been built on a foundation of forced oblivion and distorted understanding of the Jeju 4.3 events. Thus, concrete and indisputable evidence was the most effective way to defeat the endless objections and threats to the advocacy.

In addition, Korean Japanese were also actively engaged in the enactment movement in 1999 and worked to empower local activism from the outside. A few prominent figures such as Seo Seung actively participated in the later stages of the movement and represented the victims in Japan. Others organized public lectures, conferences, and memorial concerts to help publicize the Jeju 4.3 events not only to Korean Japanese but also to the Japanese public. In one conference in Tokyo in 1998, renowned historian Bruce Cumings expressed his views on US responsibility and supported the enactment movement. In his presentation he said:

> If it should come to pass that any Koreans succeed in gaining compensation from the American Government for the events of 1945 to 1953, certainly the people of Cheju [*sic*] should come first. For it was on that hauntingly beautiful island that the postwar world witnessed the American capacity for unrestrained violence against indigenous people fighting for self-determination and social justice.[58]

All of these activities served to demonstrate that the Jeju 4.3 events were not only an issue of local and national importance but were also of international importance. In a sense, Japanese senator Den Hideo's visit to the 1998 international conference was made possible by the persistent activism of the Korean Japanese.

Through all these endeavors, activists and victims achieved a significant goal: a new definition of the Jeju 4.3 events. The codification of the Jeju 4.3 events as human rights violations and state violence was the single most important achievement of the decade-long advocacy. It was especially important for the next ten years of truth commission activities, including investigations, victims' screening processes, and commemoration projects. For the conservative sector of society, the whole enactment process came as a huge surprise, since the traditional understanding of the Jeju 4.3 events stood strong for over fifty years. Their counterattack had already started in the week before the passage of the bill when twenty-three right-wing organizations took out a newspaper advertisement against the Special Law and lawmakers. The level of attack intensified as the commission's activities went forward. It was the definition of the Jeju 4.3 events in the Special Law that finally protected the proponents of the truth commission.[59]

6

The Jeju Commission, 2000–2003

In order for a law passed in the National Assembly to go into effect, it has to go through consideration by the cabinet and be approved by the president. The law goes into effect three months after its promulgation. Eight people, including six activists and two representatives of victims, were invited to the Blue House, the presidential residence, to join the ceremony of signing the Special Law. This was the first open and public signing of any law passed in the Kim Dae-jung presidency, and it indicated the president's desire to appreciate the efforts of activists and console the suffering of victims.[1] President Kim, in his address, stated, "The Special Law will be a monumental landmark in the development of human rights and democracy in our society."[2] With the president's signature, the Special Law was promulgated on 13 January 2000 and came into effect on 13 April 2000. The law mandated the government to set up two central bodies—the Jeju Commission (article 3) and the administrative committee (article 4). The Jeju Commission was designed to investigate the Jeju 4.3 events, to identify victims, and to restore the honor of victims. The prime minister led the commission, which consisted of fewer than twenty commissioners, including the governor of Jeju Province, state officials, representatives of victims, and others with knowledge and expertise. The central function of the administrative committee was to carry out practical businesses entrusted by the Jeju Commission, such as accepting applications from victims, conducting preliminary fact-finding, and administering the subsidy to victims. The governor of Jeju Province led the administrative committee, which consisted of fewer than fifteen members.

The Jeju Commission had three key mandates. First and most important, the commission had two years to collect and analyze information and evidence (article 6) and had six more months to prepare and publish an official report (article 7). Second, the commission had to receive individual applications from victims and their family members (article 10) and provide medical and financial subsidy to the victims (article 9). Finally, the commission had to carry out four commemoration projects stipulated in the law by establishing a memorial park and museum with a common graveyard and monument (article 8). In order carry out all these mandates, the enforcement ordinance first had to be legislated. However, it was not an easy process, and it took five more months to legislate the enforcement ordinance and an additional three months to launch the commission in August 2000.

These delays indicate that the creation of a truth-seeking commission was neither a smooth process nor without obstacles. On the contrary, counterattacks from opposing groups—the military and police and other anti-Communist elements in society—had already begun as activists and victims were celebrating their long-awaited victory. Immediately after President Kim singed the law, opponents started to criticize the law and to pressure the president and his administration. The conservative *Weolgan Chosun* carried opinion pieces by Lee Jin-wu, a former congressman and lawyer, and Lee Hyeon-hee, a conservative historian, arguing that the National Assembly made a fatal mistake, first, by forgetting the nature of the Jeju 4.3 "Communist rebellion" that was instigated by the Communists in the North and the Soviet Union and, second, by falsely accusing the military and police of being murderers and criminals.[3] Both made a clear statement that the Jeju 4.3 events started as a Communist riot by those who denied the legitimacy of the South Korean government. It is not surprising that they presented this view since Lee Jin-wu was a lawyer who represented Rhee In-su, adopted son of Rhee Syng-man, in his lawsuit against the *Hankyoreh* and the *Jemin Ilbo*, and Lee Hyeon-hee was a professor who contributed to history textbooks from a strong anti-Communist perspective.

At the same time, fifteen conservative leaders, including retired generals and former ministers and congressmen, filed a petition with the Constitutional Court to stop the Special Law in April 2000.[4] A similar petition signed by 322 retired generals who were in a commanding position in the South Korean military during the Jeju 4.3 events followed the first one. In addition, other anti-Communist organizations—the Korean War Veterans, the Association of Former Marine Corps Members, the Association of Former Police Officers, and the Democratic Association for Protection of Freedom—participated. The court appeals had three purposes. First, the retired generals wanted to abolish the Special Law and frustrate the commission's activities. Second, these groups wanted to exert maximum pressure on the prime minister who was heading the commission to reflect their position. Finally, these groups wanted to provide cover fire so that commissioners and members of the investigation unit representing their point of view might have maximum power.[5] Although activists and victims had gone through a long and thorny way up to the enactment of the Special Law, the struggle was not over yet.

Creation of the Commission

The initial struggle began with the legislation of the enforcement ordinance, which defined the setup and activities of the commission and the investigation unit. A draft of the ordinance was announced in April, and it was a moment when activists realized that there were double obstacles.[6] Activists faced intense resistance from conservative media, politicians, and the military and police. On top of this resistance, activists faced other hurdles such as the administration's ignorance of the Jeju 4.3 events, public officials' tendency to blindly follow precedents and adopt expediency, red tape, and organizational self-interest.

Activists criticized the administration's draft in three aspects. First, the draft proposed that more than a half of the commissioners should be state officials. The law already included the prime minister and the governor of

Jeju, but the administration added seven other ministers—the ministers of justice, defense, public administration and security, health, finance, policy coordination, and government legislation—to the list. Furthermore, for the remaining nine commissioners, the draft, primarily with pressure from the defense department, added a military historian along with "the representatives of victims and others with knowledge and expertise" stipulated in the law. Thus, at least ten out of twenty commissioners had to be either state officials or a military historian. This composition was unacceptable to activists, who initially proposed an independent body to carry out the investigation with objectivity and neutrality. It was less likely that high-level officials and military historians would be sympathetic to the victims. A few activists further argued that it was "absurd to have so many commissioners from the military, who were responsible for the massacres."[7]

Second, the law specified that the commission have a special investigation unit (article 7). However, the specific composition and function of the investigation unit were to be decided by the ordinance. In the draft, the administration proposed a unit with fifteen members with two expert advisers, who were to actually carry out the investigation and draft the report. Activists objected to the composition, first, because it was unrealistic that fifty-year-old facts about civilian deaths of thirty thousand people could be thoroughly investigated by only two experts. People in Jeju already had a realistic estimate of the time and resources needed for a full investigation after their local investigation, which had seventeen full-time investigators. The conflict over the number of experts was mainly a fight between activists who wanted a commission with a certain scale and public officials who wanted to reduce expenses.[8] The administration proposed that nine out of fifteen members should be director-level public officials—including a military historian. Thus, the draft stated that two core bodies—the commission and the investigation unit—must consist mostly of those who were ignorant of the Jeju 4.3 events.

Third, the draft ordinance allowed for only four months for victims to apply for their case to the commission, which then verifies and confirms the case and creates the victims' registry. In addition, family members were narrowly defined as spouses and lineal descendants with official family certificates. Activists first argued that at least one year should be given to victims and their families, considering the long duration of the events and the magnitude of state violence. Local activists knew very well that the registration of victims at the provincial level took a couple of years. In addition, activists objected to the lineal descendant rule and family certificate requirement on the grounds that stringent requirements would discourage victims from applying. Local activists already had seen cases where an entire family was killed and no lineal descendants survived to apply for victims' registry. Moreover, it was a nationwide practice to report a newborn child in a family registry only after a couple of years due to the high infant mortality rate. It was highly likely that victims under one or two years old would not be recorded if the strict requirements were pursued.

Activists and victims were once again on the street protesting against the draft ordinance. Through rallies, proponents of the commission wanted to demonstrate the organized power of the Jeju people behind the law and to frustrate the resistance from the conservatives. Victims and activists issued a statement threatening that they would not participate in the commission if the current draft was passed without revision.[9] Activists again lobbied politicians and congress members. Both Congresswoman Choo and the Chief Presidential Secretary Han Gwang-ok expressed their concerns about the draft ordinance, and those who helped to enact the Special Law such as Kim Seong-jae and Kim Sang-bae also played a role.[10] Choo strongly urged that a specialist on the Jeju 4.3 events, not a military historian, should be included in the commission and the investigation unit.[11] Choo further pointed out that the current proposed composition of the investigation unit, with only two experts, should be revised.[12]

Reflecting the will of local citizens and sympathetic politicians, the ordinance was passed in the cabinet on 2 May 2000 with a few important revisions. First, the number of public officials was considerably reduced from ten to eight in the commission and from nine to five in the investigation unit. Second, as per the request of victims, the specific requirement to have a military historian was deleted, and the number of experts in the investigation unit was increased from two to five. Third, the ordinance allowed six months for victims to apply, allowing two more months, and the strict family certificate requirement was loosened.[13] Immediately, the local government drafted a provincial ordinance in which the most important aspect was the formation of the administrative committee. Thus, three key legal structures—a special law, an enforcement ordinance, and a provincial ordinance—were set up by June 2000. Nevertheless, it was yet another beginning of the battles over *who* should be included on the commission and *how* the commission and committee should function.

Based on the legal structures, the highest deliberative body—the Jeju Commission—was created on 28 August 2000. The commission was composed of twenty members of which eight members were state ministers and twelve were selected from civil society.[14] Among the twelve appointed, Kim Jeom-gon, Han Gwang-deok, and Lee Hwang-wu represented the military and police, but the overall composition was considered fair and impartial since many figures sympathetic to victims were also included. Victims and activists were satisfied with the balanced composition, which was designed to avoid a potential bias in the commission's work. Following the commission, the administrative committee was set up in September, encompassing both supporters and those in opposition.[15] The process of appointing commissioners was relatively smooth because both the prime minister and the governor were responsive to victims' demands, and victims accepted that it was inevitable to have military personnel and conservative scholars on the commission and that the current composition of the commission with public officials and opponents would, in the end, empower the commission's activities by increasing its reputation as an ideologically balanced institution.

The process of setting up the investigation unit, however, was bumpier than the process of setting up the commission. The ordinance stipulated the investigation unit should be composed of fifteen members and an expert advisory group should be composed of five experts and fifteen staff members. Five expert advisers were appointed, mainly from the *Jemin Ilbo* and the Jeju 4.3 Research Institute, which had the most expertise on the Jeju 4.3 events.[16] However, the process was delayed when Lee Sang-geun from the National Institute of Korean History was appointed as head of the investigation unit. Activists opposed the decision because the institute was a government-funded body that had traditionally viewed the Jeju 4.3 events as a Communist rebellion. Again, victims organized a rally and activists paid visits to government offices and the administration; and activist accepted a compromise when the "relatively neutral" Park Won-soon, a renowned human rights lawyer, was appointed as the head.[17] The investigation unit finally started its operations on 17 January 2001, more than a year after the bill passed the National Assembly.[18]

Investigation

The Special Law stated that the first purpose of the law and the commission was to investigate the truth about the Jeju 4.3 events (article 1). The initial two and a half years of the commission's work focused mainly on the investigation and writing up the report. Other functions of the commission—the registration of victims and the commemoration project—concurrently proceeded, but key decisions were made after the release of the report. The investigation proceeded in three steps. First, the investigation unit conducted preliminary research for six months between September 2000 and February 2001. The expert group created a list of a vast array of primary and secondary sources; selected interviewees including victims, police, and military personnel, insurgents, scholars, and lawyers; and shortlisted relevant government branches and organizations to investigate. In addition, the unit had several workshops and education sessions to which they invited not only historians but also experts from other institutions who addressed the human rights violations in Gwangju and Nogunri.

Immediately, a heated debate started on *what to investigate* regarding the Jeju 4.3 events and civilian massacres.[19] The law mandated the commission to investigate the Jeju 4.3 events defined as: "an armed conflict in Jeju, which started from 1 March 1947, culminated in the disturbance on 3 April 1948, and ended on 12 September 1954, and the subsequent civilian sacrifice in the course of counterinsurgency operations." It was up to the investigation unit to decide *which aspects* of the Jeju 4.3 events should be investigated. After several debates, the members of the unit agreed to investigate sixteen aspects of the Jeju 4.3 events, which roughly fell into four categories.[20] The first was an investigation of the armed conflict itself, including the characteristics and the causes of the conflict, the role of the South Korean Labor Party, and the activities of insurgents. The second was the scope and level of civilian sacrifice, including the total number of victims, the composition of perpetrators, atrocities committed by the insurgents, abuses of state power, the role of the Northwest Youth Association, and destroyed villages and other material losses. The third was the legality of state action and the responsibilities. Here, the members decided to investigate the legality of the military court that tried civilians during the conflict, the legality of the 1948 martial law, the chain of command in the mass killing cases, and the role of the US military. Fourth, the commission examined two additional aspects—the history of transitional justice over fifty years and human rights violations of families of victims during the authoritarian regimes.

Thus, equal attention was given to the armed conflict and the subsequent civilian massacres, and it was unacceptable for members representing the military and police to put an exclusive emphasis on the armed conflict and not on human rights violations.[21] The head of the unit, Park Won-soon, a long-time proponent of human rights, defended the balanced approach on the grounds that the definition of the Jeju 4.3 events in the Special Law emphasized both the conflict and the massacres. As a human rights lawyer, Park firmly believed that human rights should be the most important focal point of the commission's activities, and he skillfully led the ideologically divided investigation unit to reach a consensus.[22] Kang Chang-il, executive secretary of the unit, strongly supported Park's position of focusing on human rights violations, even arguing that defining the characteristics of the armed conflict was "a secondary matter."[23]

The investigation unit then collected data from domestic and international sources and conducted interviews between March 2001 and August 2002. For one and a half years, the investigation unit, with support from the expert group, collected 10,594 written and recorded documents from nineteen domestic institutions and organizations and nine countries.[24] The Special Law granted the commission the right to request access to government files (article 6). None of the government organizations explicitly rejected the commission's request to access the files, and expert advisers had direct access to several key institutions such as the National Archives, the Institute for Military History Compilation, and the National Institute for Korean History. The investigation unit also focused on collecting data from records from the military and police related to the counterinsurgency operations. However, in many cases, critical evidence of the Jeju 4.3 events was already destroyed or lost by the time of investigation.[25]

In addition, since the commission did not have further enforcement power, it had to depend on the good will of these organizations. For example, the police only handed over a list of 122 policemen killed in combat, and the list of the local police chief during the Jeju 4.3 events.[26] The police explained that most of the files were lost during the 1960s or destroyed in the 1980s. The police were the most uncooperative body. The experts visited the police three times, but the information they got was "almost none."[27] The commission was only able to secure a written statement from the police that they no longer had any documents.[28] The situation was a little better with the military, and the experts were able to find a few internal documents such as personal files of commanders stationed in Jeju, personnel appointment records, and military court documents. However, critical information—such as a daily record of military operations or detailed information about military positions in Jeju—was still missing.[29] The situation was not much different for other government branches, and the commission evaluated: "The practice of managing government documents was simply poor, and most of documents were destroyed in the course of political upheavals such as the 4.19 revolution and 5.16 military coup."[30]

The Special Law also granted the commission the right to conduct private interviews to gather information (article 6). Interviews were the primary and critical source of information due to a lack of previous studies and documentation. The investigation unit came up with a list of 2,870 possible interviewees and later narrowed it down into 503 interviewees, representing both victims and perpetrators. Interviewees were dispersed by region: 353 interviewees were from Jeju; 60 from Seoul, 50 from other regions in the country, and 40 from outside the country. However, unlike later truth commissions that had minimum enforcement power, the Jeju Commission did not even have the power to issue fines for failing to co-operate.[31] The most difficult interviewees were former military officers who had been in commanding posts. Many rejected the interview request on the grounds of "illness" or "not in a mood for testimony."[32] The commission sent an official document requesting interviews and put additional pressure on a few critical witnesses. For example, Seo Jong-cheol, a retired general who served as an assistant commander, consistently rejected the commission's requests, and the commission strongly pressured him by saying that his name and the fact that he rejected several interview requests would be stated in the final report.[33] Although Seo eventually appeared before the commission, he deliberately avoided answering any questions for an hour by saying, "I do not have any recollection of that time."[34]

The Report

The next step was to draft a report analyzing the documents and testimonies. The written documents were a critical source of information regarding the background and process of the armed conflicts and counter-insurgency operations. Oftentimes, official documents provided the details of persons involved in the counterinsurgency operations and court documents provided the details of victims. However, written documents were incomplete, first, because information on mass killings was seldom recorded and, second, because many key documents were lost and destroyed under the previous regimes. Information from interviews filled in the gap left by the scarcity of written documents and provided the voice of victims, but information was "often inaccurate and suffered from selective memory of the past."[35] Five experts in the advisory group drafted the report, dividing up the sections, and then fifteen members of the investigation unit reviewed the report.[36] (Later in the review process, the division of labor became an issue when Na Jong-sam, representing the military, expressed his disapproval of other sections of the report. He further complained that it was impossible for him to have a say in other sections due to the division of labor.) Despite minor disagreements, experts generally agreed on three points: first, following the practice of the *Jemin Ilbo*'s special reports, the report should only contain those facts that went through a thorough verification process; second, the Jeju 4.3 events should be investigated within the national and international political context; and finally, a comprehensive historical truth, rather than individual and fragmented facts, should be revealed.[37]

In the course of drafting the report, two important events took place that empowered the commission's activities. First, on 27 September 2001, the Constitutional Court dismissed both petitions of the former generals and conservative politicians. The majority—seven out of nine judges—ruled against the petition arguing the Special Law was constitutional because it was enacted through democratic procedures in order to support the principle of liberal democracy. The judges reached the ruling after two oral proceedings and further investigation lasting more than a year and a half. (However, at the same time, the court strongly recommended the commission not to consider executives of the South Korean Labor Party, the leaders of the insurgents, and those who committed murder or arson as victims.[38]) Second, Roh Moo-hyun, a longtime proponent of transitional justice, won the presidential election in December 2002. Roh, as a human rights and labor rights lawyer, sympathized with the victims and understood the commission's activity as "the development of human rights."[39] During his campaign, Roh expressed his view that the commission would set an important "precedent and model for other human rights violations cases" and pledged to apologize as a president if the commission found abuse of state power.[40] (Roh kept his promise in 2003 by delivering an apology on his visit to Jeju immediately after the release of the report.)

However, despite these favorable circumstances, drafting the report was not an easy process due to the resistance from within. The debate became intense as the members started to discuss the table of contents, and the earlier debate over the focus of investigation resurfaced. For example, Ha Jae-pyeong and Ryu Jae-gap, representing the military, proposed to entirely leave out the detailed discussion of the armed conflicts and counterinsurgency operations.[41] In a sense, it was strange because the military initially advocated focusing only on the armed conflict and not on human rights violations. However, in the course of investigation, the undeniable reality of the massacres was disclosed and the military could no longer maintain their previous position. Instead, the military now wanted to totally leave out the investigation of the armed conflict so that the traditional understanding—a Communist rebellion—could be preserved. Park, the head of the investigation unit, however, defended the original plan stating, "The Special Law clearly mandates the commission and the investigation unit to investigate both armed conflict and civilian massacres."[42]

The military wanted to put more emphasis on revealing the Communist Party's involvement in the Jeju 4.3 events, while activists wanted to focus on investigating the massacres and identifying perpetrators.[43] Yang Jo-hoon testified that there was a clear divide between the two sides, and experts in the investigation unit made a strong effort to hit on a balance between the two.[44] In addition, members continued to debate the content of the report, titles and subtitles, and the use of specific terms. For example, Ha Jae-pyeong, a military historian, argued that terms like "a period of bloodshed" or "scorched-earth operations" were biased against the military.[45] The members in the unit scrutinized terms and concepts used in the draft and agreed to use ideologically neutral or value-free terms as much as possible. The members also agreed to write both viewpoints in parallel for ideologically volatile issues, such as the characteristics of the Jeju 4.3 events, the causes of the armed uprising, the roles of the South Korean Labor Party and the US military, the proportionality of violence used in the course of military operations, the legality of the martial law of 1948 and the military court, and the responsibility for the massacres. For example, instead of reaching a verdict on the illegality of the martial law and the military court during the conflict, members decided to simply state that there was controversy about the legality of these practices.

The meetings lasted over three hours, and the heated debates between the two sides even turned into brawls on several occasions. Ryu Jae-gap, representing the military, incited members by saying, "Some members of the investigation unit are negating the legitimacy of the Republic of Korea [national identity] . . . by trying to turn South Korean history upside down!"[46] It was mainly Ryu, representing the military, who attacked representatives of victims (Kang Jong-ho) and activists (Kang Chang-il).[47] In one session, Kang even scolded Ryu Jae-gap and Ha Jae-pyeong:

> You two should not have been included in the commission in the first place. People in Jeju accepted the representatives from the military and police to make the commission and its report more neutral and objective. Why are you so petty and nibble at my words? A great number of people were killed by the abuse of state violence during the Jeju 4.3 events![48]

Eventually, after debates in twelve sessions, in February 2003 a draft was finalized in a quasi-unanimous opinion.[49] Park Won-soon, as a head of the investigation unit, tried to find a consensus, but he was ready to vote even if a consensus was not reached.[50] At the same time, he tried hard to rationally persuade members from the military. For example, in one session, Park rebutted members representing the military and police by stating:

> The military is not only yours, Ryu Jae-gap and Ha Jae-pyeong. It is our military, too. How can admitting to past wrongs only defame the military? As in the cases of Geochang and Gwangju, we can reach reconciliation, and the military can regain public trust after revealing the truth.[51]

The members representing the military and police reluctantly approved the draft because of Park's threat to vote without them, but exactly the same debate was repeated in later sessions in which the twenty commissioners reviewed the draft.

Review Process

The report, which was drafted by the investigation unit, was submitted to the commission in early March 2003 for review. In a review session led by Prime Minister Ko Geon, the exact same debate started between those representing the military and police and those representing victims and activists.[52] The military and police were determined to obstruct the review process led by the prime minister. Commissioner Han Gwang-deok, a retired general, prepared a memo denouncing the value of the report in the very first meeting:

> This is not a report on the truth but a report written in order to justify the Communist rebellion and condemn the Korean military. It does not fully explain the activities of the South Korean Labor Party in Jeju. . . . The report intentionally waters down the relationship between the South Korean Labor Party and the Communist insurgents in Jeju. The Communist riot on 3 April 1948 was definitely a premeditated rebellion against the nation. . . . The report contains so much distortion of the truth and biases. . . . Thus, I propose that the head of the investigation unit, Park Won-soon, and members of the special investigation unit should be subject to investigation by the Board of Audit and Inspection.[53]

At the same time, the military, especially the defense minister, tried to "intentionally delay" the review process by suggesting getting a new advisory board or subcommittee to redraft the report.[54]

On the other side, many commissioners, including Minister of Justice Kang Geum-sil, urged the commissioners to immediately make a decision. Minister Kang clearly understood the intention of the military and police to frustrate the committee's efforts:

> The Special Law, in articles 6 and 7, clearly stipulated that the commission had two years to collect and analyze information and evidence and prepare and publish a report within six months from the end date of investigation. Since a two and a half year period already expired one month ago, we are obviously violating the law. If we need more time to investigate, we certainly have to revise the law. Moreover, having an advisory board or a subcommittee should also come after the revision of the law since we do not have a legal ground to institute such a committee.[55]

The session, which originally was scheduled for one hour, lasted over two hours, and despite Kang's urge to vote, Prime Minister Ko suggested the creation of a subcommittee to review the report.[56]

The subcommittee was composed of four ministers and three civilian commissioners.[57] The subcommittee held three meetings and revised twenty-four places in the draft report reflecting the complaints from the military.[58] It was the military—the minister of defense and Commissioner Kim Jeom-gon—who mostly raised objections, and the investigation unit—Park Won-soon and Yang Jo-hoon—responded to the criticism. In the course of discussion, the retired generals asked the prime minister to abandon the current version of the report because "it characterizes the military operations as state violence and seriously defames the legitimacy and honor of the military."[59] In the same spirit, one of the commissioners representing the military, Kim Jeom-gon, resigned because "the report focuses too much on the excessive use of force by the military and police in the course of counterinsurgency operations."[60] The conservative groups pressured the commission; the opposition party expressed their concerns about the draft report; and the conservative media carried news reports on the controversies around the draft report.[61]

Three terms in the draft report were at the center of the debate in the subcommittee meetings: "scorched-earth operations" (*chotohwa jakjeon*), "mass killing" (*jipdan salsang*), and "armed uprising" (*mujang bonggi*). First, the military demanded removing "scorched-earth operations" from the draft report because the military did not officially have such an operation named in their field manual.[62] The defense minister instead requested using "the use of excessive force during suppression" (*gwaing jinap*) or "counterinsurgency operations" (*tobeol jakjeon*). However, Yang Jo-hoon and others strongly objected to this view and argued that although it may not have been in the manual, numerous witnesses, including former military generals Kim Jeong-mu and Yu Jae-hong, testified to the operation and even the military historians used the term.[63] Kang Chang-il supported Yang's view by showing that the term is in the dictionary although it may be not in the military field manual.[64] In the end, both sides agreed not to use the term when describing the military operations but used the term when describing the consequences of the operations. In other words, the report could say "the counterinsurgency operations left scorched earth in the mountain villages" but not "the military decided to carry out scorched-earth operations in the mountain villages."[65]

Second, the military suggested using "massive life sacrifice" (*jipdan inmyeong huisaeng*) instead of "mass killing" (*jipdan salsang*) in the report.[66] Ryu Jae-gap made an argument that individuals who were suspected of being Communists and their supporters were killed *individually* not as a mass so "mass killing" was not an accurate term to use.[67] In addition, by using a word, "sacrifice" (*huisaeng*), the military wanted to emphasize that the civilian deaths were *collateral damages* to the military operations, not purposeful atrocities. However, it certainly shows ignorance or intentional distortion of the facts from the military side, since evidence of purposeful civilian massacres—such as the killing of children, women, and elderly and also mass murders of all residents in the villages—was presented to the commissioners on several occasions.[68]

Third, the military further suggested that describing the armed protest on 3 April 1948 as an "armed uprising" (*mujang bonggi*) was reflecting the Communist view.[69] However, Yang firmly stood behind the term suggesting that "uprising" (*bonggi*) is a neutral term that objectively describes "the status of violent upheaval similar to a swarm of bees" without any ideological connotation.[70] The military side was persuaded and both terms—"mass killing" and "armed uprising"—were retained.

Other issues were debated. The draft report specifically named commanders of the 9th and 2nd Regiments as responsible for the massacres. The military wanted to remove the names, but activists and victims stood firm because naming the perpetrators is one of the key elements in truth seeking.[71] Both parties reached a compromise when they decided to state those responsible as "the commander of the 9th (or 2nd) Regiment" without naming names.[72] However, their names—Song Yo-chan and Ham Byeong-seon—were already mentioned in the previous section, so readers who wanted to know the details could easily find the names in the report. Also, the report further stated, "The United States is not free from responsibility for the outbreak of the Jeju 4.3 events and subsequent counterinsurgency operations." However, Prime Minister Ko pointed out that the statement was too broad and lacked critical evidence. Thus, the sentence was revised to pinpoint the subject of responsibility, not as the United State but as "the US military government and military advisers in South Korea." In some cases, the military wanted to remove the name of Rhee Syng-man in the text and simply state "the government" and this suggestion was partly adopted.[73] In another case, the military wanted to emphasize who initiated the armed protests by qualifying "the armed conflict" with the phrase "initiated by the Jeju committee of the South Korean Communist Party" in every sentence.[74] Around thirty items were discussed in the subcommittee, and finally it was up to the commission to make the final decision.

The revised draft was resubmitted in a plenary session, and the head of the investigation unit, Park Won-soon, again urged commissioners to approve the report since "the report went through a thorough reexamination."[75] However, commissioners representing the military and police, Lee Hwang-wu, Ryu Jae-gap, and Han Gwang-deok, strongly pushed Prime Minister Ko to examine the report for another six months, this time in consultation with experts from outside, and Prime Minister Ko was persuaded by the proposal. In addition, due to the fierce debate, even commissioners who maintained a neutral position such as Shin Yong-ha suggested further review.[76] On the other side, commissioners representing victims and activists strongly urged the commission to approve and release the report. In addition, Minister of Justice Kang Geum-sil once more strongly urged Prime Minister Ko and the commissioners representing the military and police to approve the report, again arguing, "The Special Law has a specific date to deliver the report, and it is a serious breach of the law to delay the review process."[77] However, Prime Minister Ko insisted on having another session, and the commissioners tentatively approved the report under the condition that if new evidence were to be found in six months, the commission would revise the report.[78]

Since the report was tentatively approved in the session, the draft report was now in view of the public, and it had to go through further scrutiny between 1 May and 28 September 2003.[79] Another subcommittee was set up to solicit objections from the public and reexamine the report.[80] Over six months, 376 objections from twenty individuals and organizations, mostly representing the police and military, were submitted. The police submitted 20 and the military 54 objections, and other conservative organizations—for example, retired veterans and retired police—also submitted 143 objections. However, most of the revision requests from the military and police came from committee insiders. For example, Na Jong-sam, one of the expert advisers in the investigation unit, drafted several revision requests himself and provided this insider's information to right-wing organizations.[81] In addition, organizations representing victims and activists also submitted 77 petitions. In addition, eight individuals submitted 66 objections.[82] However, most of the 376 objections had already been dealt with during the previous fierce debates. Four review sessions were held, and the subcommittee decided to revise 33 items out of 376 objections, of which 21 were simple revision of wordings, phrases, and expressions. Ten were about the details of individual cases (date, name, and place), and two were revisions suggested by new evidence.[83] Of the 33 revisions, 30 items were complaints made by the military and police and other right-wing groups.[84]

The revised report was again on the table at the 8th plenary session for final approval. Again, a heated debate started between the military and the victims' sides, and exactly the same arguments were made by the military as previously, which can be summarized in four points made by the vice-minister of defense:

> First, regarding whether the Jeju 4.3 events was a Communist rebellion or armed uprising, most of the military see it as a rebellion, and even President Kim Dae-jung, in his interview with CNN stated that the events started as a "riot". . . . Second, the report does not reflect the fact that the South Korean Labor Party was actively involved in the Jeju 4.3 events. . . . Third, the United States did not have wartime operational control over the South Korean Army at that time, and it is too much to blame the US military for causing the armed protest. . . . Fourth, the 3.1 shooting incident is a separate incident, and it is too much exaggeration to see the 3.1 shooting incident and the armed protest of 3 April 1948 as part of one event. [85]

Prime Minister Ko finally realized that the fundamental differences between two groups could not be reconciled through debate, and the report was finally approved by a majority vote.

Four Conditions Leading to Success

The final report was published in October 2003, almost three years since the creation of the commission in August 2000. The truth seeking was a tedious process with twelve plenary sessions of the investigation unit, eight plenary sessions of the commission, and nine review sessions of the subcommittee. The military and police and the conservative element of society consistently challenged the commission's activities both from inside and outside the commission. A small number of commissioners and expert advisers representing the military almost dominated sessions, reiterating the anti-Communist perspective on the Jeju 4.3 events.[86] On several occasion, two or three members representing the military and police dominated nearly two-thirds of the meeting time. At the same time, retired generals and right-wing politicians consistently attempted to thwart the commission's activities by filing court complaints and directly pressuring the prime minister. The Jeju Commission, nevertheless, survived a myriad of these challenges. How was this possible?

I found four factors that led to the success of the commission's truth-seeking project. First, the Special Law and the definition of the Jeju 4.3 events provided a strong foundation for combating conservative challenges. In the law, the Jeju 4.3 events were defined both as an armed conflict and human rights violations that started with the police's shooting incident on 1 March 1947. This definition was achieved after fifty years of activism and research, and throughout negotiations with the opposition party activists held fast to this definition. Although activists and victims knew the importance of this definition, they did not expect it would eventually provide an almost invincible shield against a series of conservative and anti-Communist attacks in the course of the investigation.[87] Furthermore, the law mandated the commission to find comprehensive and historical truth instead of individual and factual truth, and the law provided for two and a half years to finish the report. These clauses, which could be seen as imposing a straitjacket, actually helped facilitate the review process by pressing both the head of the investigation and the prime minister to finalize the report.

Second, as with the process of the transitional justice movement, it was also a success based on the evidence. One of the key contributions of the investigation unit was its twelve-volume collection of data archives, with 3,019 items covering 5,848 pages. The investigation unit made it clear that all the members of the unit should share all the documents collected by individual investigators. Documents and testimonies were systematically organized and turned into a database, where information could be easily retrieved whenever there were debates and controversies.[88] One of the expert advisers—Kim Jong-min—struggled hard to get this collection released to the public. The law stipulated that the commission publish a report, but there was no further requirement for it to release collected data and archives. However, Kim saw the value of the collected data and persuaded the commissioners to publish the data.[89] Some critical documents were released to scholars in the course of investigation, and their analysis further strengthened the commission's activities.

Third, the commission made excellent use of the existing local human resources. Two and a half years was not sufficient time to investigate the fifty-year-old massacres of over thirty thousand civilians. It was almost impossible to investigate the massacres with only five expert advisers and fifteen permanent staff members. It was only possible because thirteen years of accumulated knowledge and expertise in Jeju—especially that gathered by the local newspaper and the Research Institute—was absorbed by the commission. In addition, the province-wide investigation in the mid-1990s by the local council provided critical guidelines for the national investigation. Furthermore, the commission benefitted from consistent local attention. The local news media closely followed the investigation and review process, and local movement groups demonstrated the organized power of victims and activists whenever there were obstructions from conservatives in the larger society or a deadlock within the commission.

Finally, and rather ironically, the conservatives' challenges and consistent attacks contributed to the success of the commission's activities. The challenge from inside and outside the commission made the members of the investigation unit more attentive to the details of the report and made them firmly base the report on concrete and indisputable evidence. This was very similar to the process in which police and intelligence agents' interference during the special reports of the *Jemin Ilbo* in the 1990s helped, in the end, to strengthen the report. Since both commissioners and the members of the investigation unit representing the military continuously challenged the report in every detail, the expert advisers made every effort to make the report objective and reliable. At one point, Prime Minister Ko also read the summary of the report line by line and asked expert advisers to provide concrete evidence for almost every sentence.[90] In addition, although complaints against the Special Law filed in the Constitutional Court put heavy pressure on the expert advisers, the ruling in favor of the Special Law, in turn, empowered the investigation and the report.

7

The Impact of the Jeju Commission

The Jeju Commission worked for three years and released its final report on 16 October 2003.[1] At the same time, the commission released seven policy recommendations: first, issue an apology; second, declare a memorial day; third, use the report to educate students and the general public; fourth, establish a memorial park; fifth, provide essential living expenses to bereaved families; sixth, support excavations of mass graves; and seventh, continuously support further investigation and commemoration projects.[2] Activists and victims mostly welcomed the report and recommendations even though some activists thought that the commission conceded too much to the demands of the military and police.[3] Victims demanded further government actions once the report was confirmed and the atrocities officially acknowledged. Victims and activists demanded further mandatory policy measures. For example, activists pushed to have the head of state issue the government apology. In addition, victims pushed for a mandatory revision of history textbooks and the establishment of a permanent foundation.[4] At the same time, the conservatives launched a counteroffensive by releasing a public statement that the report portrayed a Communist rebellion as state violence, repeating their previous position.[5] They tried to denigrate the report by calling the findings of the commission ideologically biased and tried to frustrate follow-up measures.

Therefore, the release of the report was not the end but the beginning of another battle between those who wanted to maximize the impact of the commission and those who wanted to minimize it. As of now, the former has been more effective than the latter, and the situation seems less likely to be reversed in the near future. Scholars, lawyers, and journalists view that the commission's activities and follow-up measures have been successful, especially compared to other commissions.[6] Three pieces of critical evidence, which I will explain more in detail, support this view. First, with the exception of declaring a memorial day, the government has started to implement all policy recommendations. Second, the Special Law went through a progressive revision in 2007, redefining the victims more widely and providing a legal basis for government-funded excavation projects and the permanent research and memorial foundation. Third, all major challenges to the commission's activities ventured by the conservatives were unsuccessful.[7]

Two recent incidents also demonstrate the influence of the commission. The first one occurred in January 2011 when the 16th plenary session of the commission recognized four thousand additional victims and bereaved family members, and approved 12 billion won ($11 million) for further commemoration projects.[8] The decision was a surprise since it was the first meeting held under the administration of President Lee Myung-bak, who had been highly critical of the government spending money on unearthing past history.[9] On assuming office in 2008, Lee slashed the budgets of the truth commissions and proposed merging the Jeju Commission with other commissions.[10] Victims and activists organized rallies and urged local and national politicians to prevent the dissolution of the commission. Eventually, they not only succeeded in frustrating the government plan but also pushed the government to take a further step. On top of this, the commission published a white paper in 2008 on its activities and achievements that was distributed nationwide despite strong objections from public officials.[11] The commission, backed up by civil society, demonstrated its strength and resilience even under a conservative government that basically opposed it.

The second incident occurred in April 2012 during the National Assembly election. The ruling Saenuri Party, formerly the Grand National Party, nominated Lee Young-jo as a candidate for the Gangnam district, the party's traditional stronghold. (Lee Young-jo was a university professor and head of the Truth and Reconciliation Commission of the Republic of Korea (TRCK) under the Lee Myung-bak administration. Although he served as the head of the commission, the commission's activity went downhill under his leadership. He was blamed for hurriedly closing down the commission, which could have worked two more years.) However, in a few days, the party had to withdraw its nomination after a controversy triggered by Lee's use of terms like "rebellion" and "revolt" when referring to the Jeju 4.3 events in a conference paper.[12] Politicians and public officials are now more cautious in their speech and use terms and vocabularies reflecting a more balanced and neutral understanding of the Jeju 4.3 events. Simple denial or ignorant dismissal of the past abuses is no longer legitimate in public discourse. The Jeju Commission played an essential role by giving official legitimation to the facts of the civilian massacres, which can no longer be dismissed as mere opinion or antigovernment agitation.

What Kinds of Truth?

Comprehensive Truth

How was this success possible? In order to understand the impact of the commission, we first have to look carefully into *what kinds of truth* the Jeju Commission revealed and acknowledged in the course of investigation. The first three years of the commission's activities resulted in a report that revealed the comprehensive and historical truth. The report aimed at revealing the facts of both the armed conflict and civilian massacres. The report contributed to the truth of the armed conflicts and counterinsurgency operations in three ways. First, new documents and testimonies were discovered, and previously unknown aspects of the armed conflicts were revealed. For example, the commission discovered the minutes of the cabinet meeting on 21 January 1949 in which President Rhee Syng-man ordered "harsh suppression" of the insurgency. It also discovered new articles from twenty-two discontinued newspapers covering this period.[13] In addition, the commission found a copy of Executive Order No. 31 (17 November 1948) that declared martial law in Jeju with the original signature of President Rhee and his cabinet members; this document provided indisputable evidence that the martial law declared in Jeju was not legally founded on the Martial Law Act of 24 November 1949.[14] Interviews also provided new facts. Lee Sam-ryong, a former local Communist Party member, revealed evidence about the Sinchon meeting in which nineteen local party executives voted for an armed protest by twelve to seven after a fierce debate between the hardliners and the moderates. He further revealed that the local executives originally planned a short-term insurgency targeting only the police and rightist youth group members.[15]

Second, for over fifty years, the authorities suppressed the knowledge of the Jeju 4.3 events other than its existence as a "Communist rebellion." Official documents and history textbooks had distorted the facts.[16] This was problematic because the inaccurate information had been reproduced over and over with the same inaccurate sources continuously cited. The commission found several examples of these errors. For example, an argument that the armed uprising on 3 April 1948 was directly ordered by the center of the South Korean Labor Party was primarily based on the testimony of Park Gap-dong, a former member of the party, that appeared in the newspaper in 1973. However, in his interview with the expert advisers, Park testified, "A series of testimonies appeared in the *Joongang Ilbo* that were not really mine. Someone from outside the newspaper changed my testimony," meaning it was censored and manipulated by the intelligence agency.[17] Similarly, the report also found that the weaponry and military force of the insurgents had been exaggerated in government documents that stated that the insurgents were heavily armed with machine guns and artillery, which was not true.[18] Furthermore, the report revealed that the police and military documents doubled or sometime quadrupled the number of Communist insurgents, oftentimes in order to justify their harsh suppression and collateral damage.[19]

Finally, the report also reinterpreted or reframed previously known facts by revealing the political context of the documents, especially the US government and military documents. Although scholars have used these critical primary sources, not many had yet considered why and with what purpose the US occupation forces and military recorded such reports in the first place.[20] In its report, the commission disclosed that some of the information was gathered with a political intention and that certain aspects of intelligence were added, deleted, or sometime intentionally leaked for political purposes. For example, rumors about mysterious vessels with either North Korean or Soviet Union flags near Jeju were rampant immediately before the full-scale operation in November 1948. Newspapers carried the report that benefitted the military and the US military advisers, justifying the harsh suppression.[21] The commission revealed that although the source of information was "least credible," the US military intentionally leaked the information to the newspapers, suggesting that dubious information leaked by the US military was one of many ways to control the political and military situation. At the same time, the report unearthed the systematic and gruesome human rights violations committed mainly by the military, the police, and rightist youth groups but also by the Communist insurgents. As explained in detail in chapter 1, the report documented three key categories of human rights violations—civilian massacres, illegal detention and imprisonment, and torture. In addition, the report also identified material damages in three categories: destruction of villages, destruction of public institutions such as schools and public offices, and destruction of industry. Around three hundred villages were razed in the course of the military operations, and twenty thousand houses were destroyed; seventy-seven schools were damaged; and industries were destroyed so that Jeju suffered from a record high unemployment rate of 28.8 percent in 1949.[22]

Importantly, the commission decided to report the human rights violations of victims' families under the authoritarian regimes. The commission reported this additional category of human rights violation on top of the atrocities committed during the conflicts: the suffering of victims' families, often referred to as the guilt by association. In a commission survey, 86 percent of victims' families and relatives were found to have experienced discrimination and unfair treatment. Although family members were not directly punished, their names were kept in the intelligence division, and family members were discriminated against in employment, promotion, state examinations, and international travel. In some instances, not only direct descendants of victims but also nephews or other distant relatives became the target of structural violence.[23] Although it was not explicitly stated, the commission showed that the past tragedy was reproduced over time and the pain of the Jeju 4.3 events was not temporally limited to the suffering that occurred between 1947 and 1954.

Individual Truth

In addition to revealing the gruesome atrocities of the past and present, the Jeju Commission had a mandate to identify individual victims and their family members. The Special Law defined victims as "anyone who is deceased, missing, or injured due to the Jeju 4.3 events" and their family members as "a spouse or immediate family members."[24] Identifying victims was a necessary step to restoring the honor of victims and thus to achieving reconciliation. Between 2000 and 2007, the commission received 15,100 applications from victims and 32,403 applications from bereaved family members. Victims first submitted their applications to the administrative committee in Jeju, and the committee went through a basic fact-checking process and transferred applications to the commission in Seoul for final approval.[25] The commission made the first decision in November 2002 on 1,715 victims and made its most recent decision in January 2011.[26] In total, the commission identified 14,033 individual victims and 31,255 family members.

The commission created the subcommittee to review applications, headed by Park Jae-seung, a respected lawyer and former president of the Korean Bar Association.[27] The subcommittee had sixty-eight plenary sessions between 2001 and 2008 and played a key role in guiding the commission's decisions.[28] The first task for the subcommittee was to set up clear criteria to evaluate and screen victims, which was not an easy task.[29] Due to a fierce debate between the two sides representing the victims and the military, it took five full sessions to reach an agreement.[30] Both sides agreed to use the Constitutional Court's 2001 decision as a guide, in which the court recommended that the commission not include executives of the South Korean Labor Party, the leaders of the insurgents, and those who committed a murder or arson as victims.[31] Both sides agreed to exclude two groups—party executives and insurgency leaders—but decided to review those who were convicted of murder or arson with scrutiny.[32] Although the military side argued that those convicted were all active insurgents, other members persuaded them that even convicts could be victims of structural violence.[33]

The screening process went smoothly until the subcommittee was left with 2,494 victims convicted in either civilian or military courts. The decisions on those who were convicted in the civilian courts—463 victims (20%)—were relatively easy since verdicts were available and sentences were usually light.[34] The subcommittee became embroiled in a longer debate over those who were convicted in a makeshift military court.[35] Most of them were convicted of high treason and espionage, got heavy sentences, and were hastily imprisoned or executed without there being any written verdicts.[36] Most members argued that these people should also be identified as victims, since the military court during the conflict was acting without due process and a proper legal ground.[37] On the other hand, the members representing the military strongly objected to the idea and requested a thorough and long-term reinvestigation of the military court.[38] A stalemate lasted about two years; a key breakthrough was made when the commissioners finally approved the report, which explicitly drew the conclusion that actions of the military court "cannot be viewed as a trial that followed a proper process defined by the law."[39]

Based on this conclusion, the subcommittee members decided in April 2003 to include eighteen injured people who had been convicted.[40] However, the subcommittee's effort failed when the prime minster decided to reverse the decision due to the fierce debate within the commission.[41] The issue now came back to square one, and it took another twelve sessions, until June 2004, for the subcommittee to decide that those convicted and given relatively light sentences (fifteen years' imprisonment or less) were victims.[42] However, it took more than a year to reach this decision, and a few members opposed the decision on the ground that the issue was too "fundamental" to be addressed by the subcommittee.[43] A list of 606 imprisoned victims was introduced in the 10th plenary session of the commission for final approval.

Immediately, Defense Minister Yoon Gwang-wung urged Prime Minister Lee Hae-chan to reexamine the subcommittee's decision, and Ryu Jae-gap, the commissioner representing the military, questioned the commission's authority to make such decisions. Furthermore, prospects seemed not so bright when Justice Minister Kim Seung-gyu supported this position. However, commissioners Lim Mun-cheol, Seo Jung-seok, Kim Sam-wung effectively argued against the position, based on the spirit of the Special Law, the official report, and presidential apology.[44] The role of Park Jae-seung, head of the subcommittee, was critical in tipping the scale toward the victims' side by proving the illegality of the military court with twelve specific pieces of evidence.[45] At the same time, Prime Minister Lee was sympathetic to the victims and decided to reach a conclusion in order to achieve reconciliation.[46] Thus, a decision was made regarding the 606 imprisoned victims in the 10th plenary session, which led to further decisions on 1,250 victims in the 11th session.[47]

The final group of victims consisted of those who were sentence to death or life imprisonment in the military court.[48] It took another year and a half for this issue to get on the agenda and still another year to reach a decision by the subcommittee members, which shows the sensitivity of the issue. The subcommittee had ten sessions exclusively on this issue between December 2005 and January 2007, where the agenda had been introduced, suspended, and reintroduced. The debate was so intense that in a few sessions, the subcommittee considered only a couple of individuals and their family members.[49] The subcommittee finally decided to present a list of 630 prisoners who were sentenced to death (319) or life imprisonment (239) for final approval,[50] and the commission approved all of them as victims in March 2007, concluding the long journey of finding truth about individual victims.[51]

Implementing Policy Recommendations

Based on both comprehensive and individual truth, the commission pushed for the implementation of policy recommendations. However, it was again a bumpy road with obstructions from conservatives in society and explicit and implicit resistance from the administration. In this section, I examine the impact of the commission by tracing the implementation of its policy recommendations. The impact of a truth commission can be evaluated using diverse criteria. Some scholars focus on the role of the commission in bringing personal healing to individual victims or peace, unity, or reconciliation to a divided society; others see the quality or popularity of the final report as a criterion; and still others measure the success as to whether perpetrators named in the reports have actually been prosecuted and convicted.[52] Here, I focus on how many of the commission's recommendations have actually been implemented by the government and through which processes. The recommendations are closely related to the root causes of human rights violations and are considered as the best measures to achieve the purported goals of the truth commission, such as human rights, democracy, peace, national unity, and reconciliation.[53]

Immediately after the release of the report, President Roh Moo-hyun made an apology to the victims, families, and Jeju islanders in his visit to Jeju on 31 October 2003.[54] President Roh officially stated:

> In response to the recommendations from the Jeju Commission, I, in my capacity as President, would like to apologize for the wrongdoings of the previous government and express my sincere condolences to the victims and the bereaved. May their innocent souls rest in peace. The government will actively support the implementation of the commission's recommendations such as building a memorial park and honoring the victims at the earliest time. . . . By applying the valuable lessons that we have learned from the Jeju 4.3 Incident, we should try to promote universal values such as peace and human rights. We should cease the confrontation and division in this land and open a new era where everyone in Northeast Asia and the world lives in peace.[55]

This was significant in that it was the first apology issued by a head of state in South Korea regarding human rights violations caused by state violence.[56] Moreover, in 2006 President Roh visited Jeju Island to participate in a memorial service for the victims, at which time he issued another apology.[57] This also was the first time the president has attended a memorial service in Jeju. Thus, the first recommendation of the commission was implemented swiftly, paving the way for implementing the rest of the policy recommendations.

Nevertheless, resistance from the military and conservative groups was resilient. Two members representing the military and police—Han Gwang-deok and Lee Hwang-wu—resigned immediately after the presidential apology as a protest. The conservative groups, including former lawmakers, heavily criticized the presidential apology, condemning it as an "act of denying the legitimacy of South Korea."[58] In six months, the conservative groups filed another complaint, with 185,689 signatories, to the Constitutional Court, claiming that the report of the commission and the presidential apology were in breach of the Constitution of the Republic of Korea.[59] The conservative groups further created the National Committee to Correct the Distortion of the Jeju 4.3 Events and pushed the commission to revise the report. However, all this resistance ended in failure when the court quickly dismissed the case in about a month.[60]

The commission also recommended that the report should be used to educate students and the general public about peace and human rights. The report was distributed to public offices, research institutions, high schools, and libraries nationwide.[61] Education offices in Jeju published an education manual for the Jeju 4.3 events and decided to teach the conflict and atrocities.[62] In addition, the narratives and descriptions in government documents and high school history textbooks have changed since the release of the report. Most textbooks and encyclopedia entries no longer characterize the events as a Communist rebellion and provide a more balanced description of the armed uprising and civilian sacrifices.[63] The 2005 revised version of a high school history textbook explained in detail about the Jeju 4.3 events, including the background of the armed uprising, the abuses of state violence, and the activities of the Jeju Commission.[64]

Nevertheless, the military and police consistently refused to change their viewpoint. In July 2004, the Institute for Military History Compilation, a research institution under the defense department, published and released its 2004 edition of *The History of 6.25* in which the Jeju 4.3 events were described using the traditional anti-Communist view, completely ignoring the findings and conclusions of the commission.[65] None of the new evidence discovered by scholars and the commission was reflected in it, and the book suffered from thirty obvious errors.[66] Activists and victims organized rallies and local politicians demanded an apology from the defense minister and urged the minister to discontinue the book's distribution.[67] Faced with strong resistance, the military issued an apology from the head of the research institution and temporarily discontinued its publication and revised the section to reflect the findings of the commission.[68]

However, this was not the first time that activists frustrated the authority's efforts to continuously paint the Jeju 4.3 events as a Communist rebellion. In 2000 local Jeju society was embroiled in a similar controversy initiated by the release of *The History of the Jeju Police*. The police referred to the Jeju 4.3 events as a Communist rebellion and concluded, "It is beyond a doubt that the Jeju 4.3 events were committed by local Communists by the order of the South Korean Labor Party."[69] The police further expressed their objection to the commission's activities by stating: "It is truly regrettable that the Jeju 4.3 events are thoughtlessly studied and distorted after fifty years by people who neither know nor have actually experienced the events."[70] Victims and local politicians pressured the police, and in a few weeks, the police decided to withdraw the book in order to revise the section. A similar incident occurred in May 2003 when victims found that a government-funded research institution published an encyclopedia of cultural history that repeated the former understanding of the Jeju 4.3 events. A lawmaker representing Jeju demanded the change, and the institution agreed to revise the entry. In addition, some of the texts in the Korean War Memorial also have been revised to reflect the findings of the commission.[71]

In accordance with recommendations, the government supported the establishment of the Jeju 4.3 Peace Memorial Park and Museum with 59.5 billion won ($55.2 million).[72] The memorial park was opened in March 2003, and the 2004 annual memorial service was held at the new place. It took another five years to finish the museum, which was opened to the general public in March 2008. The conservative groups consistently obstructed the process and defamed the memorial park and museum. Right-wing social organizations released several newspaper advertisements opposing the opening of the museum and submitted a written petition to government offices and ministers openly urging ministers and public officials not to attend the opening ceremony and calling the memorial park a "park for rioters."[73] Despite the objections, however, around 124,000 people visited the museum within the first year of its opening, and the number is increasing. In 2009 there were138,000 visitors, and in 2010 there were 202,000.[74]

Thus, the initial step of implementation was taken with the presidential apology and participation in a memorial service, the revision of official documents and history textbooks, and the establishment of the memorial park and museum. However, as victims and activists pushed for the implementation of the commission's recommendations, the limitations of the nonbinding recommendations started to become an issue. Despite President Roh's official apology and promise of full support for follow-up measures, activists have faced three obstacles: (1) outright objections from conservatives, including not only the military and police but also right-wing civil society groups and former lawmakers; (2) public officials' lukewarm, conservative, and overly prudent approach toward implementing new policy measures;[75] and (3) the innate defect of the Special Law of 2000, which was a political compromise between the ruling and opposition parties.

For example, the commission recommended declaring every 3rd of April a memorial day in order to appease the souls of victims and make the past atrocities a lesson for the future. The administration, however, expressed its caution in implementing this recommendation because the government already had forty-two memorial days with decisions on forty-five other commemoration days still pending. Also, a minimum level of monetary subsidy was given to the victims who have been suffering illnesses, but only after a strict investigation. The medical advisory board consisting of medical doctors, lawyers, and forensic scientists selected only 132 victims who had physical and mental illness directly caused by the conflict and provided only 382 million won ($340,000) in total.[76] Moreover, supporting those who have been suffering economic hardship has been practically impossible since the administrative ordinance prohibited duplicate payments for those who were already receiving a living allowance from the government, which covered the majority of eligible victims. At the same time, many large-scale projects, such as the excavation of the mass murder sites, discovering historical sites, and the establishment of the permanent foundation, were pending due to a lack of sufficient funding.[77] Victims and activists strongly believed that the progressive revision of the Special Law was the most effective way to overcome these obstacles.[78]

Kang Chang-il, a history professor and former director of the Jeju 4.3 Research Institute, led the revision movement as soon as he was elected as a congressman in May 2004.[79] Congressman Kang and his team prepared a draft for the revision of the law and had the first public hearings in November 2004 in Seoul and Jeju.[80] The bill, which included six important changes, was submitted to the National Assembly in October 2005. First, the law had a specific clause on making every 3rd of April a memorial day; second, it had a revised definition of the Jeju 4.3 events according to the report of the commission; third, it expanded the scope of victims to include those who were convicted and imprisoned; fourth, it explicitly codified the establishment of the Jeju 4.3 Peace Foundation to be created and supported by the government; fifth, it required the government to embark on the excavation project of the mass murder sites; and finally, it required provision of an extra monetary subsidy in addition to their ordinary living allowance to those victims having economic hardship.[81]

However, as soon as the bill was proposed to the National Assembly, the conservative groups again submitted petitions to individual lawmakers urging them not to vote for the revision.[82] In addition, the progressive ruling party and the conservative opposition party could not reach an agreement on a couple of revisions. The opposition fiercely objected to the declaration of a memorial day, and the administration also noted that it should be balanced with other similar cases. In addition, an intense debate was ongoing about providing living expenses to the victims in addition to the regular benefit. Thus, it took another year to adjust the details, and the revised bill finally passed the National Assembly on 22 December 2006.[83] The revised law contained three important changes: first, redefining victims to include people who had been convicted, second, supporting the creation of the permanent foundation, and finally, launching an excavation project.[84] Three items—declaration of a memorial day, redefinition of the Jeju 4.3 events, and an extra subsidy for those victims below the poverty line—were dropped in the course of negotiations.

The revised Special Law provided a strong legal basis for implementing two important recommendations of the commission. First, the Jeju local government launched a long-term excavation project in 2006 to discover mass graves and find the remains of victims. By 2010, with government funding of 4.3 billion won ($3.7 million), eight mass murder sites were unearthed, uncovering the remains of 396 victims. The largest excavation took place at murder sites at the Jeju International Airport. Many witnesses testified that hundreds of civilians were taken to the airport and forced to dig several trenches and eventually shot to death and buried in the trenches. Two trenches were discovered—one with 123 remains of the dead and the other with 261. The bereaved family members went through a DNA test to identify victims, and it turned out that the remains belonged to those victims who were convicted in the military court.[85] Another critical evidence of civilian massacre was discovered, and the evidence attested to the lack of due process in the military court. Due to its importance, the remains of the dead were enshrined in a separate building in the memorial park, and a replica of the murder trenches is now displayed.

Second, the Jeju 4.3 Peace Foundation was created to promote peace and human rights by maintaining the museum and memorial park, and conducting additional research and investigation.[86] Having a permanent institution in place is highly important because a truth commission is only a temporary organization; its work and legacy can and must be continued in a permanent institution. Through the research and memorial foundation, other projects such as the follow-up investigation, the revision of the law, and the excavation project can continue. In addition, through the continuation of truth-seeking efforts, the research and memorial foundation can lay the foundation for the long-term goals of reconciliation and achieve historical, political, and legal justice.[87]

In May 2012, the Jeju 4.3 Peace Foundation launched a project headed by Park Chan-sik, a long-time researcher and activist, to further investigate the armed conflicts and civilian massacres. The follow-up investigation is necessary because there is a gap between the number of victims estimated by the commission in its report (25,000 to 30,000) and the number of victims identified (14,033). In addition, some scholars have noted that the commission's report did not fully reveal the involvement of the US military in the counterinsurgency operations.[88]

Evaluation of the Impact: A Comparison

The Roh Moo-hyun administration saw the Jeju Commission as "a successful case that illustrates how the investigation of past atrocities and restoration of the honor of victims can pave the way for the future."[89] Furthermore, President Lee Myung-bak from the conservative party even stated, "The evaluation of the Jeju 4.3 events has been properly done, and we should acknowledge the investigation."[90] The success of the Jeju Commission becomes more apparent when we compare the commission with the TRCK. The two commissions share many similarities in terms of the work environments they encountered. First, both commissions are mandated to mainly investigate atrocities that occurred between 1945 and 1954. What this means is that, first of all, most of the key witnesses are already dead or too old to give testimonies. In addition, most of the key documents have been either destroyed or lost by the time of investigation. Second, the most frequent form of human rights violations was personal integrity rights violations, more precisely, massacres and disappearances. Third, both cases were ideologically controversial because the previous anti-Communist regimes suppressed the truth, painted the victims as Communists, and justified the crimes of the military and police. Both commissions met with strong resistance from the conservative and anti-Communist part of society, especially from the military and police. These challenges existed before, during, and after commission activities, and in both commissions, attacks came from both inside and outside.

The TRCK's recommendations, in contrast to those of the Jeju Commission, have fared less well. Although the TRCK's final report was released only in December 2010, the TRCK had by then already published seven interim reports, including recommendations on individual cases. By June 2010, the TRCK announced 855 recommendations on individual cases.[91] The government even set up the Recommendations Follow-Up Board in 2007 to monitor the implementation process. The TRCK and the board worked closely: the TRCK delivered the policy recommendation on individual cases to the board, and the board had relevant ministers draft detailed implementation plans. In turn, the ministers reported on the progress of the implementation every quarter to the board, and the board reported it back to the TRCK biannually.

The recommendations were divided into four categories: (1) measures to recover the honor of victims; (2) measures to prevent the recurrence of human rights violations; (3) measures to achieve reconciliation and to promote democracy; and (4) measures to educate and publicize the past history.[92] Specific recommendations included: apology, correction of government records, revision of textbooks and government documents, legislation and revision of the relevant laws, human rights education, support of the memorial projects, reparations, and retrials for those who were falsely convicted.[93]

The TRCK recommended that the government apologize for 179 human rights violations, and 52 official apologies have been issued.[94] Local police chiefs and low-profile military commanders issued the most apologies. Furthermore, most of these apologies were not apologies in a strict sense,[95] since most expressed their "regrets" or "condolences" while delivering an address at the memorial services.[96] The only exception was President Roh Moo-hyun's apology to the victims of civilian massacres during the Korean War. However, even this message was not delivered in person, as in the Jeju case, but was given via a videotaped message.[97] The overall implementation of the individual recommendations appears to be not so disappointing since, according to the TRCK's report, 361 out of 855 recommendations (42%) were implemented.[98] However, when we look more closely, almost half of the implemented recommendations were things that do not require much effort, such as placing the TRCK's report in local government offices (117 cases) or supporting and participating in memorial services (55 cases).[99] The *Hankyoreh*, a progressive newspaper, referred to these actions as the "less expensive or less controversial" measures.[100]

The picture becomes even gloomier when we consider the final and comprehensive policy recommendations of the TRCK. Based on the individual human rights cases, the TRCK made three policy recommendations in 2009.[101] First, the TRCK recommended that the government and the National Assembly enact a special law to make reparations to victims of civilian massacres that took place during the Korean War. Second, the commission recommended that the government establish a permanent research foundation in order to continue the investigative work of the TRCK and to promote reconciliation. Finally, the commission recommended that the government continue to unearth mass murder sites and collect and properly bury the remains of the victims. Unfortunately, none of these three key policy recommendations have been implemented as of May 2013. In addition, the prospect for the future implementation of these recommendations is not so bright either.[102] The conservative powers in society vehemently counterattacked the TRCK when it announced the plan to create a research foundation. Major conservative newspapers criticized the commission for "trying to extend the work under a new title";[103] they accused commissioners and staff of being "people who are trying to benefit from the research foundation with 800 billion won of taxpayer's money."[104]

The Power of Comprehensive Truth

Although we have to bear in mind that the Jeju Commission released its report containing policy recommendations for the government a full seven years earlier than the TRCK (2003 and 2010, respectively), the successful implementation of the Jeju Commission's recommendations and the comparable lack of progress in implementing the TRCK's recommendations is noteworthy.[105] What accounts for this difference? I found one answer in the power of the officially acknowledged truth itself.

Truth commissions are created to investigate the truth. However, there are different notions of truth: factual or forensic truth, personal or narrative truth, social or dialogic truth, and healing and restorative truth.[106] The South Korean TRCK, despite being modeled after the South African truth commission, was designed to focus on the factual or forensic truth of individual cases only.[107] Thus, the process was that individual victims would submit their applications, then an individual investigator would examine each case, and then commissioners would make the final decisions. This approach is different from the Jeju Commission where they decided to work together to create a comprehensive and historical truth about the civilian massacres besides the individual truths.[108] This direction was first debated within the special investigation unit headed by Park Won-soon and was later approved by the commissioners.[109]

Thus, in the Jeju case, the final report had a single and historical story to tell to society, while the TRCK report on individual cases did not have a master narrative. For the TRCK, every truth existed as defragmented facts without a strong narrative to organically connect the individual cases.[110] In order to have an impact on the society as a whole, individual truth and comprehensive truth must be combined. I see this as the fundamental factor that led to the success in the implementation process of the Jeju Commission's recommendations. Individual truth is the initial step leading to a comprehensive and holistic truth. These facts are the basic building blocks to achieve comprehensive truth. However, although they are a necessary element, they are never a sufficient one. A mere "collection" or "sum" of individual truths is not equivalent to the comprehensive truth. Another stream of investigation must be accompanied that reveals the historical and political structure, political, social, and ideological context, and the chain of command of the massacres.[111]

Conclusion

In this book I answered two research questions focusing on the Jeju Commission. First, why and through what process did South Korea set up the Jeju Commission in 2000 to acknowledge the massacre of thirty thousand Jeju islanders that occurred between 1947 and 1954? Second, what has the Jeju Commission accomplished and how has it affected South Korean society? The purpose of this concluding chapter is threefold. First, it summarizes my findings on both research questions and explains the theoretical contributions of my research. I focus on the two key factors that led to the success of the commission: strong and persistent local activism and the power of officially acknowledged truth and narratives. Second, I elaborate on one factor that I did not fully address in the previous chapters: the power of the ghosts. Third, I canvass the potential policy implications of my research. I first provide practical advice for South Korean society to further enhance and continue the impact of the Jeju Commission through internationalizing the successful experience of the Jeju Commission.

I then focus on the policy lessons of the Jeju Commission for other truth commission initiatives both inside and across the border.

The Theoretical Implications

The Belated Adoption of Truth Commissions

Why is there a growing tendency for states to create truth commissions to investigate human rights violations that occurred in the distant past? I have identified several factors that led to the success of the movement in different stages: strong and persistent civil society activism, mature democracy, sympathetic leadership, similar experience in a neighboring country, global diffusion of human rights norms, critical evidence, cultural artifacts symbolizing the massacres, and the role of diaspora populations. By closely examining the fifty years of activism in South Korea, I conclude that local social justice and human rights activists, students and scholars, and journalists, who were mainly motivated by the pursuit of the truth, a sense of justice, empathy and compassion, and historical consciousness, were the pillars of this long-running advocacy. Certainly, there was a range of significant domestic and international factors, but these factors would not have come into play if not for the persistent struggle of local activists. Second, local activists made the most of these domestic and international opportunities to create a truth commission by means of various timely and effective strategies.

My findings suggest that social movement theory and transnational advocacy networks theory provide useful conceptual frameworks for capturing the process of delayed truth commission establishment.[1] These theories explain social phenomena using three key conceptual elements: the presence of an agent (advocacy networks), structures (domestic and international), and strategic interaction between agent and structures. Advocacy networks are organizations characterized by voluntary, reciprocal, and horizontal patterns of communication exchange and fluid, open relationships between committed and knowledgeable actors working on specialized issues to promote causes, ideas, and norms.[2] Advocacy networks are usually motivated by core values and beliefs, such as empathy, altruism, or ideational commitment, and their goal is to secure the establishment of a truth commission by influencing the government and the general public.[3] Structures are "those consistent dimensions of the political environment that provide incentives for or constraints on people undertaking collective action."[4] Structures constitute a powerful set of constraints and opportunities that affect advocacy networks. Sometimes structures *facilitate* the formation and development of the advocacy, and other times structures *limit* its development. There are generally two types of structures affecting advocacy networks: domestic and international.

Finally, advocacy networks pursue various strategies in order to achieve their intended goals within given opportunity structures. Margaret Keck and Kathryn Sikkink provide a useful categorization of the strategies used by advocacy networks: information politics, symbolic politics, leverage politics, and accountability politics.[5] Information politics refers to the ability to quickly and credibly generate politically useful information and move it to where it will have the most impact; symbolic politics refers to the ability to call upon symbols, actions, or stories that make sense of a situation for an audience; leverage politics refers to the ability to call upon powerful actors to affect a situation in which weaker members of a network are unlikely to have influence; and accountability politics refers to the effort to hold powerful actors to their previously stated policies or principles.

In the Jeju case, local advocacy networks were the most important actors in the transitional justice process, facilitating favorable domestic and international conditions, taking advantage of the positive factors and fighting hard against constraints and obstacles. Their conscious strategic efforts to create and change the domestic and international structures allowed a space to open up. Structures are not fixed entities but constantly changing environments. Local activists have clearly shown that domestic and international structures—both opportunities and constraints—can be made, remade, and unmade through consistent activism and effective and timely strategies. Sometimes small but innovative first steps, such as the 1993 petition movement and the 1960 private investigation by local students, can make a big difference. At other times, timely and effective strategies, such as the 1992 strategic announcement of the discovery of the Darangshi cave, local investigative journalism, the introduction of the Taiwanese case to Jeju, and the deliberate use of human rights discourse to overcome ideological divides and draw national attention to the massacres, can change the prevailing dynamics and turn a hostile structure into a conducive environment.

Traditionally, scholars have frequently used decision-making models of political elites in order to explain the creation of truth commissions or the adoption of other transitional justice measures.[6] The elite model looks at the decision-making process of elite groups and treats the demand for truth and justice from civil society as one of many elements that affect the elites' decision-making process. However, by focusing on the decision makers, this approach neglects the dynamics and history of grassroots advocacy and therefore cannot adequately explain the way in which the demand for truth and justice becomes increasingly effective over time. Moreover, since the characteristics of elites are idiosyncratic, such studies are often reduced to an examination of the political environment that leaders face in their decision making. In addition, a decision-making model sets the a priori goal of decision makers as stability, power, survival, or peace, and approaches truth commissions in terms of their instrumental value in achieving or obstructing these objectives. Such an approach generally disregards the intrinsic value of truth commissions and the voices of victims and activists. My findings support social movement theory and transnational advocacy networks theory and thus draw our attention to the role of nonelite actors in shaping the transitional justice process.

However, my theoretical findings also depart from transnational advocacy networks theory, which emphasizes the importance of combining domestic and international pressure—oftentimes, confrontational pressure—to induce change. The South Korean case shows that most action starts with domestic or even local actors and that these local actors call for international pressure. In addition, local activists combine both confrontational protests and demands with negotiations and compromise in a timely manner. As seen in chapter 4, the Special Law was successfully enacted after local activists and lawmakers decided to make a strategic and provisional concession.

The Impact of Truth Commissions

The Jeju Commission revealed not only the comprehensive and historical truth about the Jeju 4.3 events and civilian massacres but also individual truths by identifying victims and bereaved family members. The commission officially acknowledged two types of truth—both comprehensive and individual truth. The commission discovered new documents and testimonies and revealed previously unknown aspects of the armed conflict and civilian massacres. It also exposed and corrected inaccurate, distorted, or exaggerated "facts" about the past. In addition, the commission further revealed the political context of formerly known facts and disclosed political intentions of past authorities. Through all these processes, individuals, including those who were convicted, cleared themselves of the false accusation of being Communist guerrillas, and the honor of individual victims has been restored.

At the same time, the commission revealed systemic human rights violations of victims' family members under the authoritarian regimes and how the authorities, for over forty years, intentionally tried to destroy the truth.[7] The commission showed that a past tragedy can be reproduced over time if not properly addressed by the government and that the suffering of the Jeju 4.3 events are not temporally limited to events that occurred in the past. In addition, the commission explicitly showed the resilience of the truth even under conditions of harsh repression and overt menace. The commission itself and the report it produced were the critical evidence demonstrating that it was impossible for the authoritarian regimes to totally cover up the traces of atrocities and indefinitely silence the victims. The power of the truth itself was remarkable, and at least one visionary brought up the past atrocities at every possible opportunity in every possible way. The repression of these individuals did not end up in silencing them but left further evidence of state violence as we have witnessed in case of the Park Chung-hee's destruction of the memorial sites in 1961 and in the government suppression and manipulation around the discovery of the Darangshi cave in 1992. In both cases, another layer of state violence was added on top of the original atrocity, and the truths became more and more resilient as the authoritarian regime attempted to destroy them more and more completely.

The truth exerted a strong influence over South Korean society when it was eventually codified in the Special Law in 2000 and when it was officially acknowledged in the final report of the commission in 2003. Most of the commission's policy recommendations have been implemented, and major challenges to the commission's activities ventured by conservatives ended in failure. The government and society have experienced important changes since the release of the report, such as the presidential apology and participation in a memorial service, the revision of history textbooks and official documents, the progressive revision of the Special Law, excavations and reburials, and the creation of a permanent institution for research and commemoration. Even the regime change to the conservative party in 2008 could not stop the progress of the Jeju Commission, as we have witnessed in several illustrative cases. Even the conservative president Lee Myung-bak visited the memorial park to pay respect to the victims during his presidential campaign in 2007, and his prime minister decided to further recognize the victims and support additional funding for the commemoration projects in 2011.

My finding of the positive impact of the Jeju Commission adds another piece of evidence to the debate over the positive and negative impact of truth commissions on the future of human rights and democracy. In particular, I found a symbiotic relationship between truth commissions and democratic consolidation, each one strengthening the other. Mature democracy, which guarantees checks and balances, the decentralization of power, and democratic leadership, is a prerequisite for a successful truth commission. In turn, effective truth commission activities enhance the legitimacy of the government by dissociating the current regime from the past and bolstering the core values of democracy such as justice, equality, human rights, and the rule of law.

My case study further advances the knowledge about truth commissions by identifying five factors contributing to their success. First, the binding Special Law and the clearly codified definition of the Jeju 4.3 events provided a strong ground to overcome conservative challenges. Second, as with the case for the movement process, the investigation also required strong and indisputable evidence. Third, the commission made full use of existing local human resources and their expertise in the commission. Previously accumulated knowledge and expertise in the local newspaper and civil society was transferred to the commission, making the commission highly efficient. Fourth, the conservatives' challenge and persistent attacks ironically contributed to the success of the commission. The conservative challenge made the commissioners more attentive to details and forced them to firmly base their report on concrete evidence. Finally, the success of the commission also lies in the power of truth itself, especially when the comprehensive and historical truth is combined with detailed individual truths.

Ghosts

In this section, I explore a rather unconventional but critical element in motivating and inspiring the movement and truth commission activities—the beliefs about ghosts, that is, the spirits of the dead. It may not be a proper social science explanation, but numerous interviewees addressed the issue and strongly believed in the existence of ghosts. Thus, I decided to address ghosts in this concluding section. It is a unique feature of the South Korean case that the beliefs about the dead victims and their ghosts played a significant role in the transitional justice process. My interviews revealed that activists and surviving victims actually believed that the ghosts had helped them in the following five ways.

First, local activists strongly believe that ghosts helped them to find decisive and important evidence of the civilian massacres, a case in point being the Darangshi cave. Even a witness who had lived in the cave could not find the entrance to the cave, but a member of the Jeju 4.3 Research Institute discovered the cave while the team was having a rest time. If the witness had discovered the cave, it might not have had the same dramatic impact since the information might have been leaked. Activists who were on the research trip strongly believed that they were mysteriously guided and that the discovery would not have been possible if it were not for the help of ghosts.[8] In addition, local journalists for the *Jemin Ilbo* admitted that they had felt the guiding hand of the dead in the course of preparing their special reports.[9] Both Yang Jo-hoon and Kim Jong-min testified that their reports would not have been as complete if the dead had not helped them to find critical evidence and witnesses, such as the late Colonel Kim Ik-ryeol's memoir.[10]

Second, ghosts were said to have prompted people to act on behalf of victims in the first place, sometimes forcibly. Yang Jo-hoon was a key member of the transitional justice movement and also in the commission. He led a team of reporters who intensively reported on the Jeju 4.3 events for over nine years and was a leader of the solidarity organization that represented Jeju civil society in the enactment movement. Most of all, he was in charge of drafting the report of the commission. It is almost impossible to discuss the truth commission process without mentioning his name. This important figure stated that while he was still hesitating, he had been moved to act by ghosts.[11] He testified that ghosts of the victims haunted him every night, prompting him to take charge of the reporting team and take his step into the whole movement.

Third, victims, inspired by their duty as children and siblings of the dead, even risked arrest or torture.[12] Victims strongly believed that it was the dead who made them move forward, and in some cases it was the final words of the dead that prompted them to resiliently act, despite state terror.[13] In South Korea, innocently murdered souls are believed to be unable to enter the next world unless their distress and rancor is resolved. Descendants and survivors saw it as their duty and responsibility to resolve their ancestors' innocent deaths. Appeasing the souls and restoring their honor were two essential elements of this process. In many cases, this duty extended to those who were not blood relations of the victims. At times, a village or a larger community felt a sense of obligation to the dead.

Fourth, local activists argue that ghosts appeared in their dreams and those of their family members to alert them of an upcoming danger or suppression. It happened to Ko Chang-hoon while he was the head of the Jeju 4.3 Research Institute at the time of discovery of the Darangshi cave. Professor Ko received a phone call from his mother one day saying that she had a mysterious dream where he was marching with his face covered by a piece of cloth and followed by several coffins.[14] She knew that the dream was ominous, alerting her either to her son's death or to unjust accusations against him. The next day, she had exactly same dream, but the cloth that covered her son's face was lifted up and she was able to see his eyes, which she thought suggested that her son would barely escape death.[15] Ko strongly believes that it was the ghosts of victims who appeared in his mother's dream and let him know of the upcoming danger. Shortly after the dream, Ko received a threat from the Jeju police chief to stop taking the follow-up measures. Similar mysterious cases were examined in which the dead appeared in a dream guiding, communicating, and sometimes correcting directions to a burial location. The dead were sometimes said to be appearing in the dreams of the bereaved members of the family, telling them exactly where they were buried.

Finally, it was a memorial service that first provided the basis for ideologically diverse groups to even consider the possibility of working together. The very act of commemorating and cherishing the souls of the dead provided the ground for reconciliation among the living. Two ideologically opposed camps agreed that the dead were ideologically neither left nor right, and this agreement provided the basis for their future cooperation. Another example is the traditional ritual of exorcism, in which the dead and the living communicate. Many surviving victims and their family members decided to come forward and testify to their experiences after having a supernatural experience. In sum, it is no exaggeration to state that people's beliefs about the ghosts of the dead was one of the many core elements of the transitional justice movement.

The Practical Implications

What practical lessons can we learn from the experience of the Jeju Commission? In this section, I draw policy implications of my research for current and future truth commissions both in South Korea and overseas. The policy advice for South Korea focuses on the effective implementation of truth commissions' policy recommendations, since many South Korean truth commissions have already finished their terms. The lessons for overseas cases, on the other hand, place the focus on how effectively civil society and victims can create truth commissions to address human rights violations of the distant past. However, before considering other cases, I consider one suggestion for the South Korean and Jeju local society to enhance and continue the impact of the Jeju Commission through internationalizing the successful experience of the Jeju Commission.

Internationalization of the Jeju Experience

What steps does South Korean society have to take in order to maximize the impact of the Jeju Commission and continue its legacy? Scholars and practitioners have suggested many important projects, such as follow-up investigations, the excavation of murder sites and the preservation of historic sites, or the further revision of the law to provide for individual reparations to the victims and their family members. All measures are important, and each proposed project certainly perpetuates the legacy of the Jeju Commission. The Jeju 4.3 Peace Foundation aims at pursuing these projects in the future, and the first step has been taken with the creation of the follow-up investigation team in May 2012. However, I suggest one further measure that has not yet been considered seriously: the internationalization of the Jeju 4.3 events and the Jeju Commission activities.

In order to internationalize the Jeju 4.3 events, we first have to consider which aspects of the Jeju 4.3 events should be internationalized. Since the enactment of the Special Law in 2000, the Jeju 4.3 events have been understood using two conceptual frameworks.[16] The first is to see the Jeju 4.3 events as a legitimate uprising against the repressive US occupation forces and the South Korean government. From this perspective, the Jeju 4.3 events are a unification movement because the insurgents explicitly objected to having a separate election in the southern part of the Korean peninsula. The second, which is a more dominant perspective, is to view the Jeju 4.3 events as a civilian massacre and mass sacrifice of Jeju residents in the course of the conflict between the government and the Communist insurgents. The Jeju 4.3 events, from this perspective, are a major human rights crisis, which some would further refer to as genocide. In general, the former perspective is seen as a bright, active, and glorious portrait of the Jeju 4.3 events while the latter is seen as a dark, passive, and shameful one.

However, each perspective represents the partial truth, since the Jeju 4.3 events contain Communist insurgency, harsh counterinsurgency operations, and a mass human rights tragedy. I thus suggest one additional view, which sees the Jeju 4.3 events as a social movement, in other words, a successful movement to reveal the truth and restore justice in the midst of harsh suppression by the consecutive anti-Communist authoritarian regimes. Indiscriminate mass murder of civilians committed in the name of counterinsurgency operations is a clear case of a crime against humanity. What happened in Jeju is not simply local or domestic but an internationally significant event that has huge ramifications for people living today and the generations to come. The story I told in this book is a story where victims and activists have successfully addressed the past wrongs through fifty years of long and painful activism and twelve years of difficult commission activities. This proud and encouraging story, including the ups and downs of the process, must be told to the victims of similar atrocities worldwide.

The first and foremost urgent project is to translate the official report of the commission and distribute the report to major national and university libraries around the world. In addition, the white paper of the commission's activity should also be translated and distributed for international audiences. At the same time, the Jeju 4.3 Peace Foundation, which now is the center of advocacy, should facilitate networks with other truth commissions and human rights NGOs overseas. The expertise and lessons of the Jeju Commission can be transferred to other commissions, while Jeju society can also learn from other bodies. In addition, close relations with international bodies, such as the UN Office of the High Commissioner for Human Rights and international human rights NGOs such as the International Center for Transitional Justice, will further facilitate the dissemination of the Jeju experience.

Lessons for Other South Korean Truth Commissions

South Korea made remarkable progress in establishing truth commissions under Presidents Kim Dae-jung (1998–2003) and Roh Moo-hyun (2003–8). The truth-seeking process, however, has been neither smooth nor without negative side effects. Because so many initiatives were launched, opponents and supporters alike have questioned whether all these truth-seeking projects could effectively be carried out with the limited budgetary and human resources available.[17] Even proponents of these processes have worried that the multiplicity and breadth of truth-seeking efforts might cause public fatigue with truth commissions or that it could precipitate a severe backlash by opponents of these efforts.[18] Some special laws were too narrow in their scope, addressing individual incidents rather than a pattern of abuses.[19] At other times, special laws were passed to investigate historically remote events, such as the Donghak peasant uprising of 1894. The mandates of the various commissions frequently overlapped.

Many of the concerns about backlash were realized in 2008 when President Lee Myung-bak began to publicly criticize the truth commissions immediately on assuming office, giving the conservative element a powerful voice in the transitional justice debate. His administration proposed slashing the budgets of the myriad commissions, both by merging them and by rejecting their requests for renewal.[20] As many scholars and practitioners have already noted, it is extremely unlikely that South Korea will have another truth commission in the near future. The prospect is even more discouraging since Park Geun-hye, leader of the conservative Saenuri Party and daughter of Park Chung-hee who regards the TRCK's finding as a "personal offensive" against her,[21] won the presidential election in December 2012. Most of her supporters in the conservative political groups think of the activities of the TRCK as "score-settling" by leftists.[22]

By the end of 2011, the major activities of the various truth commissions had reached an effective end, leaving a multitude of policy recommendations behind for implementation by the South Korean state and broader civil society. As we have seen in the case of the TRCK, however, the current government has not given serious consideration to most of their policy recommendations. What lessons can the other South Korean truth commissions, the TRCK in particular, learn from the Jeju Commission, especially in implementing their policy recommendations? A key difference between the Jeju Commission and the TRCK is that the TRCK failed to create a permanent memorial and research foundation, which is clearly stipulated in the framing act.[23] The TRCK made a move in this direction, but the conservatives have effectively blocked all their efforts, most of which came after the inauguration of Lee Myung-bak.[24] In the Jeju case, activists and victims had to struggle hard for over eight years to revise the Special Law to include this very article, and eventually they created the foundation.

Nevertheless, the creation of a research foundation for the TRCK is still feasible when the TRCK experience is compared to that of the Jeju case. Most important, there remains a group of passionate activists, researchers, and victims who strongly believe that the work of the TRCK has not yet finished with the closing down of the commission.[25] Although the government is lukewarm about adopting the TRCK's policy recommendations, victims and civil society have taken the initiative and launched a movement to create the research foundation. In 2010, human rights activists and former TRCK staff members created the Forum on Truth and Justice to continue the legacy of the TRCK.[26] Such civil society movements will positively work to implement the TRCK's recommendation. One clear lesson from the Jeju case is that as long as this group of passionate and devoted activists and victims exists, the future is still bright.

Second, South Korean scholarship, mainly in the field of history, is paying more and more attention to contemporary history and past atrocities due to the work of truth commissions.[27] Once forbidden topics in academia, they are now relatively freely discussed among a new generation of scholars due to the work of various commissions.[28] This is where there is great potential for future development. The Jeju experience proved the power of truth and evidence. As more and more evidence is discovered, the advocacy becomes more and more effective. In addition, scholarly research can provide a level of comprehensive and historical truth that the TRCK could not achieve.

Lessons for Establishing a Belated Truth Commission

What further lessons can we learn from the Jeju Commission, especially for establishing delayed truth commissions? From the Jeju case, I found both limitations and advantages to the delayed establishment of truth commissions. Certainly, the destruction of critical evidence and the death of key witnesses were difficult obstacles for the activity of the commission. At the same time, earlier and premature truth-seeking efforts made under the weak and insecure democracy ended in failure. Thus, the key is to minimize the limitations and maximize the advantages of the situation.

The development of democracy and its consolidation was an important precondition for the Jeju case. The movement gradually achieved its purported goal as democracy consolidated in South Korea. A key breakthrough occurred in 1993 when the self-governing system, which included the localization of state power, was instituted. The creation of the highly important Special Committee on 4.3 was possible within this political context. The local committee was a stepping-stone to the national commission. Moreover, the very existence of the local committee marked a new era because many believed that the Jeju 4.3 events were officially no longer taboo. A lesson could be learned that, if atrocities occurred at the local level as is the case with the most overseas events, it is a good strategy to use the local government to strategically introduce interim transitional justice measures. The local government tends to be more attentive to the demands of activists and victims, and it is much easier to move local politicians than national politicians and lawmakers. In addition, the findings from local investigations can be used as additional evidence, and the local process provides realistic estimates of the national process.

In addition, two factors are especially important in the case of belated truth commissions. First, the Jeju case was a victory of the indisputable evidence of the civilian massacres that tipped the scale in favor of activists and victims whenever there was a deadlock or confrontation. The discovery of out-of-print local newspapers, the excavation of the Darangshi cave, and the disclosure of the list of those who were convicted in the military court provided evidence beyond dispute, and this was an indispensable factor in advancing the movement. Thus, the role of the research sector and investigative journalism is extremely important in the case of belated commissions.

Second, the role of culture has proved to be critical in making both victims and the general public pay more attention to the suppressed past. Cultural activism can bring forgotten discourses and lost memories back to life. Cultural artifacts such as visual art, songs, poems, literature, plays, TV dramas, and traditional exorcism are easily accessible to the victims and the general public. In addition, in many countries, the cultural sector receives relatively less interference from government suppression and surveillance and thus a breakthrough can be made in that area, as when Hyun Gi-yeong's "Aunt Suni" opened the floodgates for advocacy in South Korea.

Notes

Introduction

1. These measures are often referred to as transitional justice, which is "the conception of justice associated with periods of political change, characterized by legal responses to confront the wrongdoings of repressive predecessor regimes." Ruti G. Teitel, "Transitional Justice Genealogy," *Harvard Human Rights Journal* 16, no. 1 (2003): 69. For more details about the legal and philosophical foundation of transitional justice, see Teitel, *Transitional Justice* (Oxford: Oxford University Press, 2000); and Jon Elster, *Closing the Books: Transitional Justice in Historical Perspective* (Cambridge: Cambridge University Press, 2004).

2. Priscilla B. Hayner, *Unspeakable Truths: Transitional Justice and the Challenge of Truth Commissions*, 2nd ed. (New York: Routledge, 2011).

3. In 2009, Mauritius, Solomon Islands, Togo, Canada, and Kenya each started a new truth commission. For the full list of the thirty-five truth commissions, see Eric Wiebelhaus-Brahm, *Truth Commissions and Transitional Societies: The Impact on Human Rights and Democracy* (New York: Routledge, 2010); Geoff Dancy, Hun Joon Kim, and Eric Wiebelhaus-Brahm, "The Turn to Truth: Trends in Truth Commission Experimentation," *Journal of Human Rights* 9, no. 1 (2010).

4. In Korea, major historic events are remembered by the date when they occurred or began. For example, the Korean War, which broke out on 25 June 1950, is widely referred to as the "6.25 War." Following this tradition, the armed conflicts in Jeju are commonly referred to as the Jeju 4.3 events. Jeju 4.3 events differ from one-off events such as the 1972 "Bloody Sunday" shootings in Northern Ireland.

5. There are only a handful of English-language articles, book chapters, and dissertations, including two of my own works, that discuss this. See Hun Joon Kim, "Expansion of Transitional Justice Measures: A Comparative Analysis of Its Causes" (PhD diss., University of Minnesota, 2008) and Kim, "Seeking Truth after 50 Years: The National Committee for Investigation of the Truth about the Jeju 4.3 Events," *International Journal of Transitional Justice* 3, no. 3 (2009); Tae-Ung Baik, "Justice Incomplete: The Remedies for the Victims of the Jeju April Third Incidents," in *Rethinking Historical Injustice and Reconciliation in Northeast Asia: The Korean Experience*, ed. Gi-Wook Shin, Soon-Won Park, and Daqing Yang (London: Routledge, 2007); and Jieun Chang, "National Narrative, Traumatic Memory, and Testimony: Reading Traces of the Cheju April Third Incident, South Korea, 1948" (PhD diss., New York University, 2009).

6. For more details, see Renée Jeffery and Hun Joon Kim, eds., *Transitional Justice in the Asia Pacific* (Cambridge: Cambridge University Press, forthcoming).

7. As the Transitional Justice Database Project reveals, of the 1,520 country-specific studies of transitional justice published, only 78 (5%) are on countries in the Asia-Pacific region. By contrast, there have been 629 studies (41%) on transitional justice in Africa, 474 (31%) on Europe, and 336 (23%) on Latin America. Transitional Justice Database Project, http://www.tjdbproject.com/ (accessed 1 March 2013).

8. For the Gwangju massacres, see George N. Katsiaficas and Kan-Chae Na, *South Korean Democracy: Legacy of the Gwangju Uprising* (New York: Routledge, 2006); In-Sup Han, "Kwangju and Beyond: Coping with Past State Atrocities in South Korea," *Human Rights Quarterly* 27, no. 3 (2005); Henry Scott-Stokes, Jae-Eui Lee, and Dae Jung Kim, *The Kwangju Uprising: Eyewitness Press Accounts of Korea's Tiananmen* (Armonk, NY: M. E. Sharpe, 2000); Gi-Wook Shin, ed. *Contentious Kwangju: The May 18th Uprising in Korea's Past and Present* (Lanham, MD: Rowman & Littlefield, 2003); Jung-seok Seo, *Jeonjaeng sok-eui ttodareun jeonjaeng* [Another war within the war] (Seoul: Seonin, 2011); and James West, "Martial Lawlessness: The Legal Aftermath of Kwangju," *Pacific Rim Law & Policy Journal* 6, no. 1 (1997).

9. Gi-Wook Shin, Soon-Won Park, and Daqing Yang, eds., *Rethinking Historical Injustice and Reconciliation in Northeast Asia: The Korean Experience* (London: Routledge, 2007); Dong-Choon Kim, *The Unending Korean War: A Social History* (Novato, CA: Tamal Vista Publications, 2009); Philip D. Chinnery, *Korean Atrocity! Forgotten War Crimes 1950–1953* (Barnsley, UK: Pen & Sword Military, 2009); Jae-Jung Suh, "Truth and Reconciliation in South Korea," *Critical Asian Studies* 42, no. 4 (2010); Charles J Hanley, "No Gun Ri," *Critical Asian Studies* 42, no. 4 (2010); Seung-Hee Jeon, "War Trauma, Memories, and Truths," *Critical Asian Studies* 42, no. 4 (2010); Kuk Cho, "Transitional Justice in Korea: Legally Coping with Past Wrongs after Democratization," *Pacific Rim Law & Policy Journal* 16, no. 3 (2007); Dong-Choon Kim, "Beneath the Tip of the Iceberg: Problems in Historical Clarification of the Korean War," *Korea Journal* 42, no. 3 (2002); Dong-Choon Kim, "The Long Road toward Truth and Reconciliation," *Critical Asian Studies* 42, no. 4 (2010).

10. Robert A. Scalapino and Chong-sik Lee, *Communism in Korea*, vol. 2, *The Society* (Berkeley: University of California Press, 1972); Glen D. Paige, "Korea," in *Communism and Revolution: The Strategic Uses of Political Violence*, ed. Cyril E. Black and Thomas P. Thornton (Princeton: Princeton University Press, 1964).

11. John Merrill, "The Cheju-do Rebellion," *Journal of Korean Studies* 2, no. 1 (1980); and Merrill, "Internal Warfare in Korea, 1948–1950: The Local Setting of the Korean War," in *Child of Conflict: The Korean-American Relationship, 1943–1953*, ed. Bruce Cumings (Seattle: University of Washington Press, 1983).

12. Cumings argues that the fundamental cause of internal armed conflicts such as those in Jeju is deep-rooted social and economic inequality between elites and the masses, which was further exacerbated by the misrule of the US military government. See Bruce Cumings, *The Origins of the Korean War,* vol. 2, *The Roaring of the Cataract, 1947–1950* (Ithaca: Cornell University Press, 2004), 250–59.

13. Kyengho Son, "The 4.3 Incident: Background, Development, and Pacification, 1945–1949" (PhD diss., Ohio State University, 2008); Allan R. Millett, *The War for Korea, 1945–1950: A House Burning* (Lawrence: University Press of Kansas, 2005).

14. Samuel P. Huntington, *The Third Wave: Democratization in the Late Twentieth Century* (Norman: University of Oklahoma Press, 1991); Guillermo A. O'Donnell and Philippe C. Schmitter, eds., *Transition from Authoritarian Rule* (Baltimore: Johns Hopkins University Press, 1986).

15. Kathryn Sikkink, *The Justice Cascade: How Human Rights Prosecutions Are Changing World Politics* (New York: W. W. Norton, 2011).

16. Ibid.; Thomas Risse, Stephen C. Ropp, and Kathryn Sikkink, eds., *The Power of Human Rights: International Norms and Domestic Change* (Cambridge: Cambridge University Press, 1999); Martha Finnemore and Kathryn Sikkink, "International Norm Dynamics and Political Change," *International Organization* 52, no. 4 (1998).

17. Hun Joon Kim, "Structural Determinants of Human Rights Prosecutions after Democratic Transition," *Journal of Peace Research* 49, no. 2 (2012).

18. This point has also been made and referred to as a localization process. See Amitav Acharya, "How Ideas Spread: Whose Norms Matter? Norm Localization and Institutional Change in Asia Regionalism," *International Organization* 58, no. 2 (2004).

19. Martha Minow, *Between Vengeance and Forgiveness: Facing History after Genocide and Mass Violence* (Boston: Beacon Press, 1998); Naomi Roht-Arriaza, ed., *Impunity and Human Rights in International Law and Practice* (New York: Oxford University Press, 1995); Hayner, *Unspeakable Truths*.

20. Elster, *Closing the Books*; Eric Brahm, "Uncovering the Truth: Examining Truth Commission Success and Impact," *International Studies Perspectives* 8, no. 1 (2007); Tricia D. Olsen, Leigh A. Payne, and Andrew G. Reiter, *Transitional Justice in Balance: Comparing Processes, Weighing Efficacy* (Washington, DC: United States Institute of Peace Press, 2010).

21. John H. Herz, ed. *From Dictatorship to Democracy: Coping with the Legacies of Authoritarianism and Totalitarianism* (Westport, CT: Greenwood Press, 1982); Minow, *Between Vengeance and Forgiveness*; Tricia D. Olsen et al., "When Truth Commissions Improve Human Rights," *International Journal of Transitional Justice* 4, no. 3 (2010).

22. Huntington, *The Third Wave*; O'Donnell and Schmitter, *Transition from Authoritarian Rule*.

23. Minow, *Between Vengeance and Forgiveness*; Jo M. Pasqualucci, "The Whole Truth and Nothing but the Truth: Truth Commissions, Impunity, and the Inter-American Human Rights System," *Boston University International Law Journal* 12, no. 2 (1994); Hayner, *Unspeakable Truths*.

24. Robert B. Weyeneth, "The Power of Apology and the Process of Historical Reconciliation," *Public Historian* 23, no. 3 (2001); Juan E. Méndez, "In Defense of Transitional Justice," in *Transitional Justice and the Rule of Law in New Democracies*, ed. A. James McAdams (Notre Dame, IN: University of Notre Dame Press, 1997).

25. Oskar N. T. Thoms, James Ron, and Roland Paris, "State-Level Effects of Transitional Justice: What Do We Know?" *International Journal of Transitional Justice* 4, no. 3 (2010); David Mendeloff, "Truth-Seeking, Truth-Telling, and Postconflict Peacebuilding: Curb the Enthusiasm?," *International Studies Review* 6, no. 3 (2004).

26. Hayner, *Unspeakable Truths*, 215.

27. Ibid.

28. Dancy, Kim, and Wiebelhaus-Brahm, "The Turn to Truth."

29. I explored three libraries—the National Assembly Library, Yonsei University Library, and Jeju National University Library—between September and December 2005 and in May and December 2011. I also collected documents from organizations such as the 4.3 Research Institute and the Jeju Commission. I obtained the confidential documents of the Jeju National University Student Association from former presidents who wanted to remain anonymous; rare documents

including a diary and notes from Professor Ko Chang-hoon's personal collection; and rare and confidential government documents.

30. Interviews were conducted, first, between January and April 2006 and, second, between April and May 2011. Most interviews were conducted in the interviewee's office, house, or in a café and lasted no longer than two hours. But, in a few cases, interviews lasted longer than three hours, and three interviews lasted five hours. I conducted several follow-up interviews, and additional e-mail exchanges and phone interviews were frequent. Interviews were neither open-ended nor structured but a focused interview where I used prepared questions with key topics listed but in no fixed order.

31. Jeju Commission, *Jeju 4.3 sageon jinsang josa bogoseo* [Report of the truth about the Jeju 4.3 events] (Seoul: Jeju Commission, 2003). 15.

32. Note that for Korean names, the surname is given first, followed by the hyphenated given name.

1. The Jeju 4.3 Events

1. Jong-min Kim, "4.3 Ihu 50 nyeon [50 years after 4.3]," in *Jeju 4.3 Yeongu* [A study of Jeju 4.3], ed. Jeju 4.3 Research Institute (Seoul: Yeoksa Bipyeong, 1999).

2. Jeju Commission, *Hwahae-wa sangsaeng: Jeju 4.3 wiweonhoe hwaldong baekseo* [Reconciliation and coexistence: White paper on the activities of the Jeju Commission] (Seoul: Jeju Commission, 2008), 187.

3. Ibid., 186.

4. Merrill, "Cheju-do Rebellion," 183.

5. Jeju Commission, *Jeju 4.3 sageon jinsang josa bogoseo*, 379–80.

6. Ibid., 387.

7. Ibid., 389 and 391.

8. Ibid., 409–10.

9. Ibid., 394–95.

10. Ibid., 414–15.

11. In the following year, Hyun published a book of short stories he had written on the theme of the Jeju 4.3 events. Gi-yeong Hyun, *Suni Samchon* [Aunt Suni] (Seoul: Changbi, 1979).

12. Michael E. Robinson, *Korea's Twentieth-Century Odyssey*, 6th ed. (Honolulu: University of Hawaii Press, 2007). 43.

13. Gregory Henderson, *Korea: Politics of the Vortex* (Cambridge: Harvard University Press, 1968), 114.

14. The Korean Provisional Government was established in 1919 and was widely supported as the legitimate governing body of the Korean people during the colonial period. For more details, see Robinson, *Korea's Twentieth-Century Odyssey*, 48.

15. Ji-yeon Sim, *Hanguk hyeondae jeongdang-ron: Hamindang yeongu 2* [Korean modern political parties: A study of the Korean Democratic Party, vol. 2] (Seoul: Changjak-gua Bipyeong, 1984).

16. Seung-heum Kim, "Jeongdang jeongchi-eui taedong-gua jeongae [The birth and development of party politics in Korea]," in *Hankuk-eui Hyeondae Jeongchi 1945—1948 Nyeon* [Modern Korean politics 1945—1948], ed. Research Institute for Korean Politics (Seoul: Seoul National University Press, 1993), 203.

17. Se-kyoon Kim, "Haebang chogi minjung undong [Minjung movement in early liberation years]," in *Hankuk-eui Hyeondae Jeongchi 1945—1948 Nyeon*, 68.

18. Bruce Cumings, "American Policy and Korean Liberation," in *Without Parallel: The American Korean Relationship since 1945*, ed. Frank Baldwin (New York: Pantheon, 1974), 53–54.

19. For more details about the trusteeship debate, see Sang-Yong Choi, "Trusteeship Debate and the Korean Cold War," in *Korea under the American Military Government, 1945–1948*, ed. Bonnie B. C. Oh (Westport, CT: Praeger, 2002).

20. Cumings, *Roaring of the Cataract,* 218.

21. Henderson, *Politics of the Vortex*, 135.

22. For more details on the policies of the US military government, see Kim, "Minjung Movement in Early Liberation Years," 74–75; Han-mu Kang, "United States Military Government in Korea, 1945–1948: An Analysis and Evaluation of Its Policy" (PhD diss., University of Cincinnati, 1970); Chan-Pyo Park, "The American Military Government and the Framework for Democracy in South Korea," in *Korea under the American Military Government*; Kwang Sung Song, "The Impact of US Military Occupation" (PhD diss., University of California, 1989).

23. In October 1945, the governor of the military government stated: "There is only one government in the southern part of the Korean peninsula. . . . The so-called Korean People's Republic is entirely without any authority, power or real entity." In addition, in December 1945, Gen. John R. Hodge declared that the US military government was the only legitimate government and stated that if any other party claimed to be the rightful government, the military government would treat this as an illegal act. *Maeil Sinbo*, 11 October 1945; Park, "American Military Government," 125–26.

24. Henderson, *Politics of the Vortex*, 117, 18–19.

25. Song, "Impact of US Military Occupation," 147.

26. Hye Sook Lee, "State Formation and Civil Society under American Occupation: The Case of South Korea," (paper presented at the Annual Meeting of the American Sociological Association, New York, August 1996), 5.

27. George M McCune, "Occupation Politics in Korea," *Far Eastern Survey* 25, no. 3 (1946): 35.

28. John Lie, *Han Unbound: The Political Economy of South Korea* (Stanford: Stanford University Press, 1998). 9.

29. Bertram D. Sarafan, "Military Government: Korea," *Far Eastern Survey* 15, no. 23 (1946): 394.

30. In the course of the negotiations, there had been an effort by the US military government to encourage a coalition of moderates from both the Right (Kim Gyu-sik) and the Left (Yeo Un-hyeong). However, this effort ended in failure. For more details, see Henderson, *Politics of the Vortex*, 134.

31. Hae-gu Jung, *10-weol immin hangjaeng yeongu* [A study of the October people's uprising] (Seoul: Yuleumsa, 1989).

32. Henderson, *Politics of the Vortex*, 143.

33. Cumings, "American Policy and Korean Liberation," 47.

34. Merrill, "Cheju-do Rebellion," 149.

35. Henderson, *Politics of the Vortex*, 127; Merrill, "Cheju-do Rebellion," 151–52.

36. Merrill, "Cheju-do Rebellion," 183.

37. Inspired by President Woodrow Wilson's principle of self-determination, thirty-three representatives declared independence from Japan in 1919, sparking peaceful public demonstrations nationwide. Japanese reprisals resulted in 7,500 people being killed, 15,000 injured, and 45,000 arrested. The movement had a significant legacy, including the establishment of the provisional government in China. For more details, see Robinson, *Korea's Twentieth-Century Odyssey*: 48.

38. Cumings sees that Rhee Syng-man and his followers, around this time, intentionally sent members of youth groups into villages and towns with strong leftist leadership and sympathizers. Jeju certainly was a place where leftists were highly influential. See Cumings, *Roaring of the Cataract*, 247.

39. Bruce Cumings, *The Korean War: A History* (New York: Modern Library, 2010), 122; Myeong-lim Park, "Jeju-do 4.3 minjung hangjaeng-e guanhan yeongu [A study on the Jeju 4.3 popular uprising]" (master's thesis, Korea University, 1988), 13.

40. Merrill, "Cheju-do Rebellion," 142.

41. Initially, it was leftist groups that formed these political and agitation groups such as the Korean Communist Young Men's Association. However, following the failure of the US-USSR joint commission in August 1947, rightist youth groups were created under the protection of the occupation forces and rightist politicians. The Great Korea Democratic Young Men's Association, the Korean Independence Youth Association, the Korea National Youth Association, and the Daedong Youth Corp were set up by rightist groups in the South and the Northwest Youth Association was created by young people who had escaped from the Communists in the North. According to Henderson, thirty-four such bodies were registered in 1947. For more details, see Cumings, *Roaring of the Cataract*, 193–203; Henderson, *Politics of the Vortex*, 140–41; Cumings, "American Policy and Korean Liberation," 85.

42. Bong-hyeon Kim and Min-ju Kim, "Jeju-do inmindeul-eui 4.3 mujang tujaengsa [A history of the Jeju people's 4.3 armed struggle]," in *Jeju minjung hangjeang* [Jeju people's uprising], ed. Arari Research Institute (Seoul: Sonamu, 1988).

43. Merrill, "Cheju-do Rebellion," 168.

44. Dong-man Kim, "Yeoksa jaehyeon-eitseo yeongsangjaryo-eui jaehaeseok-gua hwalyong-e guanhan yeongu [A study of the reinterpretation and application of film footage in the historical reappearance]" (master's thesis, Sejong University, 2003).

45. Park, "Jeju-do 4.3 minjung hangjaeng-e guanhan yeongu."

46. Cumings, *Korean War*, 131.

47. Merrill, "Internal Warfare in Korea," 144.

48. Merrill, "Cheju-do Rebellion," 181.

49. Deuk-jung Kim, *'Ppalgaengi'-eui tansaeng: Yeosun sageon-gua bangong gukga-eui hyeongseong* [The birth of the "reds": The Yeosun events and the formation of the anti-Communist state] (Seoul: Seonin, 2009), 353.

50. Merrill, "Cheju-do Rebellion," 183–84.

51. Jeju Commission, *Jeju 4.3 sageon jinsang josa bogoseo*, 293.

52. Jeong-sim Yang, *Jeju 4.3 hangjaeng: Jeohang-gua apeum-eui yeoksa* [The Jeju 4.3 uprising: A history of resistance and pain] (Seoul: Seonin, 2008), 18; Chang-hoon Ko, "4.3 minjung hangjaeng-eui jeongae-wa seonggyeok [The process and characteristics of the 4.3 democratic uprising]," in *Haebang jeonhusa-ui insik 4* [A study of the Korean liberation period, vol. 4], ed. Jang Jip Choi (Seoul: Hangilsa, 1989).

53. Ko, "4.3 minjung hangjaeng-eui jeongae-wa seonggyeok; Yang, *Jeju 4.3 hangjaeng*; Park, "Jeju-do 4.3 minjung hangjaeng-e guanhan yeongu."

54. Seok-kyun Jeong, "Jeju 4.3 sageon-ui jinsang [The truth of the Jeju 4.3 events]," *Gunsa* 41 (2000).

55. Chang-hoon Ko, "US Government Responsibility in the Jeju April Third Uprising and Grand Massacre—Islanders' Perspective," *Study of Regional Government* 8, no. 2 (2004).

56. Hae-gu Jeong, "Jeju 4.3 hangjaeng-gua migunjeongcheong yeongu [The Jeju 4.3 uprising and the policies of the US military government]," in *Jeju 4.3 Yeongu*.

2. Suppressed yet Stubborn Truths

1. Robinson, *Korea's Twentieth-Century Odyssey*, 122.

2. Rhee designed his *ilminjueui* (ideology of one people) by skillfully combining anti-Communism with nationalism. He proposed that the Korean people had always been one throughout history and thus the Communist state in the North was illegitimate and South Koreans must achieve national unification through a northward advance. This anti-Communist nationalism was the basis of Rhee's unification policy and provided firm grounds for his objection to the 1953 armistice to end the conflict on the Korean peninsula. For more details, see Gi-Wook Shin, *Ethnic Nationalism in Korea: Genealogy, Politics, and Legacy* (Stanford: Stanford University Press, 2006).

3. For more details, see Geochang County Council, *Hanguk jeonjaeng-jeonhu Geochang-gun-guannae minganin huisaengja jinsang josa bogoseo* [Report of the civilian victims in Geochang during the Korean War] (Geochang: Geochang County Council, 2003).

4. For more details on the special court, see Jong Heo, *Banmin teukui jojik-gua hwaldong* [The organization and activities of the Special Committee for Investigation of the Pro-Japanese Collaborators] (Seoul: Seonin, 2003); and Kang-su Lee, *Banmin teukui yeongu* [A study of the Special Committee for Investigation of the Pro-Japanese Collaborators] (Seoul: Nanam, 2003).

5. Kim, "4.3 Ihu 50 nyeon."

6. Jung-seok Seo, *Cho Bong-am-gua 1950-nyeondae (ha)* [Cho Bong-am and the 1950s, vol. 2] (Seoul: Yeoksa Bipyeong, 1999), 713.

7. Personal interview, Lee Mun-gyo, a former leader of Jeju National University's student movement in 1960, Jeju, 22 April 2006.

8. For more details on the Second Republic, see John Kie-chiang Oh, *Korea: Democracy on Trial* (Ithaca: Cornell University Press, 1968); and Sungjoo Han, *The Failure of Democracy in South Korea* (Berkeley: University of California Press, 1974).

9. Personal interview, Lee Mun-gyo, 22 April 2006.

10. Ibid.

11. Gi-jin Kim, *Ggeutnaji aneun jeonjaeng, gukmin bodo yeonmaeng* [Unfinished war: Civilian massacres during the Korean War] (Seoul: Yeoksa Bipyeong, 2002), 119.

12. Initially, to the disappointment of the people of Jeju, the massacres in Jeju were excluded since the Congressional Committee originally limited its mandate to the civilian massacres that occurred during the Korean War. However, the Jeju 4.3 events finally got included in the agenda due to the efforts of three congressmen from Jeju—Ko Dam-ryong, Hyun Oh-bong, and Kim Du-jin.

13. Personal interview, Lee Mun-gyo, 22 April 2006.

14. Ibid.

15. *Jeju Sinbo*, 13 June 1960.

16. In parallel, victims set up the victims' association and openly expressed their demand for truth and justice. The first victims association was created in Daejung, and the first street rally demanding truth and justice took place there. *Jeju Sinbo*, 31 May 1960.

17. *Jeju Sinbo*, 18 June 1960.

18. *Jeju Sinbo*, 1 June 1960.

19. Jeju Commission, *Jeju 4.3 sageon jaryojip 4* [Jeju 4.3 events archive, vol. 4] (Seoul: Jeju Commission, 2002).

20. *Jeju Sinbo*, 24 June 1960.

21. Kang Hee-cheol filed a complaint against Shin Hyeon-jun, a retired lieutenant general in the South Korean Marine Corps, for killing his father. *Jeju Sinbo*, 25 June 1960.

22. Shin, *Ethnic Nationalism*, 103; John Kie-chiang Oh, *Korean Politics: The Quest for Democratization and Economic Development* (Ithaca: Cornell University Press, 1999), 52.

23. Won-soon Park, *Gukga boanbeop yeongu 1: Gukga boanbeop byeoncheonsa* [A study of the National Security Law, vol. 1, The development of the National Security Law] (Seoul: Yeoksa Bipyeong, 1994).

24. The Revolutionary Court is a special court designed to try those suspected of high treason, espionage, and grand corruption. Committee on the History of the Revolutionary Court, *Hanguk hyeokmyeong jaepansa* [The history of the Revolutionary Court's rulings] (Seoul: Committee on the History of the Revolutionary Court, 1962).

25. Kim, *Ggeutnaji aneun jeonjaeng*.

26. Ibid., 282.

27. Personal interview, Ko Yeong-wu, vice-president of the Baekjo Ilson Yujokhoe and son of Ko Jeong-ha, former president of the association, Jeju, 26 October 2006.

28. Personal interview, Ko Yeong-wu, 26 October 2006.

29. *Hankook Ilbo*, 11 November 1961.

30. Personal interview, Lee Mun-gyo, 22 April 2006.

31. Kim, "4.3 Ihu 50 nyeon."

32. Personal interview, Lee Mun-gyo, 22 April 2006.

33. Personal interview, Ko Yeong-wu, 26 October 2006.

34. Personal interview, Yang Bong-cheon, president of the Hyunui Victims Association, Jeju, 19 October 2005.

35. Personal interview, Ko Yeong-wu, 26 October 2006.

36. Personal interview, Anonymous, a victim of the Jeju 4.3 events, Jeju 2 April 2006.

37. Sang-ik Hwang, "Euihaksajeok cheukmyeon-eseo bon 4.3 [The Jeju 4.3 events as medical history]," in *Jeju 4.3 Yeongu*, 326.

38. *Jemin Ilbo* 4.3 Chuijaeban, *4.3-eun malhanda 2* [4.3 Speaks, vol. 2] (Seoul: Jeonyeoweon, 1994).

39. Ibid., 413.

40. Seo, *Cho Bong-am-gua 1950-nyeondae (ha)*, 715; Kim, "4.3 Ihu 50 nyeon," 317.

41. Sporadic attempts are found in the historic record or the autobiographies of politicians. For instance, a director in the Jeju Prosecutors Office addressed the possibility of investigating the Jeju 4.3 events on 8 August 1961; Congressman Kim Seong-suk compiled a report on civilian deaths and submitted it to the 5th National Assembly in December 1961; and Congressman Hyun Oh-bong held a meeting at which Lee Seong-cheol suggested restoring the stone monument destroyed by the police on 12 January 1966.

42. Gi-yeong Hyun, *Suni Samchon*.

43. Kim, "4.3 Ihu 50 nyeon."

44. Gi-yeong Hyun, *Suni Samchon*, 74.

45. The short story also showed that "although victims and their families such as the narrator and Aunt Suni tried hard to escape the fearful memory of the massacres, they never succeeded and were haunted by it." Jae-yong Kim, "Pokryeok-gua gweonryeok, geurigo minjung [Violence, power, and people]," in *Jeju 4.3 Yeongu*, 277.

46. Gi-yeong Hyun, "Nae soseol-eui motae-neun 4.3 hangjaeng [The motif of my short story is the 4.3 uprising]," *Yeoksa Biyeong* 20, no. 1 (1993).

47. Ibid., 167.

48. Ibid., 168.

49. Personal interview, Oh Seung-guk, secretary-general of the 4.3 Research Institute and former president of the Jeju Cultural Movement Association, Jeju, 7 April 2006.

50. Personal interview, Ko Chang-hoon, professor at Jeju National University and former director of the 4.3 Research Institute, Jeju, 24 March 2006.

51. Despite the continuous challenge to his rule by dissidents and political opponents, the elites and public generally accepted Park's claims of political legitimacy. Urban middle-class and working-class citizens temporarily acquiesced to the dictatorship for the sake of "the historic modernization mission of the time" (*joguk geundaehwa*). Citizens accepted the government's stand that Korean society did not have the luxury of choosing both economic development and liberal democracy. See Jang Jip Choi, "Political Cleavages in South Korea," in *State and Society in Contemporary Korea*, ed. Hagen Koo (Ithaca: Cornell University Press, 1993).

52. Oh, *Korean Politics*, 83.

53. Merrill, "Cheju-do Rebellion."

54. Yong-sam Kang and Gyeong-su Lee, *Daeha silrok Jeju 100-nyun* [One hundred years of the history of Jeju] (Jeju: Taekwang, 1984).

55. Personal interview, Yang Bong-cheon, 19 October 2005.

3. From Oblivion to Social Attention

1. Personal interview, Yang Jo-hoon, a former editor of the *Jemin Ilbo*, Seoul, 24 November 2005; personal interview, Oh Seung-guk, 7 April 2006.

2. Personal interview, Yang Dong-yun, a former chairperson of the Provincial Solidarity for the Investigation of the Truth and Restoration of Honor for the Jeju 4.3 Events, Jeju, 1 October 2005.

3. Chung-in Moon and Sunghack Lim, "The Politics of Economic Rise and Decline in South Korea," in *Understanding Korean Politics: An Introduction*, ed. Seung-heum Kil and Chung-in Moon (Albany: State University of New York Press, 2001), 209.

4. Personal interview, Yang Dong-yun, 1 October 2005; personal interview, Yang Jo-hoon, 24 November 2005.

5. Yeong-beom Kim, "Gieok tujaeng-euiroseoeui 4.3 munhwa undong seoseol [Introduction: The 4.3 cultural movement as a struggle for memory]," in *Gieok tujaeng-gua munhwa undong-eui jeongae* [A struggle for memory and the development of the cultural movement], ed. Kan-Chae Na, Keun-sik Jung, and Chang-il Kang (Seoul: Yeoksa Bipyeong, 2004), 35.

6. *Jemin Ilbo*, 3 April 1991.

7. Personal interview, Ko Yeong-wu, 26 October 2006; personal interview, Kim Chang-hu, former director of the 4.3 Research Institute, Jeju, 12 April 2006.

8. Bong-hyeon Kim and Min-ju Kim, "Jeju-do inmindeul-eui 4.3 mujang tujaengsa."

9. For example, according to the minutes of the National Assembly, Congress members Hwang Myeong-su and Kang Bo-seong in 1988 and Congress members Kang and Choi Gi-seong in 1989 addressed the Jeju 4.3 events during the session.

10. Minutes of the National Assembly, 1990.

11. Personal interview, Lee Jung-heung, a victim whose father was murdered by the military, Jeju, 2 April 2006.

12. Seong-man Ko, "Jeju 4.3 damron-eui hyeongseong-gua jeongchijeok jakyong [The formation and political process of the Jeju 4.3 discourse]" (master's thesis, Jeju National University, 2005).

13. Personal interview, Yang Dong-yun, 1 October 2005.

14. Huntington, *Third Wave*, 215.

15. Kim Seok-beom, Kim Min-ju, Moon Guk-ju, Hyeong Gwang-su, and Kim Gyu-chan set up the organization in 1987.

16. Personal interview, Park Gyeong-hun, one of five leaders who prepared the memorial service in 1989, Jeju, 5 April 2006.

17. Personal interview, Oh Seung-guk, 7 April 2006.

18. Personal interview, Yang Dong-yun, 1 October 2005.

19. Personal interview, Oh Seung-guk, 7 April 2006.

20. Personal interview, Kang Deok-hwan, former journalist, writer, and secretary-general of the Special Committee on 4.3, Jeju, 21 March 2006.

21. Personal interview, Park Chan-sik, former secretary-general of the Jeju 4.3 Research Institute, Jeju, 6 April 2006.

22. Personal interview, Oh Seung-guk, 7 April 2006.

23. Kim, "Gieok tujaeng-euiroseoeui 4.3 munhwa undong seoseol."

24. Personal interview, Park Gyeong-hun, 5 April 2006.

25. Personal interview, Yang Jo-hoon, Seoul, 15 March 2006.

26. Jo-hoon Yang, "4.3 chuijae 6-nyeon: Muchamhi oegokdoen yeoksa [Six years of reporting on the Jeju 4.3 events: A severely distorted history]," *Yeoksa Bipyeong* 25, no. 2 (1994).

27. Personal interview, Yang Jo-hoon, 15 March 2006.

28. Ibid.

29. Personal interview, Kim Jong-min, former reporter for the *Jemin Ilbo*, Seoul, 25 May 2006.

30. Personal interview, Yang Jo-hoon, 15 March 2006.

31. Ibid.

32. Under Chun Doo-hwan's regime, only one local newspaper existed in Jeju—the *Jeju Sinmun*—due to Chun's policy of allowing only a small number of mass media in the nation to maintain easier control. Mun-gyo Lee, *Jejų eonronsa* [A history of Jeju media] (Seoul: Nanam, 1997).

33. Personal interview, Yang Jo-hoon, 15 March 2006.

34. Ibid.

35. Personal interview, Kim Jong-min, 25 May 2006.

36. Lee, *Jeju eonronsa*.

37. Gui-suk Kwon, "Jeju 4.3-eui daehang gieok-gua yeongsang [Alternative memory of the Jeju 4.3 events and visual images]," in *Gieok̦ tujaeng-gua munhwa undong-eui jeongae* [A struggle for memory and the development of the cultural movement], ed. Kan-Chae Na, Keun-sik Jung, and Chang-il Kang (Seoul: Yeoksa Bipyeong, 2004), 104.

38. Personal interview, Kim Jong-min, 25 May 2006.

39. Personal interview, Ko Hee-beom, former managing director of *Hank̦yoreh*, Jeju, 4 May 2011.

40. Personal interview, Kim Chang-hu, Jeju, 12 April 2006.

41. In this conference, professor Ko Chang-hoon, writer Oh Seong-chan, and poet Kim Myeong-sik gave a lecture on the Jeju 4.3 events and civilian massacres.

42. *Donga Ilbo*, 6 April 1988.

43. Kang Eun-suk, Kim Gi-sam, and Kang Tae-gweon were also a part of the team.

44. Personal interview, Kim Chang-hu, 12 April 2006; personal interview, Ko Hee-beom, 4 May 2011.

45. Personal interview, Kim Eun-hee, a founding member and senior researcher at the Jeju 4.3 Research Institute, Jeju 21 May 2006.

46. Personal interview, Oh, Seung-guk, 7 April 2006.

47. Personal interview, Kim Chang-hu, 12 April 2006.

48. *Jemin Ilbo*, 3 April 2003.

49. *Jeju Ilbo*, 25 October 1988.

50. Seong-chan Oh, *Halla-eui tonggok̦ sori* [Bitter wailing of Halla] (Seoul: Sonamu, 1988).

51. Ibid.; Lim-hwa Han, "Yonggang maeul saramdeul-eui bunno," [The anger of the residents of Yonggang village] *Sahoewa Sasang* 2, no. 1 (1989).

52. *Jemin Ilbo*, 8 April 1994; *Weolgan Jeju*, May 1990, July 1990, and August 1990.

53. Personal interview, Yang Jo-hoon, 15 March 2006; personal interview, Kim Jong-min, 25 May 2006.

54. Personal interview, Kim Jong-min, 25 May 2006.

55. *Jemin Ilbo*, 7 November 1991.

56. *Jemin Ilbo*, 7 February 1992.

57. Studies have revealed the importance of diaspora populations in the transitional justice advocacy. See Laura A Young and Rosalyn Park, "Engaging Diasporas in Truth Commissions: Lessons from the Liberia Truth and Reconciliation Commission Diaspora Project," *International Journal of Transitional Justice* 3, no. 3 (2009); and Ezekiel Pajibo, "Civil Society and Transitional Justice in Liberia: A Practitioner's Reflection from the Field," *International Journal of Transitional Justice* 1, no. 2 (2007).

58. Bong-hyeon Kim and Min-ju Kim, "Jeju-do inmindeul-eui 4.3 mujang tujaengsa"; Seok-beom Kim, *Ggamagui-eui juk̦eum* [The death of a crow] (Seoul: Sonamu, 1988) and Kim, *Hwasando* [A volcanic island] (Seoul: Silcheon Munhak, 1988).

59. Personal interview, Kim Eun-hee, 21 May 2006.

60. Ibid.

61. Gi-sam Kim and Dong-man Kim, *Darangshigul-eui seulpeun norae* [A sad song of the Darangshi cave] (Jeju: Gak, 2002), 31.

62. Ibid., 42.

63. Chang-hoon Ko, "Darangshigul balgul iyagi [A story of discovering the Darangshi cave]," (unpublished manuscript, 24 March 2006), 4.

64. Personal interview, Ko Chang-hoon, 12 April 2006.

65. Ko, "Darangshigul balgul iyagi," 10.

66. Personal interview, Kim Eun-hee, 3 May 2011.

67. Kim and Kim, *Darangshigul-eui seulpeun norae*, 86.

68. *Jemin Ilbo*, 4 April 1992.

69. Kim and Kim, *Darangshigul-eui seulpeun norae*, 98–99.

70. Personal interview, Ko Chang-hoon, 12 April 2006. According to South Korean criminal law, Ko had no legal obligation to report dead bodies since the corpses were more than ten years old.

71. Ko, "Darangshigul balgul iyagi," 6.

72. *Halla Ilbo*, 4 April 1992.

73. Kim and Kim, *Darangshigul-eui seulpeun norae*, 106–7.

74. Personal interview, Kim Dong-man, former secretary-general of the Jeju 4.3 Research Institute, Jeju, 12 April 2006; personal interview, Ko Chang-hoon, 12 April 2006.

75. *Jemin Ilbo*, 16 May 1992.

76. Ko, "Darangshigul balgul iyagi."

77. *Jemin Ilbo*, 16 May 1992.

78. Kim and Kim, *Darangshigul-eui seulpeun norae*, 108.

79. Ko, "Darangshigul balgul iyagi," 22–23.

80. Dong-man Kim, "Yeoksajeoks-euro bokweon-doeeoyahal Darangshi-gul [The Darangshi cave should be recovered]," *Jeju Jakga* 8 (2002).

81. Personal interview, Kim Dong-man, 12 April 2006.

82. Ibid.

4. The Struggle of the Periphery

1. Office of the Secretariat, Jeju Provincial Council, "Minutes of the 69th Plenary Session (No. 3)" (Jeju: Jeju Provincial Council, 1991).

2. Ibid.

3. Personal interview, Kim Yeong-hun, former chairperson of the Special Committee on 4.3 and a local Jeju council member, Jeju, 22 March 2006.

4. Members were Kang Weon-cheol, Ko Seok-hyeon, Kim Dong-gyu, Kim Yeong-hun, Yang Geum-seok, Lee Yeong-gil, and Lee Jae-hyeon.

5. Office of the Secretariat, Jeju Provincial Council, "Minutes of the 82nd Extraordinary Session (No. 2)" (Jeju: Jeju Provincial Council, 1993).

6. Special Committee on 4.3, *Jejudo 4.3 pihae josa bogoseo* [Report of the victims of Jeju 4.3] (Jeju: Jeju Provincial Council, 1997). 16; Office of the Secretariat, Jeju Provincial Council, "Minutes of the 83rd Extraordinary Session (No. 1)" (Jeju: Jeju Provincial Council, 1993).

7. Personal interview, Kang Deok-hwan, 21 March 2006.

8. Ibid.

9. Personal interview, Kim Yeong-hun, 22 March 2006.

10. Ibid.

11. Personal interview, Kang Deok-hwan, 2 May 2011.

12. Jeju Commission, *Jeju 4.3 sageon jinsang josa bogoseo.*

13. Pyeonjipbu, "4.3 huisaengja myeongdan choecho gonggae [The first publication of the list of 4.3 victims]," *Gwangwang Jeju*, April 1989.

14. Special Committee on 4.3, *Jejudo 4.3 pihae josa bogoseo.*

15. Ibid., 58–61.

16. Personal interview, Kang Deok-hwan, 21 March 2006.

17. Jeju Commission, *Jeju 4.3 sageon jinsang josa bogoseo*, 383–85.

18. This was a statement made by the speaker of the National Assembly when the council members visited and presented their report along with the petition to investigate the Jeju 4.3 events. Personal interview, Kang Deok-hwan, 21 March 2006.

19. Personal interview, Park Seo-dong, former editor of *Gwangwang Jeju* and a secretary-general of the Anti-Communist Association for the Civilian Victims' Families of the Jeju 4.3 Events, Jeju, 7 May 2011.

20. Ibid.

21. Personal interview, Kim Seong-su, a founding member of the Anti-Communist Association for the Civilian Victims' Families of the Jeju 4.3 Events and a victim of the violence committed by leftist insurgents, Jeju, 12 April 2006.

22. Personal interview, Lee Jung-heung, 2 April 2006.

23. Ko, "Jeju 4.3 damron-eui hyeongseong-gua jeongchijeok jakyong," 33.

24. Gyeong-hun Kim, "4.3 hapdong wiryeongje: Wae musan doeeotna [Why did the negotiation for the united memorial service fail?]," *Weolgan Jeju*, May 1993.

25. Personal interview, Kim Dong-man, 12 April 2006; personal interview, Park Seo-dong, 7 May 2011.

26. Two from the victims' association—chair Kim Byeong-eon and secretary-general Park Seo-dong—and four representing activists—Ko Chang-hoon, Mo Gap-gyeong, Yang Dong-yun, and Lee Yong-jung—were present. In addition, chair Kim Yeong-hun and executive secretary Lee Yeong-gil were represented on the Special Committee.

27. Kim, "4.3 hapdong wiryeongje: Wae musan doeeotna."

28. Ibid.

29. Ibid.

30. Personal interview, Kim Yeong-hun, 22 March 2006.

31. Personal interview, Yang Dong-yun, 1 October 2005.

32. Personal interview, Ko Chang-hoon, 24 March 2006.

33. A few further suggested the local government or the intelligence service, such as the Korean Central Intelligence Agency, was responsible in order to obstruct future united memorial services. Personal interview, Ko Chang-hoon, 24 March 2006.

34. Personal interview, Yang Jo-hoon, 24 November 2005.

35. Personal interview, Lee Jung-heung, 2 April 2006.

36. Personal interview, Kang, Ho-jin, president of the Jeju National University Student Association in 1996, Jeju, 22 March 2006.

37. Personal interview, Yang Jo-hoon, 24 November 2005.

38. Local students had already been working with the national association since the first nationwide student-led demonstration on the Jeju 4.3 events in 1991.

39. Ko, "Jeju 4.3 damron-eui hyeongseong-gua jeongchijeok jakyong."

40. Personal interview, Kim Nam-hun, former student activist, Jeju, 23 March 2006; personal interview, Kang, Ho-jin, 22 March 2006.

41. Personal interview, Oh Yeong-hun, former student activist and secretary-general of the Provincial Solidarity for the Investigation of the Truth and Restoration of Honor for the Jeju 4.3 Events, Jeju, 11 April 2006.

42. Personal interview, Kim Nam-hun, 23 March 2006.

43. Office of the Secretariat, Jeju Provincial Council, "Minutes of the 88th Plenary Session (No. 1)" (Jeju: Jeju Provincial Council, 1993).

44. Personal interview, Kim Yeong-hun, 22 March 2006.

45. Even before the visit, the Taiwanese experience was addressed in speeches of council members such as Jang Jeong-eon. *Jemin Ilbo*, 24 April 1993; Office of the Secretariat, Jeju Provincial Council, "Minutes of the 83rd Extraordinary Session (No. 1)."

46. Of course, it was not without obstacles. For example, similar to the South Korean case, President Lee Teng-hui initially opposed the idea of investigation, arguing, "We have to look forward, not backward. It is now the responsibility of historians to find the truth." *Jemin Ilbo*, 8 August 2011.

47. Personal interview, Yang, Jo-hoon, 15 March 2006.

48. Kim, "4.3 Ihu 50 nyeon."

49. Personal interview, Kang Deok-hwan, 2 May 2011.

50. Personal interview, Yang, Jo-hoon, 15 March 2006.

51. Personal interview, Kang Deok-hwan, 21 March 2006.

52. *Jemin Ilbo*, 11 July 2011.

53. *Halla Ilbo*, 17 December 1996

54. *Jeju Ilbo*, 18 December 1996.

55. *Donga Ilbo*, 20 March 1994.

56. *Halla Ilbo*, 22 March 1994.

57. *Donga Ilbo*, 21 March 1994.

58. Personal interview, Kim Dong-man, 12 April 2006; Sun-tae Kim, "Red Hunt-neun gwayeon ijeok pyohyeonmul inga? [Is the red hunt really benefitting the enemy?]," *Minju Beophak* 13 (1997).

59. Sun-tae Kim, "Jeju 4.3 dangsi gyeeom-eui bulbeopseong [The illegality of the martial law during the Jeju 4.3 events]," in *Jeju 4.3 yeongu* [A study on the Jeju 4.3], ed. Jeju 4.3 Research Institute (Seoul: Yeoksa Bipyeong, 1999).

60. Chang-rok Kim, "1948-nyeon heonbeop je-100-jo: 4.3 gyeeomryeong-eol tonghae bon ilje beopryeong-eui hyoryeok [The Constitution of 1948 and article 100: The effectiveness of the Japanese law based on the martial law during the Jeju 4.3 events]," *Beophak Yeongu* 39, no. 2 (1998).

61. Personal interview, Kim Jong-min, 25 May 2006; personal interview, Yang Jo-hoon, 15 March 2006.

62. Lee Yeong-hee, "The Truth about the Taiwanese 2.28 Events," *Jemin Ilbo*, 2 June 1993.

5. The Establishment of the Jeju Commission

1. Kim, "4.3 Ihu 50 nyeon," 343.

2. Ibid., 343–45.

3. Personal interview, Ko Chang-hoon, 24 March 2006.

4. For Ko's early contribution of the study of the Jeju 4.3 events, see Ko, "4.3 minjung hangjaeng-eui jeongae-wa seonggyeok."

5. Personal interview, Yang Dong-yun, 4 May 2011; personal interview, Yang Jo-hoon, 10 May 2011.

6. However, no further actions were taken beyond this investigation except for a few commemoration projects at the local level. In 2004 a special law designed to make individual reparations to the victims passed the National Assembly, but Prime Minister Ko Geon, who was acting president while President Roh Moo-hyun was waiting for the Constitutional Court's decision whether to uphold his impeachment, vetoed the bill. Ko's justification was that if individual reparations were made to the Geochang victims, other victims of state violence would soon

request reparations and this would cause "enormous financial burden to the state budget." Families of victims brought a series of lawsuits against the government for monetary compensation, but those lawsuits ended without success in 2008. *Hankyoreh*, 23 March 2004.

7. Pan National Committee, *4.3 bansegi* [Half a century since the 4.3] (Seoul: Pan National Committee, 2000).

8. Personal interview, Yang Dong-yun, 4 May 2011; personal interview, Yang Jo-hoon, 4 May 2011.

9. Jung Yun-hyeong, Hyun Gi-yeong, Kim Myeong-sik, Ko Hee-beom, Kang Chang-il, and Heo Sang-su, who were the members of the Research Group for the Issues in Jeju Society, led the movement.

10. For example, Lee Don-myeong, Ye Chun-ho, Lee Yeong-hee, Kim Jin-gyun, Baik Nak-cheong, Shin Yong-ha, Ko Eun, Shin Gyeong-lim, Moon Jeong-hyeon, Kim Jung-bae, Kang Man-gil, Kim Sang-gon, Kwon Young-gil, Park Won-soon, Choi Yeol, Seo Gyeong-seok, Seo Jung-seok, and Kwak Ro-hyeon were members of the Pan National Committee.

11. The Commemoration Committee was headed by Kang Chang-il, Kim Yeong-hun, Kim Pyeong-dam, Moon Mu-byeong, and Lim Mun-choel.

12. The committee was composed of five congress members (Kim Jin-bae as chair, Choo Mi-ae as vice-chair, Park Chan-ju, Yang Seong-cheol, and Lee Seong-jae) and four party executives (Kim Chang-jin, Jung Dae-gweon, Hong Seong-je, and Ko Jin-bu).

13. Kim Jong-min, a former reporter of the *Jemin Ilbo*, remembered that, before 1998, every April reporters from national newspapers and broadcasting agencies called or had a casual visit in search of news items. It was "the only way" that Jeju 4.3 events were presented in any national news media before the inauguration of Kim Dae-jung. Personal interview, Kim Jong-min, 25 May 2006.

14. Personal interview, Yang Dong-yun, 4 May 2011.

15. Commemoration Committee, *Je-50-junyeon Jeju 4.3 haksul munhwa saeop naekseo* [White paper on the work of the Commemoration Committee] (Jeju: Commemoration Committee, 1998), 39.

16. *Jeju Ilbo*, 2 April 1998.

17. Ibid.

18. Commemoration Committee, *Je-50-junyeon Jeju 4.3 haksul munhwa saeop naekseo*, 40–41.

19. Two other conferences were convened. One by the Pan National Committee (28 April 1998) and the other by the Commemoration Committee (9 April 1998).

20. Personal interview, Park Chan-sik, 4 May 2011; personal interview, Kang Nam-gyu, chief secretary of the organizing committee for the conference, Jeju, 8 April 2006.

21. Personal interview, Kang Chang-il, former director of the Jeju 4.3 Research Institute and a congress member, Jeju, 8 May 2011.

22. Personal interview, Park Gyeong-hun, 9 May 2011.

23. Provincial Solidarity had three cochairs, Kim Yeong-hun, Yang Geum-seok, and Lim Mun-cheol, and eight representatives from local NGOs (Kang Chang-il, Ko Seong-hwa, Kim Pyeong-dam, Yang Bo-yun, Oh Man-sik, Yoon Chung-gwang, Lee Eun-ju, and Heo Tae-jun).

24. By 28 October 1999, the Solidarity Association for the Achievement of the Jeju 4.3 Special Law was formed comprising twenty-four local organizations. This was an important organization that included most activists and social movement organizations both in Seoul and Jeju. Provincial Solidarity also was a part of the Solidarity Association and played a leading role. Jeju Commission, *Jeju 4.3 sageon jinsang josa bogoseo*.

25. Personal interview, Yang Dong-yun, 4 May 2011; personal interview, Yang Jo-hoon, 10 May 2011; personal interview, Kim Yeong-hun, 22 March 2006; *Jemin Ilbo*, 5 December 2011.

26. By this time, the Pan National Committee for the 50th Anniversary of the Jeju 4.3 Events changed its name to the Pan National Committee for the Investigation of the Truth and Restoration of the Honor of Victims of the Jeju 4.3 Events.

27. Personal interview, Ko Hee-beom, 4 May 2011.

28. Personal interview, Yang Dong-yun, 4 May 2011.

29. *Jemin Ilbo*, 12 December 2011.

30. *Jemin Ilbo*, 3 October 2011.

31. Kim, "4.3 Ihu 50 nyeon."

32. Personal interview, Park Chan-sik, 4 May 2011; personal interview, Kang Chang-il, 8 May 2011.

33. Personal interview, Congresswoman Choo Mi-ae, Seoul, 23 May 2011.

34. Mi-ae Choo, *Jeju 4.3 sageongua na: Ggeutnaji aneun jinsile daehayeo* [The Jeju 4.3 events and I: On the unending truths] (unpublished manuscript, 23 May 2011).

35. *Jemin Ilbo*, 3 October 2011.

36. Chan-sik Park, "Hanguk jeonjaeng-gi Jeju 4.3 guanryeon suhyeongin haksal-eui silsang [Truth about the massacre during the Korean War of court-martialed persons related to the 4.3 events]," *4.3-gua Yeoksa* 1, no. 1 (2001).

37. For example, the *Chosun Ilbo* known as a right-wing national newspaper published the news on their second page. It was the first time that news on the Jeju 4.3 events made it this close to the front page of their paper.

38. Personal interview, Yang Dong-yun, 4 May 2011.

39. Interestingly, facts about the massacre at Nogunri—four hundred civilian refugees killed by the US military during the Korean War between 26 and 29 July 1950—also broke on 30 September 1999. The US and South Korean government set up a joint investigation committee in October 1999, which led to a fifteen-month investigation lasting until January 2001 and confirmed the massacre and the US responsibility for it. President Bill Clinton expressed his "deep regrets," but the committee justified the killings as an act that was "not intentional or premeditated." The US government did not take any follow-up measures, and victims and activists pressed lawmakers to pass a special law to address the Nogunri massacre, which passed the National Assembly in 2004.

40. Congressman Kim Yong-gap, a renowned conservative politician, made this remark at the regular session of the 15th National Assembly in speaking against the enactment of the special law.

41. *Jemin Ilbo*, 30 December 2011.

42. *Jeju Sinmun*, 3 April 1996.

43. Previous laws, such as the special laws on the Geochang massacre and the Gwangju massacre, and the Taiwanese law on the 2.28 events were closely examined and referenced in order to draft the opposition's bill. Personal interview, Byun Jeong-il, former congressman, Jeju, 10 May 2011.

44. Byun told me that it was partly possible because he was the secretary to the leader of the opposition party where he could exert an influence over the party's politics. Personal interview, Byun Jeong-il, 10 May 2011.

45. Personal interview, Lim Mun-cheol, Catholic priest and former chairperson of Provincial Solidarity, Jeju, 9 May 2011.

46. Congresswoman Choo was head of the legal department of the Pan National Committee, and she and her legal team drafted the bill. Personal interview, Ko Hee-beom, 4 May 2011.

47. *Jemin Ilbo*, 3 November 1999; Personal interview, Byun Jeong-il, 10 May 2011.

48. The opposition party partly accepted activists' view of the period of the Jeju 4.3 events and extended the investigation period up to 22 September 1954. However, since the beginning date of the events was the core of the debate, it was not a meaningful change.

49. Personal interview, Choo Mi-ae, 23 May 2011

50. Personal interview, Choo Mi-ae, 23 May 2011; personal interview, Ko Hee-beom, 4 May 2011.

51. Personal interview, Oh Yeong-hun, 5 May 2011.

52. Ibid.

53. Personal interview, Yang Jo-hoon, 4 May 2011.

54. Another person who was indispensible at this critical period was Kang Seong-gu, who had been actively involved in the democratization movement under the military and authoritarian regimes and had worked closely with Kim Dae-jung and his supporters. With these personal connections, Kang played a critical role in connecting President Kim and activist groups. A few told me that Kang Seong-gu also had a connection with Kim Sang-geun, who was close to the president. Personal interview, Kim Jong-min, 2 December 2011; personal interview, Yang Dong-yun, 4 May 2011.

55. Personal interview, Ko Hee-beom, 4 May 2011.

56. Personal interview, Lim Mun-cheol, 9 May 2011; personal interview, Byun Jeong-il, 10 May 2011.

57. Office of the Secretariat, National Assembly. "Minutes of the 15th Assembly" (Seoul: National Assembly, 1999), 208–22.

58. Bruce Cumings, "The Question of American Responsibility for the Suppression of the Chejudo Uprising," (paper presented at the 50th Anniversary Conference of the April 3, 1948 Chejudo Rebellion, Tokyo, April 1998).

59. Personal interview, Yang Jo-hoon, 4 May 2011.

6. The Jeju Commission, 2000–2003

1. Park Chang-uk, Kim Du-yeon (victims) and Lim Mun-cheol, Yang Jo-hoon, Yang-Dong-yun, Yang Geum-seok, Ko Hee-beom, and Kang Chang-il (activists) were invited.

2. *Jemin Ilbo*, 12 January 2000.

3. Lee Jin-woo, "Gukgun-eul baesin han daehan minguk gukhoe [The National Assembly betrayed the Korean Army]," *Weolgan Chosun*, April 2000; Lee Hyeon-hee, "Jeju 4.3 sageon-eui bonjil-eul dasi malhanda [Rethinking the true characteristics of the Jeju 4.3 events]," *Weolgan Chosun,* April 2000.

4. Lee Cheol-seung, Moon Bong-je, Kim Ho-san, Kang Yeong-hun, Kim Jong-myeon, Chae Myeong-sin, Park Ik-ju, Lim Bu-taek, Baek Seon-jin, Baek Seok-ju, Choi Yeong-hee, Yang Chang-sik, Son Jin, Jung Nam-hyu, and Lee Gyeong-sik filed a complaint on 6 April 2000.

5. The Constitutional Court dismissed both cases on 27 September 2001, stating that it did not make a case. These groups, however, filed a complaint against the final report of the commission and against the apology made by President Roh Moo-hyun.

6. Personal interview, Yang Jo-hoon, 10 May 2011.

7. *Jemin Ilbo*, 21 April 2000.

8. Personal interview, Ko Hee-beom, 4 May 2011.

9. *Hankyoreh*, 18 April 2000.

10. Personal interview, Ko Hee-beom, 4 May 2011; Choo, *Jeju 4.3 sageongua na*.

11. Personal interview, Choo Mi-ae, 23 May 2011.

12. *Jemin Ilbo*, 25 April 2000.

13. Victims now could submit an application if they had three sureties who lived in their village. However, since many years had passed since the events, it was not always easy to find three people who were still alive and able and willing to testify. Thus, in later revision, the requirement was further loosened to "two sureties who are currently over sixty-five-years-old and lived or are still living in Jeju." In addition, although the initial ordinance provided six months to submit the application, it was not sufficient. Thus, the ordinance went through two additional revisions in order to accept applications for another six months (2 March to 30 May 2001 and 1 January to 31 March 2004). It turned out that activists had an exact estimate when they proposed one year to receive victims' applications. Jeju Commission, *Hwahae-wa sangsaeng*.

14. The twelve civilian commissioners were Kang Man-gil (president of Sangji University), Kim Sam-wung (chief editor of the Daehan Maeil), Kim Jeom-gon (retired general), Kim

Jeong-gi (president of Seowon University), Park Jae-seung (lawyer), Park Chang-uk (president of the Association for Civilian Victims' Families of the Jeju 4.3 Events), Seo Jung-seok (professor, Sungkyunkwan University), Shin Yong-ha (professor, Seoul National University), Lee Don-Myeong (lawyer, former president of Chosun University), Lee Hwang-wu (professor, Dongguk University), Lim Mun-cheol (Catholic priest), and Han Gwang-deok (retired general).

15. The administrative committee was composed of eleven civilian commissioners: Kim Du-yeon (victims' association), Kim Wan-song (association for retired police), Kim Chang-hu (Jeju 4.3 Research Institute), Song Seong-mun (victims' association), Yang Geum-seok (former local council member), Yang Dong-yun (social movement activist), Jang Yeong-bae (Democratic Association for Protection of Freedom), Cho Myeong-cheol (education), Cho Seong-yun (professor, Jeju National University), Jin Yeong-jin (lawyer), and Hong Ga-yun (local council member).

16. The expert group was composed of two former reporters at the *Jemin Ilbo* (Yang Jo-hoon, Kim Jong-min) and a researcher from the Jeju 4.3 Research Institute (Park Chan-sik). In addition, to meet the balance, two experts representing the military and police, Na Jong-sam and Jang Jun-gap, were included.

17. Jeju Commission, "Minutes of the 2nd Plenary Session, 28 June 2000."

18. The ten civilian members were: Kang Jong-ho (victims' association), Kang Chang-il (professor, Baejae University), Ko Chang-hu (lawyer), Kim Sun-tae (professor, Korean National Open University), Do Jin-soon (professor, Changwon University), Park Won-soon (lawyer), Oh Mun-kyun (researcher, Korean National Police University), Ryu Jae-gap (professor, Kyonggi University), Lee Gyeong-wu (lawyer), and Lee Sang-geun (director of the Department of Modern and Contemporary History at the National Institute of Korean History).

19. The debate over a truth commission's mandate is common in other cases. For example, the South African truth commission also had to resolve conflicts over the scope of its mandate and did so through a restrictive definition of "gross violations of human rights."

20. Jeju Commission, *Hwahae-wa sangsaeng*.

21. Within the investigation unit, Ryu Jae-gap and Ha Jae-pyeong representing the military advocated this position, and Na Jong-sam in the expert group also supported their positions. Special Investigation Unit, "Minutes of the 7th Plenary Session, 8 April 2002," 8.

22. *Jemin Ilbo*, 3 April 2001; personal interview, Yang Jo-hoon, 10 May 2011.

23. Special Investigation Unit, "Minutes of the 2nd Plenary Session, 28 February 2001," 7.

24. The commission requested the data mainly from the defense department, army headquarters, military intelligence services, the police department, and the National Archives. For foreign data, the commission focused on documents in the United States, Russia, and Japan.

25. Personal interview, Kim Jong-min, 2 December 2011; personal interview, Yang Jo-hoon, 4 May 2011.

26. Special Investigation Unit, "Minutes of the 4th Plenary Session, 26 June 2001," 5.

27. Ibid., 11.

28. Ibid., 12–13.

29. Ibid., 16.

30. Jeju Commission, *Hwahae-wa sangsaeng*, 79.

31. The Presidential Truth Commission on Suspicious Deaths, for example, had the power to enforce an interview by issuing warrants. The commission issued eleven warrants, including two for former presidents, Chun Doo-hwan and Roh Tae-woo. However, the commission had no stronger enforcement tools, none of the warrants was carried out, and former presidents Chun and Roh were fined 10 million won ($8,800) and 7 million won ($5,800), respectively.

32. Na Jong-sam, Special Investigation Unit, "Minutes of the 7th Plenary Session, 8 April 2002," 4.

33. Ibid., 5.

34. Personal interview, Yang Jo-hoon, 4 May 2011; Special Investigation Unit, "Minutes of the 9th Plenary Session, 11 October 2002," 6.

35. Yang Jo-hoon, Special Investigation Unit, "Minutes of the 2nd Plenary Session, 28 February 2001."

36. Jeju Commission, Subcommittee to Review the Report, "Minutes of the 3rd Plenary Session, 4 October 2003," 3. Han Gwang-deok, Jeju Commission, "Minutes of the 6th Plenary Session, 21 March 2003."

37. Truth commissions are created to investigate the truth, but there can be different faces of truth. The debate first came up in South Africa after the end of apartheid when the Truth and Reconciliation Commission allowed four faces of truth, including personal or narrative truth, social or dialogic truth, healing or restorative truth, and factual or forensic truth. There had been a debate about whether the report should be focused on the individual cases or comprehensive truth. However, the debate was easily resolved because the Special Law clearly stipulated that both individual and comprehensive truth be investigated. Special Investigation Unit, "Minutes of the 7th Plenary Session, 8 April 2002," 17–19.

38. Jeju Commission, "Minutes of the 3rd Plenary Session, 14 March 2002."

39. *Jemin Ilbo*, 29 December 2001.

40. *Jemin Ilbo*, 12 May 2002; *Jemin Ilbo*, 12 December 2001.

41. Ha Jae-pyeong, Special Investigation Unit, "Minutes of the 8th Plenary Session, 29 August 2002," 12. Ryu Jae-gap, Special Investigation Unit, "Minutes of the 11th Plenary Session, 13 February 2003," 38.

42. Park Won-soon, Special Investigation Unit, "Minutes of the 8th Plenary Session, 29 August 2002," 13.

43. Special Investigation Unit, "Minutes of the 11th Plenary Session, 13 February 2003," 16.

44. Personal interview, Yang, Jo-hoon, 4 May 2011.

45. Special Investigation Unit, "Minutes of the 8th Plenary Session, 29 August 2002," 11. Ha continuously made the similar argument in the later sessions. Special Investigation Unit, "Minutes of the 9th Plenary Session, 11 October 2002," 11; Special Investigation Unit, "Minutes of the 10th Plenary Session, 7 February 2003"; *Jemin Ilbo*, 26 February 2003.

46. Special Investigation Unit, "Minutes of the 9th Plenary Session, 11 October 2002," 18.

47. For more details, see Special Investigation Unit, "Minutes of the 10th Plenary Session, 7 February 2003," 4–6; Special Investigation Unit, "Minutes of the 11th Plenary Session, 13 February 2003," 15–16.

48. Special Investigation Unit, "Minutes of the 11th Plenary Session, 13 February 2003," 37. Lim Mun-cheol, representing activists, made a similar remark in the plenary session of the commission against Han Gwang-deok, who expressed his objection to the Special Law itself. Jeju Commission, "Minutes of the 5th Plenary Session, 20 November 2002," 33.

49. Park Won-soon, Jeju Commission, "Minutes of the 6th Plenary Session, 21 March 2003."

50. *Halla Ilbo*, 1 October 2002; Special Investigation Unit, "Minutes of the 12th Plenary Session, 25 February 2003," 27.

51. Special Investigation Unit, "Minutes of the 11th Plenary Session, 13 February 2003," 18.

52. Jeju Commission, "Minutes of the 6th Plenary Session, 21 March 2003."

53. Yoo Bo-seon, the vice-minister of defense, made a similar statement. See Jeju Commission, Subcommittee to Review the Report, "Minutes of the 4th Plenary Session, 7 October 2003," 10.

54. Jeju Commission, "Minutes of the 6th Plenary Session, 21 March 2003"; Shin Yong-ha, Jeju Commission, "Minutes of the 8th Plenary Session, 15 October 2003," 28.

55. Jeju Commission, "Minutes of the 6th Plenary Session, 21 March 2003."

56. Ibid.

57. On the government side, Prime Minister Ko Geon, Minister of Justice Kang Geum-sil, Minister of Defense Cho Yeong-gil, and Director of the Legislative Office Sung Gwang-weon were included; for civil society, Kim Sam-wung, Kim Joem-gon, and Shin Yong-ha were included, respectively representing victims, the military, and those in the middle.

58. Jeju Commission, "Minutes of the 7th Plenary Session, 29 March 2003."

59. Jeju Commission, *Hwahae-wa sangsaeng*, 97.

60. *Chosun Ilbo*, 25 March 2003.

61. *Halla Ilbo*, 25 March 2003.

62. Ha Jae-pyeong, Special Investigation Unit, "Minutes of the 9th Plenary Session, 11 October 2002," 20; Special Investigation Unit, "Minutes of the 10th Plenary Session, 7 February 2003," 11; Ha Jae-pyeong, Special Investigation Unit, "Minutes of the 11th Plenary Session, 13 February 2003," 11.

63. Yang Jo-hoon, Special Investigation Unit, "Minutes of the 10th Plenary Session, 7 February 2003," 21; Special Investigation Unit, "Minutes of the 11th Plenary Session, 13 February 2003," 21 and 14; Special Investigation Unit, "Minutes of the 12th Plenary Session, 25 February 2003," 21.

64. Special Investigation Unit, "Minutes of the 10th Plenary Session, 7 February 2003," 12–13.

65. Jeju Commission, *Jeju 4.3 sageon jinsang josa bogoseo*.

66. Jeju Commission, "Minutes of the 6th Plenary Session, 21 March 2003"; Jeju Commission, Subcommittee to Review the Report, "Minutes of the 3rd Plenary Session, 4 October 2003," 16.

67. Jeju Commission, Subcommittee to Review the Report, "Minutes of the 3rd Plenary Session, 4 October 2003," 15.

68. Ibid.

69. Special Investigation Unit, "Minutes of the 10th Plenary Session, 7 February 2003," 9; Special Investigation Unit, "Minutes of the 11th Plenary Session, 13 February 2003," 9; Jeju Commission, "Minutes of the 7th Plenary Session, 29 March 2003"; Jeju Commission, Subcommittee to Review the Report, "Minutes of the 3rd Plenary Session, 4 October 2003."

70. Special Investigation Unit, "Minutes of the 10th Plenary Session, 7 February 2003," 22.

71. Personal interview, Yang Jo-hoon, 4 May 2011.

72. Jeju Commission, "Minutes of the 7th Plenary Session, 29 March 2003."

73. Jeju Commission, Subcommittee to Review the Report, "Minutes of the 3rd Plenary Session, 4 October 2003," 22.

74. *Jemin Ilbo*, 31 March 2003.

75. Jeju Commission, "Minutes of the 7th Plenary Session, 29 March 2003."

76. Shin Yong-ha, Jeju Commission, "Minutes of the 7th Plenary Session, 29 March 2003."

77. Jeju Commission, "Minutes of the 8th Plenary Session, 15 October 2003," 31.

78. Ibid.

79. Jeju Commission, Subcommittee to Review the Report, "Minutes of the 1st Plenary Session, 26 September 2003."

80. Four public officials—the prime minister, minister of justice, minister of defense, and director of legislation office—and four commissioners—Kim Sam-wung, Seo Jung-seok, Shin Yong-ha, and Ryu Jae-gap—were on the subcommittee, headed by Shin Yong-ha.

81. Yang Jo-hoon and Na Jong-sam, Jeju Commission, Subcommittee to Review the Report, "Minutes of the 3rd Plenary Session, 4 October 2003," 4–5.

82. *Jeju Ilbo*, 30 September 2003.

83. Four review sessions were held on 26 September and 1, 4, and 7 October 2003. Jeju Commission, Subcommittee to Review the Report, "Minutes of the 4th Plenary Session, 7 October 2003," 2.

84. They were the Association for Retired Police Officers in Jeju, the National Police Agency, the Ministry of Defense, and some anti-Communist NGOs (e.g., the Association of Citizens for Liberty) and an individual scholar (Shin Sang-jun).

85. Jeju Commission, Subcommittee to Review the Report, "Minutes of the 4th Plenary Session, 7 October 2003," 11.

86. Jeju Commission, "Minutes of the 8th Plenary Session, 15 October 2003."

87. Personal interview, Yang Jo-hoon, 4 May 2011; personal interview, Kim Jong-min, 2 December 2011.

88. Personal interview, Kim Jong-min, 2 December 2011.

89. Personal e-mail correspondence, Kim Jong-min, 10 October 2011.

90. Personal interview, Yang Jo-hoon, 4 May 2011.

7. The Impact of the Jeju Commission

1. *Jemin Ilbo*, 16 October 2003.

2. Jeju Commission, *Hwahae-wa sangsaeng*, 112.

3. *Jeju Ilbo*, 16 October 2003; personal interview, Yang Dong-yun, 4 May 2011.

4. *Halla Ilbo*, 28 March 2003; *Jemin Ilbo*, 17 October 2003; *Jeju Ilbo*, 22 October 2003.

5. *Jeju Ilbo*, 28 October 2003.

6. Sang-su Huh, "Jeju 4.3 sageon-eui jinsang-gua jeongbu bogoseo-eui seonggwa-wa hangye [The truth about the Jeju 4.3 events and the achievements and limitations of the government report]," *Donghynag-gua Jeonmang* 61 (2004); Jo-hoon Yang, "4.3 jinsang bogosoe chaetaek-gua daetongryeong sagua-eui euieui [Confirmation of the 4.3 report and the meaning of the presidential apology]," *Jejudo Euihoebo* 19 (2004); Jae-Seung Lee, "Jeju 4.3 sageon jinsang bogoseo-e daehan pyeongga [Evaluation of the report of the Jeju Commission]," *Minju Beophak* 25 (2004); Sun-tae Kim, "Jeju 4.3 sageon wiweonhoe-eui hwaldong-gua pyeongga [Evaluation of the activities of the Jeju Commission]," *Minju Beophak* 24 (2003); Jung-seok Seo, "Guageosa jinsang gyumyeong-eui jeomgeom-gua hyanghu gwaje [Revisiting the truth-seeking efforts on past history and remaining tasks]," *Yeoksa Bipyeong* 80, no. 3 (2007).

7. When compared to other commissions overseas, local activists with the Jeju Commission were able to effectively overcome the challenges of the Cold War narrative. The South African truth commission softened its judgments and narrowed its analysis in response to threats of backlash, whereas truth commissions in Guatemala and El Salvador, which challenged dominant narratives, were ignored—at least in the short term—and did not see their recommendations implemented. For more details, see Hayner, *Unspeakable Truths*.

8. *Jemin Ilbo*, 26 January 2011.

9. Gavan McCormack and Dong-Choon Kim, "Grappling with Cold War History: Korea's Embattled Truth and Reconciliation Commission," *Asia-Pacific Journal* 8, no. 1 (2009).

10. *Jemin Ilbo*, 24 January 2008.

11. *Joongang Ilbo*, 10 December 2008; Jeju Commission, *Hwahae-wa sangsaeng*.

12. *New York Times*, 4 September 2009; Dong-Choon Kim and Mark Selden, "South Korea's Embattled Truth and Reconciliation Commission," *Asia-Pacific Journal* 9, no. 1 (2010). For more details, see *Korea Times*, 13 April 2012. For the original text of Lee's conference paper, see Young Jo Lee, "Commissioning the Past: South Korean Efforts at Truth and Justice after Democratization," (paper presented at the Symposium on Transitional Justice and Beyond in Korea, St. Louis, Missouri, November 2010).

13. Jeju Commission, *Jeju 4.3 sageon jinsang josa bogoseo*, 287.

14. Ibid., 279.

15. Ibid., 158–59.

16. For example, see Committee for the History of the Korean Police, *Hanguk gyeongchalsa* [The history of the Korean Police] (Seoul: Committee for the History of the Korean Police, 1972); Headquarters of the Korean Army, *Gongbi tobeolsa* [The history of counterinsurgency operations against Communist guerrillas] (Seoul: Headquarters of the Korean Army, 1954); Committee for Military History, *Hanguk jeonjaengsa: Haebang-gua Geonguk* [The history of the Korean War: Liberation and State Building] (Seoul: Department of Defense, 1967); Committee for Military

History, *Daebijeonggyujeonsa* [The history of unconventional warfare] (Seoul: Department of Defense, 1988).

17. Jeju Commission, *Jeju 4.3 sageon jinsang josa bogoseo*, 163.

18. Ibid., 161.

19. Ibid., 176.

20. John Merrill first studied the Jeju 4.3 events in the 1980s when the documents from the United States became available. Merrill's work was an important contribution since it was the first study not only in the United States but also in South Korea. However, Merrill could not see the limitations of the US documents and did not consider why and with what intentions the US military government recorded such reports in the first place. Thus, Merrill's study could not properly see the role of the United States or the US military government in South Korea. The report pointed out these limitations of earlier works. See Merrill, "The Cheju-do Rebellion" and Merrill, "Internal Warfare in Korea, 1948–1950." However, there are still studies of the Jeju 4.3 events that adopt US documents at face value. For example, see Son, "The 4.3 Incident."

21. The following newspapers carried the report: *Seoul Sinmun*, 15 June 1948; *Seoul Sinmun*, 16 June 1948; *Joseon Jungang Ilbo*, 24 July 1948; *Joseon Jungang Ilbo*, 1 September 1948; *Joseon Jungang Ilbo*, 7 September 1948; and *Donga Ilbo*, 13 October 1948.

22. Jeju Commission, *Jeju 4.3 sageon jinsang josa bogoseo*, 256.

23. Ibid., 496–508, 498, 499.

24. See article 2 of the Special Law for the Investigation of the Jeju 4.3 Events and Restoration of the Honor of Victims (Law No. 6117 of 2000).

25. Jeju Commission, *Hwahae-wa sangsaeng*, 130, 131, 136.

26. Jeju Commission, "Minutes of the 5th Plenary Session, 20 November 2002."

27. The subcommittee was composed of Park Jae-seung, Seo Jung-seok (professor), Kim Sam-wung (journalist), Park Chang-wuk (victim), Lim Mun-cheol (Catholic priest), Han Gwang-deok (former military general), and Lee Hwang-wu (professor). The resignation of Han Gwang-deok and Lee Hwang-wu was a protest against the final report, and Han Yong-weon and Bae Chan-bok replaced them.

28. Jeju Commission, *Hwahae-wa sangsaeng*, 159.

29. Jeju Commission, Subcommittee to Screen Victims, "Minutes of the 2nd Plenary Session, 7 November 2001," 25.

30. The debate over the definition and classification of victims is common in other cases. For example, in Northern Ireland, plans for a truth commission were scuttled over a conflict over the definition of "victims."

31. Jeju Commission, "Minutes of the 3rd Plenary Session, 14 March 2002."

32. Jeju Commission, Subcommittee to Screen Victims, "Minutes of the 16th Plenary Session, 25 October 2002."

33. Jeju Commission, *Hwahae-wa sangsaeng*, 159–60. The debate was between Han Gwang-deok and Lee Hwang-wu and other members of the subcommittee. Since the subcommittee's work started before the commission's final approval of the report, the resistance from the military and police was fierce. The debate occurred not only within the subcommittee but also out in the street with rallies organized by both victims and opponents. For more details see, Jeju Commission, Subcommittee to Screen Victims, "Minutes of the 3rd Plenary Session, 11 November 2001," 168; Jeju Commission, Subcommittee to Screen Victims, "Minutes of the 5th Plenary Session, 10 January 2002"; and Jeju Commission, *Hwahae-wa sangsaeng*.

34. Jeju Commission, *Hwahae-wa sangsaeng*, 161.

35. The first debate on the victims who were court-martialed started with the report on the court-martialed victims in the 16th plenary session of the subcommittee. See Jeju Commission, Subcommittee to Screen Victims, "Minutes of the 16th Plenary Session, 25 October 2002."

36. Jeju Commission, *Hwahae-wa sangsaeng*, 161.

37. Jeju Commission, Subcommittee to Screen Victims, "Minutes of the 16th Plenary Session, 25 October 2002."

38. Ibid.; Jeju Commission, Subcommittee to Screen Victims, "Minutes of the 19th Plenary Session, 7 March 2003," 37, 39.

39. Jeju Commission, *Jeju 4.3 sageon jinsang josa bogoseo,* 467.

40. Jeju Commission, Subcommittee to Screen Victims, "Minutes of the 21st Plenary Session, 10 April 2003."

41. Jeju Commission, "Minutes of the 8th Plenary Session, 15 October 2003," 22–23.

42. *Jemin Ilbo*, 28 June 2004; Jeju Commission, *Hwahae-wa sangsaeng*, 172; Jeju Commission, Subcommittee to Screen Victims, "Minutes of the 30th Plenary Session, 26 March 2004."

43. However, not all members representing the military and police were opposed to the decision. For example, Han Yong-weon supported the decision by arguing that fifteen years imprisonment is a minor offense considering that the leaders of an insurgency might have been sentenced to death. Jeju Commission, Subcommittee to Screen Victims, "Minutes of the 33rd Plenary Session, 28 June 2004."

44. Jeju Commission, "Minutes of the 10th Plenary Session, 17 March 2005," 11, 13–24.

45. Jeju Commission, *Hwahae-wa sangsaeng*, 176; Jeju Commission, "Minutes of the 10th Plenary Session, 17 March 2005," 25–31.

46. Jeju Commission, "Minutes of the 10th Plenary Session, 17 March 2005," 42.

47. Jeju Commission, "Minutes of the 12th Plenary Session, 14 March 2007," 8.

48. Jeju Commission, Subcommittee to Screen Victims, "Minutes of the 50th Plenary Session, 26 January 2006."

49. For example, see Jeju Commission, Subcommittee to Screen Victims, "Minutes of the 56th Plenary Session, 25 September 2006" and Jeju Commission, Subcommittee to Screen Victims, "Minutes of the 57th Plenary Session, 30 October 2006."

50. Jeju Commission, "Minutes of the 12th Plenary Session, 14 March 2007," 8.

51. However, the revised law provided an additional chance for those who did not submit their applications, and the commission received another 727 applications and made decisions on these victims at the 16th plenary session in January 2011.

52. For more details, see David Mendeloff, "Trauma and Vengeance: Assessing the Psychological and Emotional Effects of Post-Conflict Justice," *Human Rights Quarterly* 31, no. 3 (2009); Hugo van der Merwe, Victoria Baxter, and Audrey R. Chapman, eds., *Assessing the Impact of Transitional Justice: Challenges for Empirical Research* (Washington, DC: United States Institute of Peace Press, 2009); Hun Joon Kim and Kathryn Sikkink, "Explaining the Deterrence Effect of Human Rights Prosecutions for Transitional Countries," *International Studies Quarterly* 54, no. 4 (2010); Olsen, Payne, and Reiter, *Transitional Justice in Balance*; Sikkink, *Justice Cascade*; Hayner, *Unspeakable Truths*.

53. Hayner, *Unspeakable Truths*.

54. Jeju Commission, *Hwahae-wa sangsaeng*, 117–21.

55. For the full-text of the apology in English, see http://www.jeju43.go.kr/english/sub07.html (accessed 31 May 2013).

56. Jeju Commission, *Hwahae-wa sangsaeng*, 117.

57. Ibid., 302.

58. *Jeju Ilbo*, 3 December 2003.

59. *Jemin Ilbo*, 21 July 2004.

60. *Halla Ilbo*, 27 August 2004.

61. Jeju Commission, *Hwahae-wa sangsaeng*, 114.

62. *Jemin Ilbo*, 6 March 2004.

63. Jeju Commission, *Hwahae-wa sangsaeng*, 114.

64. Ibid., 114–15; *Jeju Ilbo*, 11 March 2004.

65. Ibid., 125; *Jemin Ilbo*, 10 July 2004.

66. *Jemin Ilbo*, 10 July 2004.

67. *Hankyoreh*, 16 July 2004.

68. *Jemin Ilbo*, 17 November 2004; *Hankyoreh*, 28 July 2004; Seo, "Guageosa jinsang g yu-myeong-eui jeomgeom-gua hyanghu gwaje."

69. *Jemin Ilbo*, 13 November 2000.

70. Ibid.

71. *Jeju Ilbo*, 24 May 2003; *Jemin Ilbo*, 25 May 2004.

72. Jeju Commission, *Hwahae-wa sangsaeng*, 115.

73. Ibid., 125; *Jejusori*, 30 March 2008.

74. *Jejusori*, 21 November 2011; *Jejusori*, 25 October 2010.

75. *Jemin Ilbo*, 6 April 2005.

76. Jeju Commission, *Hwahae-wa sangsaeng*, 114, 115.

77. *Jemin Ilbo*, 30 September 2004.

78. Personal interview, Kang Chang-il, 8 May 2011; personal interview, Yang Dong-yun, 4 May 2011.

79. *Jemin Ilbo*, 17 June 2004.

80. *Jemin Ilbo*, 2 November 2004.

81. Jeju Commission, *Hwahae-wa sangsaeng*, 41–45; *Jemin Ilbo*, 12 September 2005.

82. *Jemin Ilbo*, 7 November 2005.

83. Jeju Commission, *Hwahae-wa sangsaeng*, 44, 45, 40.

84. *Jemin Ilbo*, 23 December 2006.

85. *Jemin Ilbo*, 7 March 2011.

86. Jeju Commission, *Hwahae-wa sangsaeng*, 311.

87. Kim and Selden, "South Korea's Embattled Truth and Reconciliation Commission."

88. *Jemin Ilbo*, 10 February 2012; Jeju Commission, *Hwahae-wa sangsaeng*, 186.

89. Ibid., 321.

90. Ibid.

91. Republic of Korea, Truth and Reconciliation Commission, *Jinsil hwahae wiweonhoe choe-jong bogoseo* [The final report of the Truth and Reconciliation Commission, Republic of Korea] (Seoul: Truth and Reconciliation Commission, Republic of Korea, 2010), 201.

92. Ibid.

93. Ibid., 205–17.

94. Ibid., 203.

95. *Hankyoreh*, 7 September 2009.

96. *Hankyoreh*, 15 April 2009.

97. Chang, "National Narrative, Traumatic Memory, and Testimony," 107.

98. Truth and Reconciliation Commission, *Jinsil hwahae wiweonhoe choejong bogoseo*, 203.

99. Ibid.

100. *Hankyoreh*, 15 April 2009.

101. Truth and Reconciliation Commission, *Jinsil hwahae wiweonhoe choejong bogoseo*, 211.

102. *Hankyoreh*, 30 December 2010; *Hankyoreh*, 15 April 2009; Dong-gweon Lee, "Neurin husok jakeop [Unsatisfactory and slow follow-up processes]," *Weolgan Mal*, September 2008.

103. *Kookmin Ilbo*, 18 May 2009.

104. *Donga Ilbo*, 18 May 2009.

105. Seo, "Guageosa jinsang gyumyeong-eui jeomgeom-gua hyanghu gwaje [Revisiting the truth-seeking efforts on the past history and remaining tasks]."

106. Truth and Reconciliation Commission, *Truth and Reconciliation Commission of South Africa Report*, vol. 1 (Cape Town: Juta and Co., 1998), 110.

107. Kim, "Long Road toward Truth and Reconciliation," 547.

108. Jeju Commission, Special Investigation Unit, "Minutes of the 7th Plenary Session, 8 April 2002," 17–19.

109. Ibid.

110. *Ohmynews*, 29 August 2007.

111. Moo Yong Kim, "Jinsil hwahae wiweonhoe, guageo cheongsan undong-gua gukmin tonghapjueui noseon [The Truth and Reconciliation Commission, institutionalization of the transitional justice movement, and national unification]," *4.3-gua Yeoksa* 6 (2006): 147.

Conclusion

1. Doug McAdams, John D. McCarthy, and Mayer N. Zald, eds., *Comparative Perspectives on Social Movements* (New York: Cambridge University Press, 1996); Kathryn Sikkink, Sanjeev Khagram, and James V. Riker, eds., *Restructuring World Politics: Transnational Social Movements, Networks, and Norms* (Minneapolis: University of Minnesota Press, 2002); Margaret E. Keck and Kathryn Sikkink, *Activists beyond Borders: Advocacy Networks in International Politics* (Ithaca: Cornell University Press, 1998); Jackie Smith, Charles Chatfield, and Ron Pagnucco, eds., *Transnational Social Movements and Global Politics: Solidarity beyond the State* (Syracuse, NY: Syracuse University Press, 1997).

2. Keck and Sikkink, *Activists beyond Borders*, 8.

3. Finnemore and Sikkink, "International Norm Dynamics and Political Change."

4. Sidney Tarrow, *Power in Movement: Social Movements and Contentious Politics* (Cambridge: Cambridge University Press, 1998).

5. Keck and Sikkink, *Activists beyond Borders*, 16.

6. Geoff Dancy and Steven C. Poe, "What Comes before Truth? The Political Determinants of Truth Commission Onset"(paper presented at the Annual Meeting of the International Studies Association, San Diego, California, March 2006); Jack Snyder and Leslie Vinjamuri, "Trial and Errors: Principle and Pragmatism in Strategies of International Justice," *International Security* 28, no. 3 (2003); Huntington, *Third Wave*.

7. Jeju Commission, *Jeju 4.3 sageon jinsang josa bogoseo*, 496–508.

8. Personal interview, Kim Dong-man, 12 April 2006; Personal interview, Kim Eun-hee, 3 May 2011.

9. Personal interview, Yang Jo-hoon, 10 May 2011; personal interview, Kim Jong-min, 2 December 2011.

10. Personal interview, Yang Jo-hoon, 4 May 2011; personal interview, Kim Jong-min, 2 December 2011.

11. Personal interview, Yang Jo-hoon, 10 May 2011.

12. Personal interview, Yang Bong-cheon, 19 October 2005.

13. Personal interview, Ko Yeong-wu, 26 October 2006.

14. Personal interview, Ko Chang-hoon, 3 May 2011.

15. Ibid.

16. The traditional anti-Communist understanding of the Jeju 4.3 events as a Communist rebellion has become relatively weak in both academia and politics, as shown by the case in which the conservative Saenuri party withdrew the nomination of Lee Young-jo in 2012.

17. *Chosun Ilbo*, 1 August 2004; *Chosun Ilbo*, 3 May 2005; Jae-jeong Kim, "Daedam: Kim Dong-Choon [Interview with Kim Dong-Choon]," *Weolgan Mal*, June 2006.

18. *Joongang Ilbo*, 5 April 2004; Wung-jae Jung, "Daedam: Kim Dong-Choon [Interview with Kim Dong-Choon]," *Weolgan Mal*, September 2008.

19. For example, some laws were enacted to address the following individual incidents: abuses in Samcheong detention centers, Nogunri shooting incidents, issues related to persons on special espionage missions to North Korea, discrimination and mass killing of people with Hansen's disease, and the arrest and illegal detention of Buddhist monks. For more details, see Truth and Reconciliation Commission, *Jinsil hwahae wiweonhoe choejong bogoseo*, 13–15.

20. *Hankyoreh*, 30 December 2010; Jung, "Daedam: Kim Dong-Choon."

21. *Joongang Ilbo*, 1 February 2007.

22. *New York Times*, 11 March 2007; *Donga Ilbo*, 11 December 2006; *New York Times*, 5 January 2005.

23. See article 40, Framing Act for Clearing Up Past Events (Law No. 7542 of 2005).

24. *Korea Times*, 30 December 2010.

25. Kim, "Long Road toward Truth and Reconciliation," 550; Kim and Selden, "South Korea's Embattled Truth and Reconciliation Commission."

26. Kim and Selden, "South Korea's Embattled Truth and Reconciliation Commission."

27. Seo, "Guageosa jinsang gyumyeong-eui jeomgeom-gua hyanghu gwaje."

28. Ibid.

Bibliography

Acharya, Amitav. "How Ideas Spread: Whose Norms Matter? Norm Localization and Institutional Change in Asia Regionalism." *International Organization* 58, no. 2 (2004): 239–75.

Arendt, Hannah. "Truth and Politics." In *Between Past and Future: Eight Exercises in Political Thought*, edited by Hannah Arendt, 227–64. 1961. Reprint, New York: Penguin Books, 1993.

Baik, Tae-Ung. "Justice Incomplete: The Remedies for the Victims of the Jeju April Third Incidents." In *Rethinking Historical Injustice and Reconciliation in Northeast Asia: The Korean Experience*, edited by Gi-Wook Shin, Soon-Won Park, and Daqing Yang, 94–113. London: Routledge, 2007.

Brahm, Eric. "Uncovering the Truth: Examining Truth Commission Success and Impact." *International Studies Perspectives* 8, no. 1 (2007): 16–35.

Chang, Jieun. "National Narrative, Traumatic Memory, and Testimony: Reading Traces of the Cheju April Third Incident, South Korea, 1948." PhD diss., New York University Press, 2009.

Chinnery, Philip D. *Korean Atrocity! Forgotten War Crimes 1950–1953*. Barnsley, UK: Pen & Sword Military, 2009.

Cho, Kuk. "Transitional Justice in Korea: Legally Coping with Past Wrongs after Democratization." *Pacific Rim Law & Policy Journal* 16, no. 3 (2007): 579–611.

Choi, Jang Jip. "Political Cleavages in South Korea." In *State and Society in Contemporary Korea*, edited by Hagen Koo, 13–50. Ithaca: Cornell University Press, 1993.

Choi, Sang-Yong. "Trusteeship Debate and the Korean Cold War." In *Korea under the American Military Government, 1945–1948*, edited by Bonnie B. C. Oh, 13–39. Westport CT: Praeger, 2002.

Choo, Mi-ae. "Jeju 4.3 Sageongua Na: Ggeutnaji Aneun Jinsile Daehayeo" [The Jeju 4.3 events and I: On the unending truths]. Unpublished manuscript, 23 May 2011.

Commemoration Committee. *Je-50-Junyeon Jeju 4.3 Haksul Munhwa Saeop Naekseo* [White paper on the works of the Commemoration Committee]. Jeju: Commemoration Committee, 1998.

Committee for History of the Korean Police. *Hanguk Gyeongchalsa* [The history of the Korean Police]. Seoul: Committee for History of the Korean Police, 1972.

Committee for Military History. *Daebijeonggyujeonsa* [The history of unconventional warfare]. Seoul: Department of Defense, 1988.

——. *Hanguk Jeonjaengsa: Haebang-Gua Geonguk* [The history of the Korean War: Liberation and state building]. Seoul: Department of Defense, 1967.

Committee on the History of the Revolutionary Court. *Hanguk Hyeokmyeong Jaepansa* [The history of the Revolutionary Court's rulings]. Seoul: Committee on the History of the Revolutionary Court, 1962.

Cumings, Bruce. "American Policy and Korean Liberation." In *Without Parallel: The American Korean Relationship since 1945*, edited by Frank Baldwin, 39–108. New York: Pantheon Books, 1974.

——. *The Korean War: A History*. New York: Modern Library, 2010.

——. *The Origins of the Korean War.* Vol. 2, *The Roaring of the Cataract, 1947–1950.* Ithaca: Cornell University Press, 2004. 1990.

——. "The Question of American Responsibility for the Suppression of the Chejudo Uprising." Paper presented at the 50th Anniversary Conference of the April 3rd, 1948 Chejudo Rebellion, Tokyo, April 1998.

Dancy, Geoff, Hun Joon Kim, and Eric Wiebelhaus-Brahm. "The Turn to Truth: Trends in Truth Commission Experimentation." *Journal of Human Rights* 9, no. 1 (2010): 45–64.

Dancy, Geoff, and Steven C. Poe. "What Comes before Truth? The Political Determinants of Truth Commission Onset." Paper presented at the Annual Meeting of the International Studies Association, San Diego, California, March 2006.

Elster, Jon. *Closing the Books: Transitional Justice in Historical Perspective*. Cambridge: Cambridge University Press, 2004.

Finnemore, Martha, and Kathryn Sikkink. "International Norm Dynamics and Political Change." *International Organization* 52, no. 4 (1998): 887–917.

Geochang County Council. *Hanguk Jeonjaeng-Jeonhu Geochang-Gun-Guannae Minganin Huisaengja Jinsang Josa Bogoseo* [Report of the civilian victims in Geochang during the Korean War]. Geochang: Geochang County Council, 2003.

Han, In-Sup. "Kwangju and Beyond: Coping with Past State Atrocities in South Korea." *Human Rights Quarterly* 27, no. 3 (2005): 998–1045.

Han, Lim-hwa. "Yonggang Maeul Saramdeul-Eui Bunno." *Sahoewa Sasang* 2, no. 1 (1989): 217–41.

Han, Sungjoo. *The Failure of Democracy in South Korea*. Berkeley: University of California Press, 1974.

Hanley, Charles J. "No Gun Ri." *Critical Asian Studies* 42, no. 4 (2010): 589–622.

Hayner, Priscilla B. *Unspeakable Truths: Transitional Justice and the Challenge of Truth Commissions*. 2nd ed. New York: Routledge, 2011.

Headquarters of the Korean Army. *Gongbi Tobeolsa* [The history of counterinsurgency operations against Communist guerrillas]. Seoul: Headquarters of the Korean Army, 1954.

Henderson, Gregory. *Korea: Politics of the Vortex*. Cambridge: Harvard University Press, 1968.

Heo, Jong. *Banmin Teukui Jojik-Gua Hwaldong* [The organization and activities of the Special Committee for Investigation of the Pro-Japanese Collaborators]. Seoul: Seonin, 2003.

Herz, John H., ed. *From Dictatorship to Democracy: Coping with the Legacies of Authoritarianism and Totalitarianism*. Westport, CT: Greenwood Press, 1982.

Huh, Sang-su. "Jeju 4.3 Sageon-Eui Jinsang-Gua Jeongbu Bogoseo-Eui Seonggwa-Wa Hangye [The truth about the jeju 4.3 events and the achievements and limitations of the government report]." *Donghynag-gua Jeonmang* 61 (2004): 176–228.

Huntington, Samuel P. *The Third Wave: Democratization in the Late Twentieth Century*. Norman: University of Oklahoma Press, 1991.

Hwang, Sang-ik. "Euihaksajeok Cheukmyeon-Eseo Bon 4.3 [The Jeju 4.3 events perceived from medical history]." In *Jeju 4.3 Yeongu* [A study on the Jeju 4.3], edited by Jeju 4.3 Research Institute, 304–37. Seoul: Yeoksa Bipyeong, 1999.

Hyun, Gi-yeong. "Nae Soseol-Eui Motae-Neun 4.3 Hangjaeng [The motif of my short story is the 4.3 uprising]." *Yeoksa Biyeong* 20, no. 1 (1993): 163–70.

——. *Suni Samchon* [Aunt Suni]. Seoul: Changbi, 1979.

Jeffery, Renée, and Hun Joon Kim, eds. *Transitional Justice in the Asia Pacific*. Cambridge: Cambridge University Press, forthcoming.

Jeju Commission. *Hwahae-Wa Sangsaeng: Jeju 4.3 Wiweonhoe Hwaldong Baekseo* [Reconciliation and coexistence: White paper on the activities of the Jeju Commission]. Seoul: Jeju Commission, 2008.

——. *Jeju 4.3 Sageon Jaryojip 4* [Jeju 4.3 events archive, vol. 4]. Seoul: Jeju Commission, 2002.

——. *Jeju 4.3 Sageon Jinsang Josa Bogoseo* [Report of the truth about the Jeju 4.3 events]. Seoul: Jeju Commission, 2003.

——. "Minutes of the 2nd Plenary Session, 28 June 2000." Seoul: Jeju Commission, 2000.

——. "Minutes of the 3rd Plenary Session, 14 March 2002." Seoul: Jeju Commission, 2002.

——. "Minutes of the 5th Plenary Session, 20 November 2002." Seoul: Jeju Commission, 2002.

——. "Minutes of the 6th Plenary Session, 21 March 2003." Seoul: Jeju Commission, 2003.

——. "Minutes of the 7th Plenary Session, 29 March 2003." Seoul: Jeju Commission, 2003.

——. "Minutes of the 8th Plenary Session, 15 October 2003." Seoul: Jeju Commission, 2003.
——. "Minutes of the 10th Plenary Session, 17 March 2005." Seoul: Jeju Commission, 2005.
——. "Minutes of the 12th Plenary Session, 14 March 2007." Seoul: Jeju Commission, 2007.
Jeju Commission. Special Investigation Unit. "Minutes of the 2nd Plenary Session, 28 February 2001." Seoul: Jeju Commission, 2001.
——. "Minutes of the 4th Plenary Session, 26 June 2001." Seoul: Jeju Commission, 2001.
——. "Minutes of the 7th Plenary Session, 8 April 2002." Seoul: Jeju Commission, 2002.
——. "Minutes of the 8th Plenary Session, 29 August 2002." Seoul: Jeju Commission, 2002.
——. "Minutes of the 9th Plenary Session, 11 October 2002." Seoul: Jeju Commission, 2002.
——. "Minutes of the 10th Plenary Session, 7 February 2003." Seoul: Jeju Commission, 2003.
——. "Minutes of the 11th Plenary Session, 13 February 2003." Seoul: Jeju Commission, 2003.
——. "Minutes of the 12th Plenary Session, 25 February 2003." Seoul: Jeju Commission, 2003.
Jeju Commission. Subcommittee to Review the Report. "Minutes of the 1st Plenary Session, 26 September 2003." Seoul: Jeju Commission, 2003.
——. "Minutes of the 3rd Plenary Session, 4 October 2003." Seoul: Jeju Commission, 2003.
——. "Minutes of the 4th Plenary Session, 7 October 2003." Seoul: Jeju Commission, 2003.
Jeju Commission. Subcommittee to Screen Victims. "Minutes of the 2nd Plenary Session, 7 November 2001." Seoul: Jeju Commission, 2001.
——. "Minutes of the 3rd Plenary Session, 11 November 2001." Seoul: Jeju Commission, 2001.
——. "Minutes of the 5th Plenary Session, 10 January 2002." Seoul: Jeju Commission, 2002.
——. "Minutes of the 16th Plenary Session, 25 October 2002." Seoul: Jeju Commission, 2002.
——. "Minutes of the 19th Plenary Session, 7 March 2003." Seoul: Jeju Commission, 2003.
——. "Minutes of the 21st Plenary Session, 10 April 2003." Seoul: Jeju Commission, 2003.
——. "Minutes of the 30th Plenary Session, 26 March 2004." Seoul: Jeju Commission, 2004.
——. "Minutes of the 33rd Plenary Session, 28 June 2004." Seoul: Jeju Commission, 2004.

——. "Minutes of the 50th Plenary Session, 26 January 2006." Seoul: Jeju Commission, 2006.

——. "Minutes of the 56th Plenary Session, 25 September 2006." Seoul: Jeju Commission, 2006.

——. "Minutes of the 57th Plenary Session, 30 October 2006." Seoul: Jeju Commission, 2006.

Jeju Provincial Council. Office of the Secretariat. "Minutes of the 69th Plenary Session (No. 3)." Jeju: Jeju Provincial Council, 1991.

——. "Minutes of the 82nd Extraordinary Session (No. 2)." Jeju: Jeju Provincial Council, 1993.

——. "Minutes of the 83rd Extraordinary Session (No. 1)." Jeju: Jeju Provincial Council, 1993.

——. "Minutes of the 88th Plenary Session (No. 1)." Jeju: Jeju Provincial Council, 1993.

Jeju Provincial Council. Special Committee on 4.3. *Jejudo 4.3 Pihae Josa Bogoseo* [Report of the victims of the Jeju 4.3]. Jeju: Jeju Provincial Council, 1997.

Jemin Ilbo 4.3 Chuijaeban. *4.3-Eun Malhanda 2* [4.3 speaks, vol. 2]. Seoul: Jeonyeoweon, 1994.

Jeon, Seung-Hee. "War Trauma, Memories, and Truths." *Critical Asian Studies* 42, no. 4 (2010): 623–51.

Jeong, Hae-gu. "Jeju 4.3 Hangjaeng-Gua Migunjeongcheong Yeongu [The Jeju 4.3 uprising and the policies of the US military government]." In *Jeju 4.3 Yeongu* [A study on the Jeju 4.3], edited by Jeju 4.3 Research Institute, 180–204. Seoul: Yeoksa Bipyeong, 1999.

Jeong, Seok-kyun. "Jeju 4.3 Sageon-Ui Jinsang [The truth of the Jeju 4.3 events]." *Gunsa* 41 (2000): 1–49.

Jung, Hae-gu. *10-Weol Immin Hangjaeng Yeongu* [A study of the October people's uprising]. Seoul: Yuleumsa, 1989.

Jung, Wung-jae. "Daedam: Kim Dong-Choon [Interview with Kim Dong-Choon]." *Weolgan Mal*, July 2008, 132–35.

Kang, Han-mu. "United States Military Government in Korea, 1945—1948: An Analysis and Evaluation of Its Policy." PhD diss., University of Cincinnati, 1970.

Kang, Yong-sam, and Gyeong-su Lee. *Daeha Silrok Jeju 100-Nyun* [One hundred years of the history of Jeju]. Jeju: Taekwang, 1984.

Katsiaficas, George N., and Kan-Chae Na. *South Korean Democracy: Legacy of the Gwangju Uprising*. New York: Routledge, 2006.

Keck, Margaret E., and Kathryn Sikkink. *Activists beyond Borders: Advocacy Networks in International Politics*. Ithaca: Cornell University Press, 1998.

Kil, Seung-heum. "Jeongdang Jeongchi-Eui Taedong-Gua Jeongae [The birth and development of party politics in Korea]." In *Hankuk-Eui Hyeondae Jeongchi 1945—1948 Nyeon* [Modern Korean politics 1945—1948], edited by Research Institute for Korean Politics, 183–232. Seoul: Seoul National University Press, 1993.

Kim, Bong-hyeon, and Min-ju Kim. "Jeju-Do Inmindeul-Eui 4.3 Mujang Tujaengsa [A history of the Jeju people's 4.3 armed struggle]." In *Jeju Minjung Hangjeang* [Jeju people's uprising], edited by Arari Research Institute, 199–277. Seoul: Sonamu, 1988.

Kim, Chang-rok. "1948-Nyeon Heonbeop Je-100-Jo: 4.3 Gyeeomryeong-Eol Tonghae Bon Ilje Beopryeong-Eui Hyoryeok [The Constitution of 1948 and article 100: The effectiveness of the Japanese law based on the martial law during the Jeju 4.3 events]." *Beophak Yeongu* 39, no. 2 (1998): 477–93.

Kim, Deuk-jung. *'Ppalgaengi'-Eui Tansaeng: Yeosun Sageon-Gua Bangong Gukga-Eui Hyeongseong* [The birth of the "reds": The Yeosun events and the formation of the anti-Communist state]. Seoul: Seonin, 2009.

Kim, Dong-Choon. "Beneath the Tip of the Iceberg: Problems in Historical Clarification of the Korean War." *Korea Journal* 42, no. 3 (2002): 60–86.

——. "The Long Road toward Truth and Reconciliation." *Critical Asian Studies* 42, no. 4 (2010): 525–52.

Kim, Dong-Choon. *The Unending Korean War: A Social History*. Novato, CA: Tamal Vista Publications, 2009.

Kim, Dong-Choon, and Mark Selden. "South Korea's Embattled Truth and Reconciliation Commission." *Asia-Pacific Journal* 9, no. 1 (2010): 4–10.

Kim, Dong-man. "Yeoksa Jaehyeon-Eitseo Yeongsangjaryo-Eui Jaehaeseok-Gua Hwalyong-E Guanhan Yeongu [A study on the reinterpretation and application of film footage in the historical reappearance]." Master's thesis, Sejong University, 2003.

——. "Yeoksajeoks-Euro Bokweon-Doeeoyahal Darangshi-Gul [The Darangshi cave should be recovered]." *Jeju Jakga* 8 (2002): 1–10.

Kim, Gi-jin. *Ggeutnaji Aneun Jeonjaeng, Gukmin Bodo Yeonmaeng* [Unfinished war: Civilian massacres during the Korean War]. Seoul: Yeoksa Bipyeong, 2002.

Kim, Gi-sam, and Dong-man Kim. *Darangshigul-Eui Seulpeun Norae* [A sad song of the Darangshi cave]. Jeju: Gak, 2002.

Kim, Gyeong-hun. "4.3 Hapdong Wiryeongje: Wae Musan Doeeotna [Why did the negotiations for the united memorial service fail]." *Weolgan Jeju*, May 1993.

Kim, Hun Joon. "Expansion of Transitional Justice Measures: A Comparative Analysis of Its Causes." PhD diss., University of Minnesota, 2008.

——. "Seeking Truth after 50 Years: The National Committee for Investigation of the Truth about the Jeju 4.3 Events." *International Journal of Transitional Justice* 3, no. 3 (2009): 406–23.

——. "Structural Determinants of Human Rights Prosecutions after Democratic Transition." *Journal of Peace Research* 49, no. 2 (2012): 305–20.

Kim, Hun Joon, and Kathryn Sikkink. "Explaining the Deterrence Effect of Human Rights Prosecutions for Transitional Countries." *International Studies Quarterly* 54, no. 4 (2010): 939–63.

Kim, Jae-jeong. "Daedam: Kim Dong-Choon [Interview with Kim Dong-Choon]." *Weolgan Mal*, June 2006, 42–47.

Kim, Jae-yong. "Pokryeok-Gua Gweonryeok, Geurigo Minjung [Violence, power, and people]." In *Jeju 4.3 Yeongu* [A study on the Jeju 4.3], edited by Jeju 4.3 Research Institute, 268–303. Seoul: Yeoksa Bipyeong, 1999.

Kim, Jong-min. "4.3 Ihu 50 Nyeon [50 years after 4.3]." In *Jeju 4.3 Yeongu* [A study on the Jeju 4.3], edited by Jeju 4.3 Research Institute, 338–424. Seoul: Yeoksa Bipyeong, 1999.

Kim, Moo Yong. "Jinsil Hwahae Wiweonhoe, Guageo Cheongsan Undong-Gua Gukmin Tonghapjueui Noseon [Truth and Reconciliation Commission, institutionalization of the transitional justice movement, and national unification]." *4.3-gua Yeoksa* 6 (2006): 129–58.

Kim, Se-kyoon. "Haebang Chogi Minjung Undong [Minjung movement in early liberation years]." In *Hankuk-Eui Hyeondae Jeongchi 1945—1948 Nyeon* [Modern Korean politics 1945—1948], edited by Research Institute for Korean Politics, 57–114. Seoul: Seoul National University Press, 1993.

Kim, Seok-beom. *Ggamagui-Eui Jukeum* [The death of a crow]. Seoul: Sonamu, 1988.

———. *Hwasando* [A volcanic island]. Seoul: Silcheon Munhak, 1988.

Kim, Sun-tae. "Jeju 4.3 Dangsi Gyeeom-Eui Bulbeopseong [The illegality of the martial law during the Jeju 4.3 events]." In *Jeju 4.3 Yeongu* [A study on the Jeju 4.3], edited by Jeju 4.3 Research Institute, 147–79. Seoul: Yeoksa Bipyeong, 1999.

———. "Jeju 4.3 Sageon Wiweonhoe-Eui Hwaldong-Gua Pyeongga [Evaluation of the activities of the Jeju Commission]." *Minju Beophak* 24 (2003): 93–116.

———. "Red Hunt-Neun Gwayeon Ijeok Pyohyeonmul Inga? [Is the red hunt really benefitting the enemy?]." *Minju Beophak* 13 (1997): 317–21.

Kim, Yeong-beom. "Gieok Tujaeng-Euiroseoeui 4.3 Munhwa Undong Seoseol [Introduction to the 4.3 cultural movement as a struggle for memory]." In *Gieok Tujaeng-Gua Munhwa Undong-Eui Jeongae* [A struggle for memory and the development of the cultural movement], edited by Kan-Chae Na, Keun-sik Jung, and Chang-il Kang, 26–68. Seoul: Yeoksa Bipyeong, 2004.

Ko, Chang-hoon. "4.3 Minjung Hangjaeng-Eui Jeongae-Wa Seonggyeok [The process and characteristics of the 4.3 democratic uprising]." In *Haebang Jeonhusa-Ui Insik 4* [A study of the Korean liberation era, vol. 4], edited by Jang Jip Choi, 245–340. Seoul: Hangilsa, 1989.

———. "Darangshigul Balgul Iyagi [A story of discovering the Darangshi cave]." Unpublished manuscript, 24 March 2006.

———. "US Government Responsibility in the Jeju April Third Uprising and Grand Massacre—Islanders' Perspective." *Study of Regional Government* 8, no. 2 (Summer 2004): 123–40.

Ko, Seong-man. "Jeju 4.3 Damron-Eui Hyeongseong-Gua Jeongchijeok Jakyong [The formation and political process of the Jeju 4.3 discourse]." Master's thesis, Jeju National University, 2005.

Kwon, Gui-suk. "Jeju 4.3-Eui Daehang Gieok-Gua Yeongsang [Alternative memory of the Jeju 4.3 events and visual images]." In *Gieok Tujaeng-Gua Munhwa Undong-Eui Jeongae* [A struggle for memory and the development of the cultural movement], edited by Kan-Chae Na, Keun-sik Jung, and Chang-il Kang, 97–136. Seoul: Yeoksa Bipyeong, 2004.

Lee, Dong-gweon. "Neurin Husok Jakeop [Unsatisfactory and slow follow-up processes]." *Weolgan Mal*, September 2008, 120–21.

Lee, Hye Sook. "State Formation and Civil Society under American Occupation: The Case of South Korea." Paper presented at the Annual Meeting of the American Sociological Association, New York, August 1996.

Lee, Hyeon-hee. "Jeju 4.3 Sageon-Eui Bonjil-Eul Dasi Malhanda [Rethinking the true characteristics of the Jeju 4.3 events]." *Weolgan Chosun*, April 2000.

Lee, Jae-Seung. "Jeju 4.3 Sageon Jinsang Bogoseo-E Daehan Pyeongga [Evaluation of the report of the Jeju Commission]." *Minju Beophak* 25 (2004): 481–502.

Lee, Jin-woo. "Gukgun-Eul Baesin Han Daehan Minguk Gukhoe [The National Assembly betrayed the Korean Army]." *Weolgan Chosun*, April 2000.

Lee, Kang-su. *Banmin Teukui Yeongu* [A study of the Special Committee for Investigation of the Pro-Japanese Collaborators]. Seoul: Nanam, 2003.

Lee, Mun-gyo. *Jeju Eonronsa* [A history of Jeju media]. Seoul: Nanam, 1997.

Lee, Young Jo. "Commissioning the Past: South Korean Efforts at Truth and Justice after Democratization." Paper presented at the Symposium on Transitional Justice and Beyond in Korea, St. Louis, Missouri, November 2010.

Lie, John. *Han Unbound: The Political Economy of South Korea*. Stanford: Stanford University Press, 1998.

McAdams, Doug, John D. McCarthy, and Mayer N. Zald, eds. *Comparative Perspectives on Social Movements*. New York: Cambridge University Press, 1996.

McCormack, Gavan, and Dong-Choon Kim. "Grappling with Cold War History: Korea's Embattled Truth and Reconciliation Commission." *Asia-Pacific Journal* 8, no. 1 (2009): 6–9.

McCune, George M. "Occupation Politics in Korea." *Far Eastern Survey* 25, no. 3 (1946): 33–36.

Mendeloff, David. "Trauma and Vengeance: Assessing the Psychological and Emotional Effects of Post-Conflict Justice." *Human Rights Quarterly* 31, no. 3 (2009): 592–623.

——. "Truth-Seeking, Truth-Telling, and Postconflict Peacebuilding: Curb the Enthusiasm?" *International Studies Review* 6, no. 3 (2004): 355–80.

Méndez, Juan E. "In Defense of Transitional Justice." In *Transitional Justice and the Rule of Law in New Democracies*, edited by A. James McAdams, 1–26. Notre Dame, IN: University of Notre Dame Press, 1997.

Merrill, John. "The Cheju-Do Rebellion." *Journal of Korean Studies* 2, no. 1 (1980): 139–97.

——. "Internal Warfare in Korea, 1948–1950: The Local Setting of the Korean War." In *Child of Conflict: The Korean-American Relationship, 1943–1953*, edited by Bruce Cumings, 133–62. Seattle: University of Washington Press, 1983.

Millett, Allan R. *The War for Korea, 1945–1950: A House Burning*. Lawrence: University Press of Kansas, 2005.

Minow, Martha. *Between Vengeance and Forgiveness: Facing History after Genocide and Mass Violence*. Boston: Beacon Press, 1998.

Moon, Chung-in, and Sunghack Lim. "The Politics of Economic Rise and Decline in South Korea." In *Understanding Korean Politics: An Introduction*, edited by Seung-heum Kil and Chung-in Moon, 201–30. Albany: State University of New York Press, 2001.

National Assembly. Office of the Secretariat. "Minutes of the 15th Assembly." Seoul: National Assembly. 1999.

O'Donnell, Guillermo A., and Philippe C. Schmitter, eds. *Transition from Authoritarian Rule*. Baltimore: Johns Hopkins University Press, 1986.

Oh, John Kie-chiang. *Korea: Democracy on Trial*. Ithaca: Cornell University Press, 1968.

——. *Korean Politics: The Quest for Democratization and Economic Development*. Ithaca: Cornell University Press, 1999.

Oh, Seong-chan. *Halla-Eui Tonggok Sori* [Bitter wailing of Halla]. Seoul: Sonamu, 1988.

Olsen, Tricia D., Leigh A. Payne, and Andrew G. Reiter. *Transitional Justice in Balance: Comparing Processes, Weighing Efficacy*. Washington, DC: United States Institute of Peace Press, 2010.

Olsen, Tricia D., Leigh A. Payne, Andrew G. Reiter, and Eric Wiebelhaus-Brahm. "When Truth Commissions Improve Human Rights." *International Journal of Transitional Justice* 4, no. 3 (2010): 457–76.

Paige, Glen D. "Korea." In *Communism and Revolution: The Strategic Uses of Political Violence*, edited by Cyril E. Black and Thomas P. Thornton, 215–42. Princeton: Princeton University Press, 1964.

Pajibo, Ezekiel. "Civil Society and Transitional Justice in Liberia: A Practitioner's Reflection from the Field." *International Journal of Transitional Justice* 1, no. 2 (2007): 287–96.

Pan National Committee. *4.3 Bansegi* [Half a century since the 4.3]. Seoul: Pan National Committee, 2000.

Park, Chan-pyo. "The American Military Government and the Framework for Democracy in South Korea." In *Korea under the American Military Government, 1945—1948*, edited by Bonnie B. C. Oh, 123–49. Westport, CT: Praeger, 2002.

Park, Chan-sik. "Hanguk Jeonjaeng-Gi Jeju 4.3 Guanryeon Suhyeongin Haksal-Eui Silsang [Truth about the massacre during the Korean War of court-martialed persons related to the 4.3 events]." *4.3-gua Yeoksa* 1, no. 1 (2001): 17–51.

Park, Myeong-lim. "Jeju-Do 4.3 Minjung Hangjaeng-E Guanhan Yeongu [A study on the Jeju 4.3 popular uprising]." Master's thesis, Korea University, 1988.

Park, Won-soon. *Gukga Boanbeop Yeongu 1: Gukga Boanbeop Byeoncheonsa* [A study of the National Security Law, vol. 1, The development of the National Security Law]. Seoul: Yeoksa Bipyeong, 1994.

Pasqualucci, Jo M. "The Whole Truth and Nothing but the Truth: Truth Commissions, Impunity, and the Inter-American Human Rights System." *Boston University International Law Journal* 12, no. 2 (1994): 321–70.

Pyeonjipbu. "4.3 Huisaengja Myeongdan Choecho Gonggae [The first publication of the list of 4.3 victims]." *Gwangwang Jeju*, April 1989.

Republic of Korea. Truth and Reconciliation Commission. *Jinsil Hwahae Wiweonhoe Choejong Bogoseo* [The final report of the Truth and Reconciliation Commission, Republic of Korea]. Seoul: Truth and Reconciliation Commission, Republic of Korea, 2010.

Risse, Thomas, Stephen C. Ropp, and Kathryn Sikkink, eds. *The Power of Human Rights. International Norms and Domestic Change*. Cambridge: Cambridge University Press, 1999.

Robinson, Michael E. *Korea's Twentieth-Century Odyssey*. 6th ed. Honolulu: University of Hawaii Press, 2007.

Roht-Arriaza, Naomi, ed. *Impunity and Human Rights in International Law and Practice*. New York: Oxford University Press, 1995.

Sarafan, Bertram D. "Military Government: Korea." *Far Eastern Survey* 15, no. 23 (1946): 349–52.

Scalapino, Robert A., and Chong-sik Lee. *Communism in Korea*. Vol. 2, *The Society*. Berkeley: University of California Press, 1972.

Scott-Stokes, Henry, Jae-Eui Lee, and Dae Jung Kim. *The Kwangju Uprising: Eyewitness Press Accounts of Korea's Tiananmen*. Armonk, NY: M. E. Sharpe, 2000.

Seo, Jung-seok. *Cho Bong-Am-Gua 1950-Nyeondae (Ha)* [Cho Bong-am and the 1950s, vol. 2]. Seoul: Yeoksa Bipyeong, 1999.

——. "Guageosa Jinsang Gyumyeong-Eui Jeomgeom-Gua Hyanghu Gwaje [Revisiting the truth-seeking efforts on the past history and remaining tasks]." *Yeoksa Bipyeong* 80, no. 3 (2007): 46–79.

——. *Jeonjaeng Sok-Eui Ttodareun Jeonjaeng* [Another war within the war]. Seoul: Seonin, 2011.

Shin, Gi-Wook, ed. *Contentious Kwangju: The May 18th Uprising in Korea's Past and Present*. Lanham, MD: Rowman & Littlefield, 2003.

——. *Ethnic Nationalism in Korea: Genealogy, Politics, and Legacy*. Stanford: Stanford University Press, 2006.

Shin, Gi-Wook, Soon-Won Park, and Daqing Yang, eds. *Rethinking Historical Injustice and Reconciliation in Northeast Asia: The Korean Experience*. London: Routledge, 2007.

Sikkink, Kathryn. *The Justice Cascade: How Human Rights Prosecutions Are Changing World Politics*. New York: W.W. Norton, 2011.

Sikkink, Kathryn, Sanjeev Khagram, and James V. Riker, eds. *Restructuring World Politics: Transnational Social Movements, Networks, and Norms*. Minneapolis: University of Minnesota Press, 2002.

Sim, Ji-yeon. *Hanguk Hyeondae Jeongdang-Ron: Hamindang Yeongu 2* [Korean modern political parties: A study of the Korean Democratic Party, vol. 2]. Seoul: Changjakgua Bipyeong, 1984.

Smith, Jackie, Charles Chatfield, and Ron Pagnucco, eds. *Transnational Social Movements and Global Politics: Solidarity beyond the State*. Syracuse, NY: Syracuse University Press, 1997.

Snyder, Jack, and Leslie Vinjamuri. "Trial and Errors: Principle and Pragmatism in Strategies of International Justice." *International Security* 28, no. 3 (2003): 5–44.

Son, Kyengho. "The 4.3 Incident: Background, Development, and Pacification, 1945–1949." PhD diss., Ohio State University, 2008.

Song, Kwang Sung. "The Impact of Us Military Occupation." PhD diss., University of California, 1989.

Suh, Jae-Jung. "Truth and Reconciliation in South Korea." *Critical Asian Studies* 42, no. 4 (2010): 503–24.

Tarrow, Sidney. *Power in Movement: Social Movements and Contentious Politics*. Cambridge: Cambridge University Press, 1998.

Teitel, Ruti G. *Transitional Justice*. Oxford: Oxford University Press, 2000.

———. "Transitional Justice Genealogy." *Harvard Human Rights Journal* 16, no. 1 (2003): 69–94.

Thoms, Oskar N. T., James Ron, and Roland Paris. "State-Level Effects of Transitional Justice: What Do We Know?" *International Journal of Transitional Justice* 4, no. 3 (2010): 1–26.

Truth and Reconciliation Commission. Vol. 1 of *Truth and Reconciliation Commission of South Africa Report*. Cape Town: Juta and Co., 1998.

Van der Merwe, Hugo, Victoria Baxter, and Audrey R. Chapman, eds. *Assessing the Impact of Transitional Justice: Challenges for Empirical Research*. Washington, DC: United States Institute of Peace Press, 2009.

West, James. "Martial Lawlessness: The Legal Aftermath of Kwangju." *Pacific Rim Law & Policy Journal* 6, no. 1 (1997): 85–168.

Weyeneth, Robert B. "The Power of Apology and the Process of Historical Reconciliation." *Public Historian* 23, no. 3 (2001): 9–38.

Wiebelhaus-Brahm, Eric. *Truth Commissions and Transitional Societies: The Impact on Human Rights and Democracy*. New York: Routledge, 2010.

Yang, Jeong-sim. *Jeju 4.3 Hangjaeng: Jeohang-Gua Apeum-Eui Yeoksa* [The Jeju 4.3 uprising: A history of resistance and pain]. Seoul: Seonin, 2008.

Yang, Jo-hoon. "4.3 Chuijae 6-Nyeon: Muchamhi Oegokdoen Yeoksa [Six years of reporting on the Jeju 4.3 events: Severely distorted history]." *Yeoksa Bipyeong* 25, no. 2 (1994): 339–51.

———. "4.3 Jinsang Bogosoe Chaetaek-Gua Daetongryeong Sagua-Eui Euieui [The confirmation of the 4.3 report and the meaning of the presidential apology]." *Jejudo Euihoebo* 19 (2004): 1–9.

Young, Laura A., and Rosalyn Park. "Engaging Diasporas in Truth Commissions: Lessons from the Liberia Truth and Reconciliation Commission Diaspora Project." *International Journal of Transitional Justice* 3, no. 3 (2009): 341–61.

Index

Page numbers followed by letters *f* and *m* refer to figures and maps, respectively.